Journal of the Fantastic in the Arts
Volume 34 Number 2

I0167170

JFA

Journal of the Fantastic in the Arts
Volume 34/ Number 2

FAVIAN PRESS

Published by Favian Press
an imprint of Fiction4All
www.fiction4all.com

This edition published 2023

Journal of the Fantastic in the Arts
Volume 34/ Number 2
Whole Number 117
Supported by the
International Association for the Fantastic in the Arts.
Printed in the United States of America.

Cristina Bacchilega
Kyle William Bishop
Jim Casey
Ian Campbell
Bodhisattva Chattopadhyay
F. Brett Cox
Mame Bougouma Diene
Grace Dillon
Tananarive Due
Neil Gaiman
John Garrison
Mads Haahr
Regina Hansen
Rachel Haywood
Kathryn Hume
Obidike Kamau
Aaron Kashtan
Brooks Landon
Isiah Lavender III
Roger Luckhurst
Rob Maslen
Cheryl Morgan
James Morrow
Alec Nevala-Lee
Joy Sanchez-Taylor
Wole Talabi
Sheryl Vint
Gary K. Wolfe

COVER ART

Soovin Ahn is a multi-talented professional based in Seoul, South Korea, who excels as a graphic designer, visual artist, and planterior designer. Currently, she holds the position of CEO at Slow and Steady, a renowned planterior company. Her career, spanning 13 fruitful years, is adorned with collaborations with world-leading Korean corporations such as Hyundai Motors., SK and CJ. From 2016 to 2022, Ahn has staged numerous highly acclaimed plant styling exhibitions in Seoul, manifesting her unique style and aesthetic vision.

In the cover art for this special issue, Ahn endeavored to embody the theme, NEWtrospection, by illustrating how manipulation of a cutting-edge machine learning AI program reinterprets this historic photograph from the Korean War. The cover art features a black and white photograph provided by Noonbit Publishing Co., originally captured by the U.S. Navy in the heart of Seoul in June 1951 amidst the chaos of the Korean War. This poignant image portrays the tenacity of a young Korean woman enduring a war-torn crisis.

Ahn's visionary reinterpretation transforms the scene, depicting the woman as a Korean astronaut. This fresh perspective serves as a representation of an Asian-futuristic image, a reimagined future free from colonial constraints and steeped in feminist ideals. It symbolizes an era where Asian women play significant roles in space exploration, thereby contributing to a diverse and inclusive future.

GENERAL INQUIRIES

Inquiries and other editorial correspondence should be directed to jfa.editor@fantastic-arts.org.

SUBMISSIONS

Like the International Conference on the Fantastic in the Arts, *JFA* welcomes papers on all aspects of the fantastic in world literatures and media, as well as interdisciplinary approaches including African/Diaspora Studies, anthropology, area studies, critical game studies, disability studies, future studies, gender studies, history, Indigenous studies, music, philosophy, political science, postcolonial studies, psychology, queer studies, religious studies, science and technology studies, and sociology. All papers are made available in English and fully refereed. The journal is indexed in the MLA Bibliography.

Submissions should contain a more in-depth discussion than a conference-length paper and demonstrate a grasp of current scholarship on the subject. The length of articles generally varies from 3,500-9,000 words and ranges from 15-35 pages.

All submissions are peer-reviewed in accordance with our peer review statement and the BIPOC Anti-Racist Statement on Scholarly Reviewing Practices. If submissions are flagged at any point of the review process for the risk of promulgating potentially misrepresentative, stereotypical, ableist, or racist views, contributors will be asked to address these problems before the review process can continue.

Since the refereeing process is anonymous, the author's name should not appear anywhere on the text file itself, including the notes. No title page is needed. However, an abstract of 100-150 words must be included with each submission.

Please ensure that all citations and the Works Cited entries are in MLA style, 9th Edition. Please enter end notes manually.

Due to the need to provide the journal in multiple formats, the journal does not currently publish images/illustrations in articles.

Scholarly articles should be directed to the *JFA*'s Acquisitions and Reviews team (under Editor-in-Chief Novella Brooks de Vita at jfa.acquisitions@fantastic-arts.org). Please send your anonymized submission to the Submissions Editor, Tedd Hawks, at journal@fantastic-arts.org and include "ATTN: JFA Article Submission" at the start of your subject line. Allow thirty days for confirmation of receipt before querying.

BOOK REVIEWS

JFA also publishes reviews of scholarly works addressing the fantastic, broadly construed. Reviews of fiction are limited to reissues of speculative works with new introductions and scholarly apparatuses, and speculative works with the potential to impact scholarship in the genre. Books and other media received are advertised on the IAFA discussion list (which can be subscribed to through the IAFA homepage at www.iafa.org), and IAFA members are encouraged to suggest titles for review.

To mail book copies for review and for queries or reviews of English-language publications, please contact Book Reviews Editor-in-Chief Mailyn Abreu Toribio at jfa.bookreview@fantastic-arts.org, with a copy to journal@fantastic-arts.org.

Contents

REVIEWS

Introduction

Newtrospection: Reverse-Engineering Modernity in South Korean Speculative Fiction

Sang-Keun Yoo

1. Elephant-Shaped Hole

IN HER BOOK *Postcolonialism and Science Fiction*, science fiction scholar Jessica Langer recounts a conversation she had with SF writer Nalo Hopkinson in 2005, in which they discussed the absence of voices of color and postcolonial perspectives in the genre. Hopkinson remarked that it was like "there should be an elephant, but instead, there's an elephant-shaped hole" (1). Langer goes on to note that "the volume of science fiction in a particular language available in English is merely a fraction of a larger body of cultural production" (1).

In the intervening 17 years since Langer and Hopkinson's observation, substantial transformations have occurred within the domain of science fiction literature, progressively filling the metaphorical elephant-shaped void. The number of science fiction authors of color publishing in English and garnering prestigious accolades, including the Hugo, Nebula, and World Fantasy Awards, has witnessed a significant upswing. Concurrently, there has been an efflorescence of scholarly work encompassing Afrofuturism, Indigenous Futurism, and Chicanofuturism, authored by scholars of color and their allies. Prominent scholars, such as Ida Yoshinaga, Bodhisattva Chattopadhyay, and Isiah Lavender III, to name but a few, have made considerable contributions to the ongoing discourse. This evolving literary landscape reflects a broader cultural shift, engendering a more inclusive and diverse representation within the science fiction genre.

Simultaneously, the burgeoning popularity of South Korean K-pop artists, such as BTS and Blackpink, coupled with the widespread appeal of South Korean visual media, including Netflix dramas and films, has ushered in a renaissance of South Korean science fiction and fantasy. This resurgence can be traced back to the acclaimed film director Bong Joon-ho's seminal science fiction film, *The Host* (2006), which was followed by *Snowpiercer* (2013) and *Okja* (2017). Subsequently, an array of South Korean SF films and TV dramas spanning diverse genres have achieved success in the United States and other countries. Examples include the zombie genre with *Train to Busan* (2016), *Kingdom* (2019-2021), and *All of Us are Dead* (2022); space travel in *The Silent Sea* (2021) and *Space Sweepers* (2021); the monster/creature genre in *Sweet Home* (2020); cyberpunk and robot/cyborgs in *Memories of the Alhambra* (2018), *Dr. Brain* (2021) and *Jung_E* (2023); time travel narratives in *Goblin* (2016) and *Reborn Rich* (2022); climate fiction in *Black Knight* (2023); and ghost fantasy in *The School Nurse Files* (2020), *Hi Bye, Mama!* (2020), and *Revenant* (2023).

Furthermore, considering the multitude of science fiction and fantasy films and TV series that have garnered popularity among domestic audiences in South Korea, albeit without achieving global recognition, the list is virtually inexhaustible. It is also worth noting that while the majority of global attention on South Korean cultural products has centered on films and TV series, the market for South Korean webtoons and web novels has reached a staggering 117 million dollars, particularly captivating the interest of South Korean Generation Z readers. A preponderance of these webtoon and web novel writers in South Korea employ the diverse genre of speculative fiction, predominantly concentrating on themes of return, possession, and reincarnation (회귀, 빙의, 환생; hoegwi, pingŭi, hwansaeng).

Despite the escalating global popularity of South Korean science fiction and fantasy in visual media and web formats, a conspicuous lacuna persists in the translation and academic scrutiny of South Korean SF literature within the Anglophone world. While new South Korean science fiction films and television series continue to be released at an unparalleled pace, the availability of English translations for South Korean SF literature remains markedly constrained. This discrepancy highlights the need for further investigation and dissemination of South Korean SF literature and visual media in order to foster a more comprehensive understanding of its cultural and literary significance in the global landscape.

Nonetheless, several commendable endeavors have been undertaken in recent years to ameliorate this disparity. In 2019, *Readymade Bodhisattva: The Kaya Anthology of South Korean Science Fiction*, the inaugural anthology of South Korean SF literature in translation, was published under the editorship of USC Professor Sun-Young Park and SF translator and archivist Sang-Joon Park. Furthermore, Korean novelist Kim Bo-Young's two short story collections, *On the Origin of Species and Other Stories* (2021) and *I'm Waiting for You and Other Stories* (2022), have been translated and published in English.

English translations of other notable works include Chung Bora's *Cursed Bunny* (2017), Pyun Hye-Young's *City of Ash and Red* (2010), *The Hole* (2017), and *The Owl Cries* (2023), Bae

Myung-Hoon's *Tower* (2009; translation in 2020), *Launch Something!* (2020; translation in 2022), Choi Jin-Young's *To the Warm Horizon* (2017; translation in 2021), Dolki Min's *Walking Practice* (2022; translation 2023), and Djuna's *Counterweight* (2023). Moreover, it is pertinent to acknowledge the presence of South Korean short stories in American SF magazines such as *Clarkesworld*, as well as English works penned by American authors of Korean descent, including Yoon-ha Lee and Alice Sola Kim. The University of Hawaii Press's journal *Azalea: Journal of Korean Literature and Culture* has also published translations of Korean science fiction short stories.

Despite these strides, the extant English translations represent a mere fraction of the extensive corpus of South Korean science fiction and fantasy literature, demanding more translation and introduction of the South Korean science fiction and fantasy literature to the global world. For example, in an examination of the bestseller list for fiction on Kyobobooks, the nation's preeminent online bookstore website, it is notable that the current top two bestselling novels are fantasy works: Lee Mi-ye's *Dallergut Dream Department Store* and its sequel. Within the top 20, an additional four science fiction and fantasy novels are featured, such as Kim Cho-yup's SF anthology and hard science fiction novel, Cheon Seon-ran's *A Thousand Blues*, and Jeong Se-rang's *The School Nurse Files*. The authors of other works on the list, including Han Kang and Jeong Yu-jeong, have also engaged with science fiction and fantasy genres at various points in their careers, incorporating elements such as dreams and speculative modes within their narratives, despite the listed works of this year's bestseller not being strictly classified as science fiction or fantasy.

As the nation's literary and visual media landscape becomes increasingly saturated with science fiction and fantasy, aspiring writers from the younger generation are likewise drawn to these genres. The burgeoning interest in science fiction and fantasy among these emerging writers is best exemplified by the proliferation of literary awards specifically targeting these genres, which have been established within the past decade. Examples of such accolades include Gwacheon National Science Museum's Korean Science Fiction Award (2014–), Han Nak-won Science Fiction Award (2014–), Hubble's Korean Science Fiction Award (2016–), Arzak's Moon Yun-Sung Science Fiction Award (2021–), the Postech Science Fiction Award (2021–), Golden Leaf's Time Leap Literary Award (2016–), the Golden Dragon Award (2000–), and the ZA Literary Award (2016–). Most of these awards have relatively brief histories, with durations of less than a decade, which serves to emphasize the burgeoning interest and engagement of new writers in the realms of science fiction and fantasy over the past ten years. This trend also reflects a broader cultural shift, as science fiction and fantasy literature attain unprecedented traction and prominence within the South Korean literary landscape.

2. Disparity between South Korean Science Fiction's Global Popularity and the Scarcity of Academic Research

Numerous factors may contribute to the underrepresentation of South Korean speculative fiction and its rich history in global translations and scholarship, including a dearth of scholarly research, different genre categorizations compared to their Western counterparts, and the perceived degradation of genre literature in Korean society. Firstly, there is a notable scarcity of scholarship on Korean speculative fiction within the Anglophone academic sphere. Between 2016 and 2021, Korean language course enrollments experienced a significant increase in U.S. higher education—20.3% at two-year schools and 37.8% at four-year institutions. This growth is particularly noteworthy given that enrollment in most other foreign language courses has been on the decline during the same period ("Korean Language Study Continues to Grow"; Looney and Lusin 29-33). Despite this enthusiasm, research on Korean science fiction and fantasy continues to be limited.

Nevertheless, a few exceptional scholarly works have spearheaded this field of research. Haerin Shin's two articles, "The Curious Case of South Korean Science Fiction: A Hyper-Technological Society's Call for Speculative Imagination" (2013) in *Azalea: Journal of Korean Literature and Culture*, and "Affect in the End of Days: South Korean Science Fiction Cinema, Doomsday Book, and Affective Estrangement" from *Future Yet to Come* (2021), spearheaded this research. Additionally, Min Sung Park's "Korea's Force is Not Strong—Exploring the Definitions of Science Fiction" (2017) in *Plaridel*, Sun-Young Park's "Between Science and Politics: Science Fiction as a Critical Discourse in South Korea, 1960s–1990s" in the *Journal of Korean Studies* (*JKS*) (2018) and "Decolonizing the future: Postcolonial themes in South Korean science fiction" (2020) from the *Routledge Handbook of Modern Korean Literature*, and Dong-Won Kim's "Science Fiction in South and North Korea: Reading Science and Technology as Fantasized in Cultures" (2018) in *East Asian Science, Technology and Society: An International Journal*, all contribute to this burgeoning field of study.

Dafna Zur and Benoit Berthelier have also advanced research on North Korean science fiction. Dafna Zur has authored more than a dozen articles on Korean children's literature, encompassing both South and North Korea, as well as the interdisciplinary relationship between science and literature in Korea. Her 2014 article, "Let's Go to the Moon: Science Fiction in the North Korean Children's Magazine *Adong Munhak*, 1956–1965," published in the *Journal of Asian Studies*, represents the first attempt to analyze North Korean science fiction within the Anglophone academic sphere. Benoit Berthelier has similarly pioneered research on North Korean science fiction, as evidenced by his 2018 article, "Encountering the Alien: Alterity and Innovation in North Korean Science Fiction since 1945," published in the *JKS*. Furthermore, Dahye Kim's recent article, "Who Is Afraid of Techno-Fiction? The Emergence of Online Science Fiction in the Age of Informatization," published in the *JKS* in 2022, explores the history of Korean online fiction as it relates to the domain of science fiction.

It is noteworthy that this previous scholarship on South Korean science fiction has been presented and published within the domains of Korean studies or Asian studies, rather than in the field of science fiction studies. The Anglophone world of science fiction studies has generally overlooked Korean science fiction. Over the past forty years, there have been no papers on Korean science fiction in either *Science Fiction Studies* or the *Journal of the Fantastic in the Arts*. It was not until 2020 that the first paper exclusively focused on a Korean science fiction work appeared in *Science Fiction Film and Television*. Authored by myself, Sang-Keun Yoo, this paper examined Bong Joon-Ho's science fiction film *The Host* (2006) compared to his more recent film *Parasite* (2019).

The second reason for the lack of research and introduction of Korean science fiction in the global world can be attributed to the distinct genre categorization prevalent in South Korea. Nalo Hopkinson notes in *Whispers from the Cotton Tree Root* (2000) that "Northern science fiction and fantasy emerge from a rational and skeptical approach to the world [...] But the Caribbean, much like the rest of the world, tends to have a different worldview: The irrational, the inexplicable, and the mysterious exist side by side with the daily events of life" (xii-xiii). This statement demonstrates that the traditional genre categories, developed within the Anglophone context, may not be applicable to global cultural productions. She argues that in many parts of the world beyond the United States and modern imperial nations, the distinction between science fiction and other fantastic genres, such as those engaging with spirits and magic, does not exist. Similarly, in Korea, the boundaries between science fiction and fantasy have been consistently blurred, rendering the distinction between them largely meaningless for several decades.

Consequently, for the past several decades, numerous South Korean writers have not labeled their science fiction and fantasy works as SFF, nor have they identified themselves as SFF writers— instead, they predominantly classified themselves merely as fiction writers, rather than science fiction writers. In the interview included in this issue, Bo-Young Kim, currently one of the most famous science fiction writers, admits, "Honestly, even after my debut as a science fiction writer, I was skeptical about the potential of sustaining a professional career with this genre of novels." She attributes her skepticism to the insufficient recognition of science fiction as a distinctive genre. Kim adds, "The literary contests that gave me my debut were soon discontinued, and there weren't many science fiction magazines or awards where I could publish my work." Similarly, Bong Joon-ho's 2006 science fiction film, *The Host*, wasn't promoted or labeled as a science fiction film in Korea. Instead, it was marketed as a family drama that incorporated a profound social critique.

The historical disregard for genre literature, specifically science fiction, in South Korea mirrors past attitudes in North America, though it's arguably more intense. Genre literature has been perceived as second-rate compared to realist fiction and has been regarded as solely for young children's entertainment or scientific education or a genre for national political propaganda. Given South Korea's history, which is fraught with a series of brutal events and mass massacres stemming from Japanese colonialism, the Korean War, military dictatorship, and the Cold War, writing science fiction and fantasy was often deemed as not-serious escapism, while "serious" writers focused on addressing the "real" social problems at hand.

Additionally, certain geopolitical conditions caused South Korean writers to hesitate in exploring science fiction themes. Tae-hun Lim, in his enlightening article "A Preface to the Study of 'Geopolitical SF,'" attributes this dearth of science fiction imagination in South Korean literary history to the nation's geopolitical status. He discusses South Korea's experience with 35 years of colonialism and its subsequent influence from the Cold War conditions between global powers. He observes, "Positioned geopolitically as inferior, [Korean SF] writers' creative potential often gets overshadowed as they measure themselves against the world's central powers. This comparison leads to a sense of emptiness and anxiety, which they attempt to alleviate through a quest for recognition and international validation from these leading nations" (my translation 98). Specifically, he notes the impact of Cold War ideology on late-twentieth-century South Korea, stating, "When factors such as Cold War ideology come into play, they inevitably constrain the writers' imagination of collective identity and lead to self-censorship, thereby stifling or halting creativity and thought" (my translation 100). This indicates that the marginalization of science fiction and fantasy in South Korea throughout the twentieth century is not solely due to local readers' preference for "serious" literature. External factors such as Cold War ideology and colonialism also played a significant role, as these conditions made imagining the distant future and outer space seem absurd.

In this context, the recent upsurge of science fiction and fantasy in South Korean culture mirrors a shift in the geopolitical conditions that Lim outlined about the literary history of the twentieth century. This change has occurred as the nation's people start to conceptualize a decolonized futurity in step with the development of their own technology. The country is leading the world in certain ways, as demonstrated by globally prominent tech companies such as Samsung and Hyundai. The recent launch of a self-developed space rocket, Nuri-ho, has also been a significant event for South Korean readers. It has made imagining a science fiction future seem more tangible, rather than just a far-fetched idea.

3. Newtrospection

As the guest editors of this focused issue, we—Haerin Shin and Sang-Keun Yoo—have endeavored to address this glaring omission in recent years by organizing South Korean science fiction panels at academic conferences such as ICFA and SFRA and authoring research papers for academic journals. This focused issue on South Korean science fiction represents the first publication in English-language academic journals devoted exclusively to the nation's SFF products. Furthermore, academic journals in the fields of Korean studies or Asian studies have not previously featured a focused issue on the nation's science fiction, although Dafna Zur and Christopher P. Hanscom, as guest editors, edited a special issue on "Science and Literature in North and South Korea" with the *JKS*.

We have titled this issue *Newtrospection: Reverse-Engineering Modernity in South Korean Speculative Fiction*. The title *Newtrospection* emphasizes several distinct characteristics of South Korean science fiction and its traditions. One of the key traits of South Korean science fiction and fantasy is its persistent interest in the past and history. South Korean speculative fiction is predominantly retrospective. It may seem peculiar for science fiction works to maintain a consistent interest in the past rather than the future, and in history rather than science, especially considering that science fiction as a genre typically envisions futures with advanced science and technology. For example, one of the early South Korean science fiction films, *2009: Lost Memories* (2002), presents an alternative historical narrative that imagines a Korea that could not achieve independence from Japanese colonialism. A SF drama released last year that gained significant popularity among local audiences, *Reborn Rich*, is also a time-travel narrative in which the main character returns to the 1990s and is reborn as the youngest grandson of a wealthy CEO of a conglomerate company (presumably Samsung's founder). Netflix's fantasy series *The School Nurse Files* portrays a high school nurse who discovers a centuries-old well in the basement of a high school, and how it affects the well-being of 21st-century Korean students. Gina Kim's VR film *Bloodless* revisits the historical events of the early 1990s, employing the newly developed media technology of virtual reality film to offer a fresh perspective on representation.

Even other SF films, novels, and TV dramas that do not return to the past and instead imagine the future, such as *The Silent Sea* (2021), *Space Sweepers* (2021), and *Peninsula* (2020), consistently scrutinize South Korea's position within global politics and among powerful countries. They imagine a future South Korean government and its citizens who do not possess sovereignty as an independent country, reminding audiences of the nation's modernization history, which was influenced by foreign forces such as the Japanese Empire, People's Republic of China, and US neo-imperial military intervention. These films retrospectively examine how Koreans have arrived at their present situation and what they should do to forge different, changed trajectories in the future. The dual gaze that South Korean science fiction displays—rewriting history from the perspective of present-day insights and imagining the future informed by the lessons of the past and present—aptly captures the unique characteristics of South Korean science fiction.

Although it may seem peculiar for South Korean science fiction to focus more on the past rather than the future, it is understandable when considering that the birth of science fiction coincided with the emergence of historical fiction. Carl Freedman, in his book *Critical Theory and Science Fiction*, argues that Mary Shelley's *Frankenstein* (1818) was written around the same time as the first historical novel, Sir Walter Scott's *Waverley* (1814), and that both genres are byproducts of the European readers' initial mass experience of the French Revolution. Both historical novels and science fiction were borne from the newly-formed collective identity experienced by Europeans, which enabled them to imagine their shared past and future as part of a larger historical narrative. What is unique in South Korean science fiction and fantasy, however, is that the desire to understand and imagine this collective past and future is not divided into two separate genres but rather merged into one, making South Korean science fiction simultaneously historical and retrospective rather than solely futuristic or projective. To denote this unique characteristic of South Korean science fiction, where the imagination of the future and retrospection of the past converge within a single work, we have chosen to employ the neologism "Newtrospection" rather than "Retrospection."

The term "Newtrospection" carries an additional connotation in the context of this issue's aim. Our objective is to trace and revisit the history of South Korean science fiction literature and films through the lens of contemporary science fiction studies. As mentioned earlier, a considerable body of literary works and films produced in the past in South Korea was often not classified or categorized as science fiction or fantasy, even though they would be considered compelling examples within the current discourse of global science fiction studies. Since the distinction between hard and soft science fiction has blurred with the emergence of the New Wave in the Anglophone world, the umbrella term "speculative fiction" has become more widely circulated in science fiction studies, making it increasingly challenging to clearly delineate what is and what is not science fiction. Reexamining past literary and visual examples from South Korea through the lens of this evolved academic discourse allows us to adopt a fresh perspective for analyzing the imaginative spheres of South Korean artistic materials from the past—neither as folklore and myth, nor as second-rate, non-serious literature solely intended for children's scientific education.

To this aim, this issue presents four academic articles from leading scholars in the field. The inaugural article, penned by Ji Eun Lee, critically examines the catalysts behind the recent upsurge in South Korean science fiction novels. Lee conducts an extensive analysis of three prominent female science fiction authors' works, providing valuable insights into the sociocultural conditions that have spurred the growth of feminist science fiction. Additionally, Lee contrasts these Korean narratives with American feminist science fiction theories, notably those of Donna Haraway and Joanna Russ, to foster comparative understanding. In the second article, Se Young Kim navigates through the history of South Korea's diverse sub-genres of speculative fiction visual media in popular culture, with a particular emphasis on its relationship with Japanese cultural influence. Through a thorough analysis of the globally acclaimed Netflix series, *Squid Game*, Kim contends that the show's success is significantly influenced by Japanese culture. Furthermore, Kim demonstrates how this influence permeates various speculative fiction sub-genres of South Korea and Japan, including piloted robot series, kaiju (monster), and Tokusatsu genres. Rather than viewing this as a unilateral influence, Kim interprets it as a manifestation of hybridity, where the melding of distinct national traditions forms something entirely new.

The third contribution, authored by myself, Sang-Keun Yoo, delves into Gina Kim's recent virtual reality film *Bloodless*. I scrutinize how Kim uses newly emerging media technology to artistically revisit traumatic historical events from Korea. This analysis explores how virtual reality media serves as a potent tool to blur the boundaries between realistic and speculative modes to visualize South Korea's military sex workers's ghostly presence. In the issue's concluding article, Sang Eun Eunice Lee illuminates South Korea's current speculative media landscape through an analysis of webtoons. Focusing on the unique aspects of recent South Korean webtoons, such as cyclical rebirth and gamified existence, Lee employs *Tomb Raider King* and *Again My Life* as her primary examples to dissect how these narratives challenge covert societal hierarchies in South Korea. By illuminating the alternate future world these webtoons envision, Lee's analysis invites us to contemplate the potential of these digital narratives in challenging and dismantling entrenched social inequalities.

This issue goes beyond a traditional academic article collection to provide a comprehensive look at South Korean science fiction and fantasy, incorporating a design fiction and three insightful interviews to deepen our understanding of South Korean SFF's present. The issue presents a speculative design fiction from Seo-Young Chu, the author of the influential science fiction theory monograph, *Do Metaphors Dream of Literal Sleep?: A Science-Fictional Theory of Representation* (2010). Chu's short explanation in this issue about design fiction does not provide a single definition, but it does identify the practice as interdisciplinary and a type of storytelling with experimental artifacts. In her design fiction, Chu provides a thought-provoking exploration of South Korea's colonial history and rapid capitalist development through the lens of Korea's college entrance examination. Completing the issue are interviews with prominent figures in South Korean SFF: acclaimed science fiction novelist

Bo-Young Kim, Sung-hee Jo, the film director of Netflix's *Space Sweepers*, and Kyoung-mi Lee, the director of Netflix's fantasy series *The School Nurse Files*. The interviews were conducted remotely, with questionnaires provided to the artists in writing, and their responses also received in the same format.

While the guest editors of this issue endeavored to adopt a comprehensive approach toward the history and current state of South Korean science fiction and fantasy across diverse media and genres, we were unable to encompass the entire scope. In particular, this issue could not address North Korean science fiction and its unique traditions, despite the fact that North Korea has cultivated a distinct and rich history of science fiction that differs from that of South Korea. We also could not include young adult fiction and other various sub-genres of speculative fiction. The editors are also cognizant of the absence of research on major South Korean science fiction writers, such as Djuna, Lee Yeongdo, Bok Geo-il, Han Nak-won, and others. Furthermore, South Korean science fiction history boasts a rich tradition of feminist comics and graphic novels by female writers in the 1980s and 90s, such as Kim Jin, Shin Il-Sook, and Kang Kyung-ok, which this issue could not cover. Additionally, many American and European science fiction works have been introduced and translated into Korean since the 1920s, and the history of translating English, French, and Russian science fiction works into Korean throughout the twentieth century is an important area of research that we wished to include in this issue but could not due to the issue's limited scope. We hope that this issue serves as a starting point for further future research.

Works Cited

Freedman, Carl. *Critical Theory and Science Fiction*. Wesleyan University Press, 2000.

Hopkinson, Nalo. *Whispers from the Cotton Tree Root*. Invisible Cities Press, 2000.

"Korean Language Study Continues to Grow." *The MLA Newsletter*, vol. 55, no. 2, 2023, p. 4.

Langer, Jessica. *Postcolonialism and Science Fiction*. Springer, 2011.

Lim, Tae-hun. "A Preface to the Study of 'Geopolitical SF.'" *Journal of Bangyo Language and Literature*, vol. 63, pp. 81-118, 2023.

Looney, Dennis, and Natalia Lusin. "Enrollments in Languages Other Than English in United States Institutions of Higher Education, Summer 2016 and Fall 2016: Final Report." *MLA*, June 2019, www.mla.org/content/download/110154/file/2016- Enrollments-Final-Report.pdf.

A Radical Future: Gender and Science Fiction in Contemporary Korean Literature

Ji-Eun Lee

Prologue: Sudden Arrival of an SF Boom

IN 2017, A STUDENT OF MINE, an avid reader of science fiction, wanted to learn about Korean equivalents.[1] We found a handful of short stories translated into English through a pathbreaking special on South Korean science fiction in the 2013 issue of *Azalea*, a small pool of horror films that would qualify as broader speculative fiction, and a noticeable dearth in films that would qualify as SF. We considered two films: *Save the Green Planet* (2003, dir. Jang Joon-hwan)[2] for aliens from outer space, and *I'm a Cyborg, But That's Okay* (2007, dir. Park Chan-wook)[3] for the motif of the cyborg. Both films featured characters with psychoses and SF elements, the former as manifestation of mental confusion in a black comedy and crime thriller setting and the latter in a romantic comedy, but we both agreed that they were not works of SF in the conventional sense. Short stories included in the literary magazine *Azalea*, such as "Road Kill" by Park Min-kyu and "Art and the Acceleration of Gravity" by Bae Myung Hoon, may qualify as SF—a promising start—but even taken all together, these works did not predict the burgeoning, robust interest in the genre we see today. Compared to the Western SF tradition with its dedicated focus on science and technology, these stories came across more as critiques of the current world without showcasing a full-scale imagining of a world different from ours. And we were not the only ones noticing the scarcity of Korean SF at that time: this seeming disinterest in science fiction has been observed by researchers including Haerin Shin (2013) and Pae Sangmin (2017). In "Seeds of Korean SF," Pae did not hide his disappointment in the shoddy science and overall quality of narrative present in recent works of SF he was reviewing, and he agreed with Shin about the inherent possibilities of the genre in South Korea given its technological development, which should be fertile ground for "seeds" of SF to grow (Pae 294–305; Shin 81–2).

In less than the five years since my encounter with a disillusioned SF fan in my course, science fiction has become the most popular genre in South Korean literature,[4] and as a feminist literary scholar with little knowledge of SF, I was drawn to how this new popularity is led by women writers and a new generation of women readers who are known as "young feminists" in their 20s. Why science fiction? Why now? And what is the significance of this phenomenon in the history of South Korean women's literature? During the mid-twentieth century, before it arose as the leader in technological innovations, South Korea strove to become a global manufacturer of electronics and mundane commodities, and science fiction was perceived less as a literary genre than as educational material for boys, something that would instill nationalistic ambition given science and technology's promise as a way out of the country's poverty. Even after Korea's rise as one of the biggest economic powers on the global stage in the 1990s, SF remained a minor genre domestically. Imported space opera, fantasy, and films with space and aliens were received well along with other Hollywood blockbusters but did not seem to impact the domestic film industry much, to say nothing of literature, which kept its highbrow-lowbrow strata and marginalized speculative fiction overall as a niche lowbrow genre. Considering this humble status in the previous era's literary history, the recent rise of SF in South Korea by women writers and readers is remarkable.

Against that backdrop, this paper explores the work of several major women writers who spearheaded the new SF trend including Kim Bo-young (Kim Poyŏng, b.1975), Chung Se-rang (Chŏng Serang, b.1984), and Kim Choyeop (Kim Ch'oyŏp, b.1993), and examines the social and cultural environment in which such writers emerged. It will also reflect on two American feminist theorists of SF, Donna Haraway and Joanna Russ, who have provided important insights into how SF and fantasy may answer some feminist calls for a world differently imagined and constructed. Rather than providing exhaustive and extensive research on the origins and history of the SF genre, the main focus of this introductory essay on Korean SF and feminism is to better discern the contours of Korea's own SF impulse and the energies that motivated and constrained it. By doing so, it hopes to avoid leaning heavily on Western theories, the usual tendency in discussing women's literature, and instead views South Korea's contemporary social environment as the driver for the distinctive impulses and motivations of the country's home-grown writers and readers.5

1. A Different Origin: SF and Women's Literature in South Korea

Even for people who are not readers of science fiction, a rush of Korean films in the genre in recent years has been unmistakable. *Space Sweepers* (dir. Jo Sung-hee) was released during the COVID-19 pandemic through Netflix in 2021 and branded as the "first Korean SF film," and a parallel version in webtoon format had been serialized before the film was released to help hype expectations. Indeed, it had Korean identity markers—a spaceship with a Korean name and a crew with names like Kim Taeho, Captain Jang, and Tiger Park—and classic SF elements including space, a robot, futuristic science, and possible doom for a utopian and dystopian world. Gender role reversal (the ship's captain is a woman) and gestures toward gender fluidity through the robot Bubs (Ŏptong-i in the original)[6] added a bridge to feminist elements found in Korean science fiction that will be explored later in this paper. This was followed quickly by *The Silent Sea*, a 2021 8-part mini-series about investigating a failed mission on the Moon, and the film *Seobok* (2021), named after the main character, who is a cloned human with extraordinary powers. Added to these are horror and thriller genres with supernatural and gothic elements, which already had niche success in Korean dramas and films. In sum, we are witnessing the heyday of a Korean science fiction genre not just in literature, but in popular culture more broadly.

In some cases, success in film and drama is directly related to literature, as seen in *The School Nurse Files* (2021), a six-part drama series. Not strictly SF, but a work that belongs to more broadly defined speculative fiction, this drama was based on Chung Serang's 2015 novel featuring Ahn Eunyoung, a school nurse, who sees "jellies"—congealed harmful energy—and exorcises them with a toy gun and sword. But with or without the marketing power of the film or drama series, both science and speculative fiction by a young generation of South Korean writers—the majority of them women—have been leading bestsellers in the print book market for the last several years, a phenomenon reflected in recent English translations of Korean SF and speculative fiction including *On Origin of Species and Other Stories* (2021) and *I am Waiting For You* (2021) both by Kim Bo-young (b.1973); *Readymade Boddhisattva: The Kaya Anthology of South Korean Science Fiction* (2019); and *Cursed Bunny* (2021) by Chung Bora (Chŏng Pora, b.1976), to name just a few. And this trend is expanding as the number of writers dedicated to the genre increases. Bestselling authors Kim Cho-yeop and Cheon Seon-nan (Ch'ŏn Sŏllan), for example, both born in 1993, have been producing one SF hit after another.

Where did this sudden explosive popularity of SF come from?[7] Yi Sŏnok's research on scientism through *Sasanggye* (1953-1970), an influential periodical geared toward educated readers with a nationalistic focus on socio-political issues, and her followup research on the girls' magazine *Yŏhaksaeng*, have shown how scientism was used in nation-building during the Park Chung Hee Era (1960-1978) broadly (Yi "1960-nyŏndae kwahakchuŭi wa gender ŭi chaegusŏng" 261-302, 225-54). Similarly, Dafna Zur's work on children's literature in the first half of the 20th century in Korea observes how science became the most important topic for children and young adults and offers a glimpse of why science fiction remained an underdeveloped genre in Korea. The importance of science and technology for warfare in postwar Korea carried real-world implications in the ceasefire situation. Encouraging children ("boys") to be interested in science was directly related to the survival of the nation. Along with articles on scientific knowledge, futuristic, apocalyptic, and fictional works with scientific themes by writers like Han Nagwŏn (1924-2007) were serialized in magazines for young adults (Zur 191-214),[8] and as Ko Changwŏn's article explains, the target audience for SF— including occasional translations of foreign works—was limited to children and young adults until the 1990s (Ko 231).

Outside children's literature, however, not many works of futuristic imagination flourished in the 1960-70s[9] despite this techno-nationalism (*kisul minjok chuŭi*),[10] and the authoritarian political environment in South Korea is seen as a major reason for the dearth of a SF tradition. Repeated coups and civilian resistance in the latter half of the twentieth century left little imaginative room for Korean authors beyond fighting against fabrications produced by military dictatorship. Telling the truth—accounting accurately for casualties and giving voice to fighters and victims— was the daunting primary task for writers during the authoritarian era of the 1960-80s, and the corresponding mode of fiction writing was realism, telling a *real* story as truthfully as possible to counter the distortions and elisions of official history.[11]

It was only after the authoritarian regime ended in South Korea in 1987 that the literary scene opened itself to diverse forms and themes (Lee 358–9). Alternative history like *Searching for the Epitaph* (1987, Pimyŏng ŭl ch'ajasŏ) by Pok Kŏil (b.1943) is often associated with SF from that era.[12] It is not a coincidence that alternative history was SF's chosen form, as that impulse has significant overlap with efforts to write a "history" among earlier era writers: it continued the pursuits of a previous generation of male writers, but repackaged that effort in a way that responded to a changed political environment. Although such works represented a limited venue for alternative imaginings to grow in post-authoritarian South Korea, it took another several decades for speculative fiction to rise as a significant genre in Korean literature, as something more than experiments by authors whose works were guaranteed to be accepted in the mainstream *mundan*.[13] The authority of *mundan* and the wall it embodied between highbrow and lowbrow genres had to be chipped away before speculative fiction could thrive.[14]

The following decades, from the 1990s to early 2000s, saw the rise of women writers and feminist literature. Even if women writers from the late 80s to early 2000s did not completely break away from realism, works by women, on women, and for women from this era brought changes to the literary scene. Women writers expanded and diversified the themes and issues in literature from struggles of (male) Koreans in the post-Korean War and Cold War eras to include everyday life, individuality, and gender identity. Fights mounted by feminist groups three decades ago and their efforts at correcting legal and systematic patriarchy also affected the literary landscape. For the last three decades, shortlists for major literary awards have shown equal or majority representation by women writers. It took longer for women literary critics to gain visibility, but that eventually happened as well. Ultimately, *mundan* in 2023 is no longer a single authority that decides what gets published, which authors become famous, or sets the definition of good literature.

This is not to say that the literary scene is now free of sexism; #MeToo brought to light past sexual violence by several male writers and reports on prevalent patterns of sexual abuse and misogyny among current writers.[15] The current generation of women writers in South Korea have witnessed these fights too, especially in the form of a new "gender war," an unprecedented hostility between polarized groups regarding gender issues, which continues through on- and offline trolling and mirroring attacks by both sides.[16] While South Korea has witnessed a rapid increase in the suicide rate among young women,[17] the gender war became even more fierce as politicians used it as fodder for the presidential election in 2021.[18] What we see with the current flourishing in SF and its domination by women is a reflection of the rise of women writers over several decades, unresolved issues in systematic gender inequality, and continuing misogyny in the era of post-#MeToo. Added to that is the climate catastrophe, a widening wealth gap, and an unpredictable future despite or due to advancements in science and technology. This era, in sum, calls for radical imagination to deal with a disappointing and dangerous day-to-day reality for the young generation in South Korea and around the globe.

Feminist literature outside Korea has a much stronger tradition of women's SF and fantasy, spanning from the Gothic novels of Mary Shelley to modern-day classics by Ursula K Le Guin and Margaret Atwood. In Korea, women's SF and fantasy arose much later and from completely different socio-cultural soil, and, as we will see presently, its writers are projecting possible solutions and hopes in their cautionary tales. The three stories introduced in the following sections are yet to be published in English translation at the time of this essay. Although all three stories were published between 2019 and 2020, Kim Bo-young, Chung Serang, and Kim Choyeop were each born in a different decade, so each belongs to a slightly different generation with a different literary trajectory. In imagining new futures, however, women's literature and SF share the goal of engaging freely with radical possibilities, especially new worlds where being a woman, being different, and living as oneself are not bound by preconceived norms.

2. Kim Bo-young: *Resemblance* (2020)

In 2021, Harper Collins Voyager released the first English translation of Kim Bo-young's short stories, *I am Waiting for You and Other Stories*, one of the rare Korean works to be published by a major commercial press in America. Kim worked in the game industry as a developer, game scenario writer, graphic designer, and producer while she wrote and published her works, and this new contract finally allowed her to be a full-time writer (Kim Bo-young, interview). By then she already had avid fans who had been waiting for Kim's talent to be recognized outside a small pool of SF readers in Korea. Kim's path toward becoming an established writer has been different from conventional fiction writers. She started publishing in 2004 and in the beginning of her career, Kim submitted works to competitions for creative writing on science and contributed to web-based magazines specializing in the fantasy genre. As she earned recognition, her works became regular fare in occasional edited volumes and special issues on themes of science, fantasy, and speculative fiction. Kim has since become the face of Korean SF within Korea and beyond and has edited several anthologies of SF works.

Kim Bo-young's rise to international recognition is a result of persistence and focus, but at the same time, because of the dearth of SF, and particularly SF by women, she is frequently asked about her origins: where did she draw inspiration from, and who were her "role models"? Her interviews reveal an unorthodox path, an eclectic mix of Pak Wansŏ (1931-2011), *Demian* (1919) by Hermann Hesse (1877-1962), and Korean animations in the 1970s featuring giant combat robots. In giving these answers, she points out that she grew up in an era where there were not many translated or domestic science fiction stories, and "science fiction welcomed her (work)" when all she did was to write for herself in the way she wanted to (Kim Bo-young, interview). In one of her interviews Kim quotes Joanna Russ's statement on how those who cannot find one's own story in the existing literary tradition would seek a world different from the here and now, noting that this described her writing process exactly (Kim Bo-young, interview).

With this origin story in mind, let us now consider one of Kim's best-known works, her 2020 novella *Resemblance* (Ŏlmana talmannŭn'ga). In addition to the notion that women's SF is inherently subversive because it breaks off from a world dominated by patriarchy, this novella is one of Kim's most distinctively gender-themed works. The story is not translated into English, but a literal English translation of the title would be "how much does (A) resemble (B)" in question form, but with A and B omitted. The reader is thus set to look for "A" and "B"; given that this is science fiction with an AI as the main character, a good initial gloss is "how much does an AI resemble a human." One of the threads for this inquiry through much of the story involves the human crew harassing the AI named HUN, the spaceship's emergency management system. Although it normally exists as an interactive system in the spaceship's computer, HUN has demanded to be transferred into a shell of a humanoid body, and the novella begins as HUN wakes up in this body-shell only to discover it has amnesia, including about why it demanded a body. Finding this reason then becomes another quest for HUN and readers.

The search that becomes the major plot in this novella, however, is yet to come. HUN keeps feeling something is missing in its system and is puzzled by it from the beginning. Meanwhile, HUN, in a body of a humanoid, is immediately thrown in the middle of conflicts among crew members who are all humans. A lack of *something*, something removed or erased deliberately from its logic system, nags HUN throughout the story, and when it finally realizes what it is toward the end of the story, that "something" turns out also to be the key in understanding the real source of conflict among crew members. At the outset, crew members disagreed about whether to deviate from their course to provide aid to a deserted mine colony on a remote planet. The captain has decided to go ahead with the aid despite technical and logistical challenges and the science officer helps her plan for the mission. Meanwhile, the navigation officer and a few others oppose the decision and become violent. HUN is supposed to manage this crisis, and according to its manual, it was to accomplish this by taking the blame instead of crew members, thus resolving the conflict. That was why HUN asked to be transferred into a human shell, but the plan has not worked and conflict on board continues, leaving HUN feeling that the missing/erased information holds the key to a resolution. After repeated harassments, a failed attempt at gang rape by the navigation officer and his allies, and HUN's noticing the extreme precautions that the captain—a woman—takes for self-protection, the captain finally points out gender difference to HUN, who comes to grasp that this was what aggression from the crew was based on.[19] Hun then realizes that a whole set of information on gender inequality and discrimination (sŏngch'abyŏl) was missing from its system; a bureaucrat had decided to erase it, as if in the world of space travel and women serving as captain, gender discrimination was no longer relevant, and was thus unnecessary information for an AI (Kim "Ŏlmana Talmannŭn'ga," 324). These threads of identity-searching conclude when HUN boards a lander with supplies for the stranded miners on Titan, an altruistic mission unexpected of an AI.

Hiding the gender issue well into the plot was possible in part because of how the Korean language enables hiding the gender of a person in ordinary speech, and also because of default expectations about gender. Many women SF writers including Kim Bo-young do not indicate the biological sex of their characters linguistically, and because Korean words often do not carry gender markers—both "he" and "she" can be signified by the same word "kŭ" (그), for example—gender-neutral names like Yi Chinsŏ and Nam Ch'anyŏng may lead readers to assume crew members, including HUN in the humanoid shell, are all men. And indeed, this is what Kim Bo-young intended—that without adding specifically feminine aspects, characters look and sound like men (Sim 53). The ingenuity of this work is that when one removes gender discrimination as a possible explanation—the way an unnamed bureaucrat who erased the information from HUN did—then events of the story lose the one thing that make them cohere, leaving only the non-comprehension that manifests in HUN. Absent that vital framework of understanding, the story as a whole does not stand, for the exact same reason HUN cannot comprehend. In coalescing at the end, the novella asserts gender discrimination as something that exists whether we acknowledge it or not; it exists in space, and even an AI may not escape it. In remaining hidden for so much of the story, gender discrimination emerges as an insidious, often unseen force, evident more by its wake than its overt claims. While a reader may feel disappointed that gender discrimination and conflict figure so deeply even in an imagined future, the novella also highlights how ridiculous it is for such a thing to exist in the age of space travel. In this imagined future, AI and robots mimicking humans or having superhuman abilities (like computing power) provoke an almost instinctual animus among the male crew. Differences between AI and human in this story, however, dwindle compared to gender discrimination, in the form of crew members making unreasonable demands simply because men will not obey orders given by a ship's captain who is a woman—something the AI cannot understand until a twist near the end of the story. As this stark conflict unfolds on the ship, descriptions of the dire situation among miners on Titan appear in a different typeset several times throughout, adding irony and contrast to what is supposed to be a rescue mission: lives are put in jeopardy because of male egos.

3. Chung Serang: "Reset" (2020)

One thing I think we must know—that our traditional gender roles will not be part of the future, as long as the future is not a second Stone Age. Our traditions, our books, our morals, our manners, our films, our speech, our economic organization, everything we have inherited, tell us that to be a Man one must bend Nature to one's will—or other men. This means ecological catastrophe in the first instance and war in the second. To be a Woman, one must be first and foremost a mother and after that a server of Men; this means overpopulation and the perpetuation of the first two disasters. The roles are deadly. The myths that serve them are fatal.

Women cannot write—using the old myths.

But using new ones—? (Russ 93)

Has anyone seen a character in an apocalyptic tale happy that the world as they knew it disappeared? Readers of "Reset" by Chung Serang have. Taking the form of diary entries by four people from various time points, "Reset" tells about a world one day after giant earthworms appeared everywhere on earth and ate up everything—buildings, cars—in their path. If Kim Bo-young's *Resemblance* transposed the gender discrimination of 21st century Korea onto a future in a spaceship with an AI and used familiar settings of the science fiction genre, Chung Serang uses another typical trope of SF: an apocalypse. Chung tweaks what is already a cliché in the apocalyptic genre seen in Hollywood blockbusters—a lone survivor (often a man), a heavy dose of melancholy, and an ending that yields the birth of a hero, a repeat of an "old myth" as Joanna Russ calls it. Embracing the apocalypse in "Reset" offers a fresh perspective, an altruistic worldview that extends to other species in the world; it's the people who harm others that make the "A.R." (presumably, "After Reset") era chaotic and dangerous, and meanwhile, the first narrator calmly reflects on the nauseating hypocrisy and negligence of a human race that puts itself and an entire planet on a sure course to disaster. The arrival of earthworms is a "reset," a timely correction before the human race does even more harm to other species and themselves on earth. The first narrator falls asleep with a smile and a sense of awe, under an emergency blanket made of thin reflective material, knowing that his/her death will contribute to the lives of other species.

As the story unfolds, more elements of classic SF appear in this unusual apocalyptic story: time travel, underground cities, secret storage for crop seeds, and a young savior of the world, in this case, an eighteen-year-old daughter of two oligochaetologists, who, with her prodigious knowledge in the study of earthworms, joins a group of people who are later named "Heroes of the Reset Era." "Reset" stands out because of its audacious attitude toward the future—if this is a world not worth saving, then so be it. The reset is accomplished by a creature that is ubiquitous but unnoticed by most city-dwelling people—earthworms, except that the earthworms in "Reset" are attracted to the smell of things made of fossil fuel such as polyester fabric or plastic, and the reason cities and buildings become their targets is that they are full of man-made, fossil-fuel-based products and garbage. When earthworms gulp down and destroy buildings and the people inside are killed as collateral, the end result is giant piles of poop of fertile soil that emanates the smell of lilies. But the giant earthworms do not procreate, so after decades in which human survivors live underground, use only organic material, and produce no garbage, the story ends with earth on the right path for peaceful coexistence with all species on the planet.

Unlike the central placement of gender in Kim Bo-young's novella, "Reset" does not directly engage gender issues. Four narrators whose diary entries we read at different moments in this work seem to be women, but the plot wouldn't change much if they were men. And there are men who play important roles as well, most noticeably Oli, Ann's son and partner in the Reset plan who arrives in a spaceship made of biodegradable material, presumably to manage the Reset operation on the ground.[20] The desire for intervention into the cruelties humans exercise on one another and on animals does not have to be gendered, the story seems to say; cruelty is a human feature. A feminist reading of "Reset" is possible in how the intervention is into a world constructed predominantly by men according to masculine pursuits of expansion and exploitation. The intervention can be done by both men and women, but regardless of who does it, it will be an attempt to resist what Joanna Russ calls "the culture from a single point of view–the male" (Russ 81). Breaking away from a simple gender role switch,[21] many recent science fiction works by Korean women writers are less bound by bifurcated notions of gender.[22] What makes "Reset" a feminist work is the very premise of the story: that the world needs to be reimagined, *reset* to become free of centuries of evil and inertia built for the most part under a patriarchal world order.

4. Kim Choyeop: "My Space Hero"[23] (2019)

> The result is that these very familiar plots simply won't work. They are tales for heroes, not heroines, and one of the things that handicaps women writers in our—and every other—culture is that there are so very few stories in which women can figure as protagonists.
>
> Culture is male. (Russ 80)

What is the first image we conjure when we hear "space hero"? Real-life female astronauts come easily to mind: Sally Ride (1951-2012), the first American woman to fly in space; Christa McAuliffe (1948-1986), the teacher-astronaut whose life was lost in the tragic failed launch of the space shuttle Challenger; and Korea's only astronaut, Soyeon Yi (Yi So-yŏn b.1978).[24] Films such as *Gravity* (2013), *Interstellar* (2014), and *The Silent Sea* (Koyoŭi pada, 2021) also feature leading women in space, so the premise of female astronauts in Kim Choyeop's short story "My Space Hero" (Naŭi ujuyŏng'unge kwanhayŏ) is not new. Since the 1980s, each example of women in space has served as heroic inspiration for a younger generation. As with Chung Serang's "Reset," it is not the simple reversal of gender roles (woman astronaut) that qualifies Kim Choyeop's story as a feminist work. Rather, Kim's story questions the very structure of how a woman often becomes a hero: by achieving exactly the same things men do, and perhaps executing the mission even better than a man would. Success in the mission is defined by following the course of training and fulfilling expectations, and this seems to be gender-neutral, an equal opportunity to become a hero through a given mission regardless of which gender carries it out. But, when culture surrounding the mission and the very definition of its success are "male," how does a woman become a hero? When the expectation for a woman is not just to do what a man would do, but to be a man, which thus sets her mission up for failure, what can she do? Can or should she set her own terms of success?

The story features numerous social biases, and it shows how they operate through the life of a female astronaut, Chaegyŏng, who was believed to have perished during her mission. Several years later, Kayun, who has a daughter-niece relation to Chaegyŏng, is chosen for a re-do of a mission to travel through a "tunnel," a black-hole like passage found near Mars, to explore the universe at its other end. Chaegyŏng was an astrophysicist and, at the time of her selection for the mission, was forty-eight years old, of petite stature, and suffered chronic vestibular disorder. The scientific establishment thus deemed her inadequate to represent the human race ("inryu taep'yo") (Kim "Naŭi Uju Yŏng'ung e Kwanhayŏ," 279). Yet she was selected, and suspicions circulated through the media were that it was because she was a woman, and an Asian, and could thus address the optics of political correctness and regional and sexual balance. Interestingly, the selection was done by an AI, who calculated that her giving birth to a child was proof of her mental endurance.

The story opens with an announcement that Kayun has been selected for the Tunnel mission and it ends with her reaching the other side of the Tunnel, thus becoming the first human to survive the journey. But while Kayun fulfills the mission that her mother-aunt figure never did, Kayun ponders the significance of the "success": if humans can achieve the tunnel mission only after giving up the human body and transforming it almost entirely through a pantropic process called cyborg grinding, as both Kayun and Chaegyŏng before her did, is that a success for the human race?

The success of Kayun's journey through the tunnel is somewhat played down, perhaps to focus better on her thoughts as she processes the event. She seeks to understand Chaegyŏng's disappearance—not the accidental death they were told about, but her dive into the ocean the night before the mission launch. This reflection turns into a question regarding how a woman becomes a hero, what it means to "complete" a "mission" as a woman, for whom, and why.[25]

The woman's body emerges as a focal point in "My Space Hero." A scene in which Chaegyŏng is interviewed about her expectations for the upcoming trip is revealing: in describing her experience of being pregnant, she says that the primitive nature of it all made her imagine having a different body. When Kayun goes through the same cyborg grinding process that Chaegyŏng did years prior, she starts to understand Chaegyŏng's choice not to go through with the mission. Living in a woman's body proved to be a "handicap," a reason to disqualify Chaegyŏng from representing the human race according to media views that never fully accepted the AI's choice.[26] If one gets a new body that transcends the limitations and handicaps of the old, then why remain within the same social structure that has denied her already? Why not pursue one's own mission?

The question of body is also related to ableism, a topic frequently found in women's SF in Korea. In Kim Choyeop's case, her own hearing disorder comes up often in interviews, along with her degrees in Chemical Engineering and Biochemistry from the prestigious Pohang Institute of Technology. While Kim Choyeop is considered among the brightest stars in the current South Korean SF market, her questions regarding ableism, ageism, and unthinking pursuit of scientific discoveries, among others, reflect her own experiences of disability and her experience as a female graduate student in a STEM field. The question of body in "My Space Hero" is tied to the futility and problem of representation, namely, why must an astronaut possess qualifications deemed representative of the "human race," and why does the default representation have to be a young physically fit man? What does it matter, and to whom? Even in the midst of debating whether Chaegyŏng could indeed represent humankind, she is also seen as a representative for people pushed to the margins. As Kayun puts it, "she overrepresented and underrepresented at the same time" (297).[27]

The question of representation also expands to the question of individual choice. When a person gets a body like no other's, should her success or failure still be understood as representing a group? Kayun's answer is no. By saying "a failure by someone sometimes becomes the failure of the whole group to which the person belonged, but some other failure does not," she accepts the choice of Chaegyŏng's jumping off a cliff into the sea, an optimal environment for her body newly transformed through cyborg grinding (308). By living Chaegyŏng's experience and transformation, Kayun comes to an understanding that having that body was Chaegyŏng's goal, and reaching the deep ocean where her new body could thrive was a successful completion of *her* mission.

Kayun completes the tunnel mission despite how she, too, started to doubt its purpose—that the Tunnel was only mathematical data until value was created by the need to travel through it (315). As Chaegyŏng predicted, the other side of the Tunnel is a universe with stars and nebulas, not so different from the familiar side. Has it been worthwhile putting so many resources, including the lives of astronauts, on the line? Chaegyŏng's answer was no, and she chose her new world accordingly, a place in tune with her new body. Kayun's decision to stay on the mission thereby gains significance, not for the human race or national pride, but because she wants to see the other side of "this universe," a space that is left for Kayun to explore without burden because "Chaegyŏng took it with her to the deep sea," the burden of being an Asian woman astronaut, a suspicion that she was chosen out of consideration for minorities and not for her capabilities, and the doubt over whether she really could complete the mission (315). Such an ending is anticlimactic if one expects the main protagonist to resonate with some heroic vibe that is supposed to accompany mission success. Instead, the ending is calm: Kayun pushes buttons for her fellow astronauts to wake up, looks out the window, and thinks that if one day she meets her hero, she'll tell her the view of space on the other side was not bad. This ending seems yet another twist from Kim Choyeop, a contrast to the hero's story in a genealogy of men. Kayun inherits an unfulfilled mission from her aunt-mother, already a non-linear genealogy forged through friendship between two single mothers. On the surface, Kayun is fulfilling Chaegyŏng's unaccomplished goal, but in reality, they have been engaged in two different missions, and neither is defined as boldly reaching where no one has gone before. Chaegyŏng's goal was to have a different body that would enable her to explore a new world that was better for her, and Kayun's is to understand her hero Chaegyŏng through living Chaegyŏng's experience. Not a conventional hero's tale if that's what one expected, but in subverting cliches in narratives regarding space missions, "My Space Hero" writes a "new myth" just as "Reset" does.[28]

Epilogue

Ursula K Le Guin (1929-2018) has been critically acclaimed in SF since the late 1960s in the US, but in South Korea, the earliest translation of her work according to the National Library of Korea, was *The Left Hand of Darkness* in 1986. Several works by Le Guin were introduced in the mid 1990s under the classification young adult literature. A few more translations followed in the mid

2000s, but this time they were marketed as adult SF as they slowly gained niche readership through internet-based fan groups. Finally, a more comprehensive six-volume set of her major works was translated and published in 2014.[29] The trajectory clearly shows that domestic socio-cultural factors were important for change and growth of the SF and fantasy genres. Such factors include fall of the authority of *mundan*, a weakened boundary between lowbrow and highbrow literature, and the rise of diverse groups of writers including women and younger generation writers in the 1990s and early 2000s. It seems no mere chance that Kim Bo-young and DJUNA[30] started publishing their works on the internet during this era.

The Korean translation of *To Write like a Woman: Essays in Feminism and Science*, a collection of essays by Joanna Russ, is another case that shows the locally-driven characteristics of feminist SF in South Korea. The majority of essays in Russ's book were written in the 1970s, the rest in the 1980s, and assembled as a book in 1995. It was translated into Korean under the title "How SF became a playground for women" (SF nŭn ŏttŏke yŏjadŭl ŭi norit'ŏga toeŏtna) and was published in the summer of 2020 during a wave of intense interest in women's SF. That the collection was "discovered" several decades later from the opposite side of the globe tells us that foreign works of SF and feminist theorists of SF and posthumanism were summoned, sometimes belatedly, to explain and understand the Korean literary and social phenomenon in a wider global context. As a result, imported feminist SF theories have served as affirmations of efforts by Korean women SF writers in creating their own worlds from scratch during a time when there was no room in the literary tradition for such imagination.[31] What South Korean writers found through Le Guin's works and Joanna Russ's essays from the 1970s US confirms the shared reality women have confronted in a patriarchal literary and social world regardless of their geographic, temporal, and cultural differences. For scholars who have long observed how modern Korean literary history took shape around major impacts from early 20th-century European literature, discovering the autochthonous origin of women's SF in South Korea is almost a shock.[32] Such an original impulse deserves significant scholarly attention.

That impulse seems even more remarkable precisely because it emerged through tenacity and effort rather than magic or some alignment of stars. As Oh Ŭn'gyo notes, women's SF was no "Big Bang" or overnight success. She observes Kim Bo-young's winding career journey filled with setbacks, lack of income structure for internet-based SF writers, and sporadic SF literary competitions with meager prize money. Those headwinds required sufficient drive to produce momentum among SF writers including those working in graphic novels, which eventually resulted in a genealogy and archive of women's work in fantasy and science fiction. As Oh and Kim Bo-young herself both testify, women have been building this tradition for decades through what they have enjoyed doing despite the absence of any spotlight. Finally, the world has caught up with this effort and now shines new light on how we look at these works, an overdue development (Oh 364-80).

Along with feminist works like *The Vegetarian* by Han Kang (English translation released 2015) and *Kim Jiyoung, Born 1982* by Cho Nam-joo (English translation released in 2020)—two prominent faces in Korean literature globally—women's SF has created a space for Korean feminist voices to manifest. If *Kim Jiyoung, Born 1982*, through use of statistics from real history, laid bare the incessant and ubiquitous gender discrimination a woman faces in day-to-day life, SF allows a very different approach for giving women a voice, a Haraway-esque one that departs from and challenges dichotomy. In contrast to utopias or apocalypses created by male authors for their works, women's SF contains a "vision of freedom," Chŏng Ŭn'gyŏng argues, a vision both spawned by and a transcendence of limitations women face in the current society of strict gender binaries. In her reading of Korean feminist SF, Chŏng calls the multiple, flexible, or singular sexualities shown in these works a practice of cyborg feminism per Haraway's notion, one that offers not only a "gender utopia" but also a "humanitarian practice for liberating humanity" (Chŏng 35).

This article has focused on introducing the recent rise of women's SF in South Korea and explored three short-stories as examples. It seems fitting, and perhaps prescient, that all three stories end with a hopeful vision based in independent thinking and freedom of making one's own decision. Kim Bo-young's *Resemblance* juxtaposes two questions—the classic SF one, "What is being a human?", and the other a present-day preoccupation, "What happens if one denies the existence of gender inequality?"— transposed to a space travel setting. It ends with HUN, the AI with newly gained insights into human emotions, perceptions, and self-awareness, making the altruistic decision to descend to Titan with supplies to save people's lives. Chung Serang describes a stop-and-reset for a post-capitalistic society as it heads to self-destruction, but instead of imagining a doom or apocalypse, the "reset" turns out to be a new hopeful beginning for coexistence of all beings on earth. Kim Choyeop disrupts the typical expectation of space exploration—expansion and conquest—by showing the absurdity of such thought. The achievements of the protagonists portrayed in "My Space Hero" lie in the pursuit of freedom for them both.

SF is thus no longer an odd gap or anomaly in the literary history of Korea. Works introduced in this paper showcase how "new myth" (Joanna Russ) is being written by Korean women writers, as a caution about many challenges Koreans face and indeed humanity faces at the dawn of the Fourth Industrial Revolution, but also as a projection of hope, if we get them right. One crucial aspect of that hopeful vision is an inclusive future where differences—including among genders, species, and between human and cyborg—are embraced and appreciated. Furthermore, the radical future they suggest does not just subvert the current rules to make this world a more inclusive and equitable place. The urgency of this project lies in how radically our world gets reimagined in each story. By creating an entirely new world—and perhaps only by doing so—the human race along with its ecosystem (animals, plants) may survive on earth as we know it. Feminist SF's conventional agenda of writing a new myth thus gains another mission in this era of climate change: to save the world, literally and figuratively, through its critique of the current world and its vision for the future.

Notes

1. Science fiction in South Korea is a loosely defined term that encompasses fictional works that are apocalyptic, Gothic, superhero, supernatural, or fantastical. Genre fiction or speculative fiction (sabyŏn sosŏl) are better and more correct terms in this context, but neither of them are widely used in South Korea compared to "SF". While there is a debate among fans and writers themselves on what is "science fiction" and whether what they are writing and reading are indeed "SF," in South Korea in 2022, SF seems to have become the brand that sells. The "SF" boom in contemporary Korea is as much a social phenomenon as it is a literary one and thus, the use of the term science fiction (SF) in this paper will refer to fictional works marketed and received as "SF" in Korea, which includes what is often distinguished as fantasy in North America.

2. The McCune-Reischauer Romanization system is used in this paper. Exceptions are made for individual names as they appear in published material including books, films, interviews and articles in English, on the assumption that those published forms are preferred by the person.

3. One of the anonymous reviewers of this paper noted that *Snowpiercer* (2013) is missing from this exploration. I omitted it from present consideration because it was based on a French original graphic novel and produced in Hollywood. I do agree with the reviewer's view on the

film's contribution in triggering the trend of SF films in Korea's film industry

4. Many changes have occurred since 2017, of course, too many to list here. Among them were changes in the publishing environment in South Korea, which then supported the rise of science fiction and speculative fiction. See Yi, Yunghee (2019) and Heekyoung Cho (2021) for the role of platform companies in the South Korean mediascape. Articles included in the special issue themed "Science and Literature in North and South Korea" of *The Journal of Korean Studies* (Vol. 23, Issue 2, 2018) are a valuable source on Korean SF in general. One of the reviewers also noted several sources to help fill the gap: a 2021 blog post by Lee, Ji-Yong titled "Introducing Korean Sci-Fi!"; an article by the same author "Han'guk SF ŭi genre-jŏk kaebyŏlsŏng kwa hyŏndae-jŏk chujae ŭisik." [Genre Individuality and Modern Theme Consciousness of Korean SF]. *Han'guk yŏn'gu*, no. 8, 2021, pp. 37–68; and Kang, Ŭn'gyo's 2022 thesis from Ewha Womans University titled "A Study on DJUNA's SF as Feminist Worlding." I am grateful for these valuable suggestions.

5. Due to the limited scope of this paper, there is not much coverage on the origins and theories of feminist SF in general. I am grateful for one reviewer's suggestions for references on this topic.

6. This character turns out to be a gender-fluid figure whose voice and also function as a battle machine suggest maleness, but who buys the body of a young woman later in the film. As a side note, the Korean name means a child left at the doorway of a wealthy(-ier) family, and the common belief is that such a baby brings luck to the adoptive family. This robot character's story is not explained in the film, but the name suggests that the robot was found at a dumpster during a regular salvage business operation and was fixed and adopted as their crew, thus adding a sense of family to their relationship.

7. For an overview of the SF genre in both South and North Korea, see Yi, Chi-yong (2017) and Pak, Sang-jun (2005).

8. During research for this article, I found that the link between SF and children's literature still exists: many academic articles on SF appeared in the journal *Ch'angbi Ŏrini*, which specializes in children's literature.

9. One interesting exception is Mun Yusŏng's *Perfect Society* (Wanjŏn sahoe, 1965), a novel about a utopia ruled by women, which targeted adult readers. See Yi, Chiyong (2017), p.172.

10. See Yi, Sŏnok (2016) for more on techno-nationalism.

11. As seen in *The Dwarf* (1978, English tran. 2006) by Cho, Se-hŭi (1942-2022), a different approach to telling the truth through allegories, fables, and other flights of imagination coexisted during this time despite the strongly favored literary realism. See Youngju Ryu (2016) for a more detailed literary history under the Park Chung Hee regime.

12. Yi Munyŏl (b.1943)'s "The General and The Doctor" (1989) is another example of alternative history. See also Kim, Dahye (2022), pp. 305-327 for a change of publication venue brought on by proliferation of internet access and cases of online web-based serialized "amateur" work in this era.

13. *Mundan* is often translated as "literary world" that includes authors and critics and their activities. It is an institution in the sense that to become a member of *mundan* one must either win a competition sanctioned and refereed by people in *mundan*, or one's work must be recommended by a respected senior member of *mundan* to a prestigious literary magazine that is published or acknowledged by *mundan*. Sanctions, endorsements, acknowledgements are mostly done through tacit agreement—indeed, this kind of institutionalization through networks describes the tight-knit elite society of South Korea more broadly.

14. On lack of popularity of SF in Korea, Kim Bo-young hints at this pressure for conformity by saying that "there was a pressure to read only certain kinds of novels" in her interview given in 2017 (http://ch.yes24.com/Article/View/33852).

15. Allegations of sexual misconduct and violence started to come out in 2016. For a case that involved poet Ko Ŭn (b.1933) see Bo Seo, "The #MeToo Poem That Brought Down Korea's Most Revered Poet," available at *The Paris Review* (blog), April 30, 2018 (https://www.theparisreview.org/blog/2018/04/30/the-metoo-poem-that-brought-down-koreas-most-revered-poet/).

16. See Haeyeon Choo (2021) for differences found in the Korean #MeToo movement. Also see Kim, Yang-sŏn (2017) and Kim, Ŭn-ha

(2019) for how #MeToo and calls for a "feminism reboot" have affected efforts to rewrite a history of feminist literature in Korea.

17. According to various news reports including one on Yŏnhap News dated October 1, 2021, between 2015-2020, suicide rates among 20-year-old women grew by 64.5%, the highest among all age groups among both men and women. While overall expectations for gender equality have grown, inequality still prevails in the job market, and the lack of help in post-traumatic mental healthcare for sexual violence and violent crimes targeting this group are believed to be contributing factors. https://www.yna.co.kr/view/AKR20210930161600002

18. For example, abolishing the Ministry of Gender Equality and Family became one of the major campaign promises of the conservative candidate who subsequently became the president.

19. In Ayŏng points out that a robot is already gendered when it is designed and used to offer customized service to humans in a docile manner (50). In this sense, an assumption of female gender for HUN, regardless of the shape of its humanoid body, seems reasonable, which contradicts a more common perception of robots as male-like with its metal body and lack of emotion.

20. This mother-son pair connection is implied in Anne's remark on her own name, Anne from Annelid, given by her mothers who were both scientists studying annelids. Oli, from oligochaeta, would have been her name if she were born a boy. Anne recognizes Oli as her son when he arrives from the future because of the name. The biodegradable spaceship is the same kind of ship that brought giant earthworms and triggered the Reset.

21. As a contrast, simple role reversal has been a notable formula in Korean films for the last two decades. Examples include: *Joint Security Area* (2000) directed by Park Chan-wook, in which a male character in the original novel *DMZ* (1997) by Pak Sangyŏn was changed to Major Sophie Jang, a woman. The legendary North Korean sniper appearing in *The Frontline* (2011), directed by Jang Hoon, was played by Kim Ok-bin, a character based on a historical figure, a male sniper during the Korean War. Subsequently, a young beautiful woman with a big gun became a trope in Korean films and dramas: *Assassination* (2015) and the drama series *Mr. Sunshine* (2018) both featured women assassins for Korea's

independence. These two latter examples were not a simple sex change, but they are not entirely free from using the sex ("woman") for spectacle and shock value.

22. In such an operation, one of the peculiarities of Korean SF comes from the Korean language which often does not specify gender, so writers can easily hide the gender of a character. Pronouns are not as often used in Korean language, which instead uses names or precise words of appellation (e.g. "nuna" for older sister by a speaker who is a man, "imo" for an aunt who is a sister of the speaker's mother, etc.) to designate a relationship between the person speaking and the one referred to. The gender-unspecified third person pronoun "그" is often tied to the rise of modern literature in which characters may appear without names or without revealing relationships between people. Unlike "kǔ", the female-specific "kǔnyǒ" didn't achieve wide usage during this time. For feminist and SF writers, this linguistic feature provides room for fluidity in representing gender, and Sim Wansǒn's collection of interviews show all six writers (five women, one man) do not use "kǔnyǒ." See Sim, Wansǒn (2022).

23. The title of this story uses the generic (male) form for "hero," but in Korean language, the feminine form of a noun is made by attaching "woman" (yǒ-, yǒja-) to the default word. However, this practice is done when there is a need to indicate the sex for a contrast. The word for "heroine" would be "yǒja yǒngung", but it is completely natural to use "yǒngung" for both.

24. Yi was selected and trained by the Korean space program as one of two astronauts (the other, a male astronaut, was a backup) to be sent to space through the Russian space program. After going through training, she was chosen to board the space shuttle for a ten-day mission to the International Space Station in 2008.

25. Instead of a conventional father-son setting where a son sets out to complete an unfulfilled mission of his father, who died tragically, a woman astronaut who is not tied to the "aunt" by blood inherits the incomplete mission in this story. The gender switch (to women), the absence of biological ties between the two figures, and redefinition of mission success and failure in distinctive ways for each protagonist, can all be read as subversion of the familiar trope of a hero's tale.

26. In the context of limits of (female) body, Sunyoung Park's following comment in explaining Kim Bo-young's works seems applicable here as well: "(O)vercoming human form, in Kim's world, is not quite a way of transcending our limits, as is often the case in superhero narratives, but rather a desperate attempt to survive by the marginalized and the vulnerable" (299).

27. All translations of quoted passages from the Korean original are mine unless noted otherwise.

28. Certain elements in this short-story recall Donna Haraway's "Cyborg Manifesto," aside from the obvious pantropic process that changes a body into a super-human, a cyborg. While Haraway's manifesto is a feminist essay, it is also deeply ironic in criticizing bifurcated identity politics of feminism and suggests ways of breaking down its boundaries and structures by emphasizing embodiment, situated knowledge, and "liminal transformation". "My Space Hero" does not stage an overt intervention or subversion, and instead questions the process of how values operate in human society. The anticlimactic ending where Kayun calmly opens her eyes after successfully reaching the other side of the Tunnel and finds just another big empty space with stars as Chaegyŏng predicted, can be read as a transcendent moment not unlike what Haraway reached for in her essay.

29. According to the record available through the National Library of Korea, *A Wizard of Earthsea* (1968) and *The Tombs of Atuan* (1970) were published by Ungjin Ch'ulp'an as children's books in 1994 and 1993 respectively. Hwanggŭm kaji (est. 1996), a subsidiary of Minŭmsa, one of the biggest publishing houses in South Korea, republished *A Wizard of Earthsea* as a 3-volume series between 2002-2004. *Dispossessed* (1974) was also published in 2002 in Korean translation by the same publisher. Sigongsa, another publisher known for genre literature, published several translations of Le Guin's works including *The Left Hand of Darkness* (1969) in 2002 and *Planet of Exile* (1966) in 2005.

30. DJUNA is a pen-name of one of the first and most influential writers of SF and film criticism on the internet from the 1990s. Personal information including name and age are not available, and although it is presumed that DJUNA is a woman, DJUNA's gender was also not officially acknowledged by the writer. Although a minority view, there is

some speculation DJUNA is a group of several writers. For this reason, combined with the limited scope of this paper, DJUNA's contribution to the rise of women's SF is not discussed in this paper. For more on DJUNA, see Kang, Ŭn'gyo's master's thesis (2022).

31. Several collections of essays and interviews by Le Guin have also been translated and published in South Korea since 2019.

32. Korean SF in general was much more than just an adaptation of imported space opera or other blockbusters: it featured Korean characters with Korean names and settings congruent with Korean society. Given that the majority targeted children and young adult readers, these Korean features may be seen as related to nationalist sentiment expected in educational material. However, this may have resulted in shifting the genre toward stronger ties to its domestic roots and local characteristics.

Works Cited

Cho, Heekyoung. "The Platformization of Culture: Webtoon Platforms and Media Ecology in Korea and Beyond." *The Journal of Asian Studies*, vol. 80, no. 1, 2021, pp. 73–93.

Chŏng, Ŭn'gyŏng. "SF wa gender utopia." [SF and Gender Utopia] *Chaŭm kwa moŭm*, vol. 42, Sept. 2019, pp. 22–35.

Chung, Se-rang (Chŏng, Serang). "Reset." In *Moksori rŭl tŭrilgeyo: Chŏng Serang sosŏljip*. Seoul: Ajak, 2019.

Haraway, Donna Jeanne. "A Cyborg Manifesto: Science, Technology, and Socialist-Feminism in the Late Twentieth Century." In *Manifestly Haraway*. Minneapolis, MN: University of Minnesota Press, 2016.

Hŏ, Yun. "Ilhal su ŏpnŭn mom ŭl chŏnyu hanŭn feminist SF ŭi sangsang ryŏk—Kim Bo-young sosŏl ŭl chungsim ŭro." [Feminist SF's Imagination for 'Disabled Body'—On Kim Bo-young's novels] *Yŏsŏng munhak yŏn'gu*, vol. 52, 2021, pp. 10–35.

In, Ayŏng. "Gender ro SF hagi" [Doing SF with Gender]. *Chaŭm kwa moŭm*, vol. 42, Sept. 2019, pp. 46–58.

Kang, Ŭn'gyo. *Feminist Wordling rosŏ DJUNA ŭi SF e taehan yŏn'gu* [A Study on DJUNA's SF as Feminist Wordling]. M.A. Thesis. Ewha Womans University, 2022.

Kim, Bo-young (Kim, Poyŏng). "Ŏlmana Talmannŭn'ga." In *Ŏlmana Talmannŭn'ga: Kim Po-Yŏng Sosŏljip*. Seoul: Ajak, 2020. pp.249-339.

———. "SF sosŏl 'Ŏlmana talmatnŭnga' ŭi chŏja Kim Bo-young chakka waŭi interview." [An Interview with Kim Bo-young, the author of SF 'Resemblance'] *Marie Claire*, 14 January 2021, https://www.marieclairekorea.com/lifestyle/2021/01/how-much-does-it-resemble/.

Kim, Chonghyŏn. "Muosi 20-dae yŏsŏng ŭl chŏlbak hage hana… kŭpchŭng hanŭn kŭktan sŏnt'aek" [What Makes Women in the 20s Desperate… A Rapid Rise of Suicide]. Yonhap News, 1 Oct. 2021, https://www.yna.co.kr/view/AKR20210930161600002.

Kim, Choyeop (Kim, Ch'oyŏp). "Naŭi Uju Yŏng'ung e Kwanhayŏ." In *Uri Ka Pit Ŭi Sokto Ro Kal Su Ŏptamyŏn: Kim Ch'oyŏp Sosŏl*. Seoul: Hŏbŭl, 2019, pp. 273–319.

Kim, Dahye. "Who Is Afraid of Techno-Fiction? The Emergence of Online Science Fiction in the Age of Informatization." *Journal of Korean Studies* 27, no. 2 (2022), 305-327.

Kim, Yangsŏn. "Feminist Reboot wa 'Kim Jiyoung' hyŏnsang—'82-nyŏnsaeng Kim Jiyoung'" [Feminism Re-boot and 'Kim Jiyoung' Syndrome—Cho Namju's *Kim Jiyoung born in 1982.*" *Feminism and Korean Literature*, no. 42, 2017, pp. 283–87.

Kim, Yunju. "Kim Bo-young, SF naegae nŏmudo sarangsŭrŏun genre" [Kim Bo-young, SF is a Precious Genre for Me], *Channel YES24.* 2022, http://ch.yes24.com/Article/View/48436.

Kim Ŭnha. "Munhak chŏngchŏn ŭi haech'ae wa chae kusŏng" [The Decomposition and Reorganization of Literary Anthology: Finding the Origin and Identity of Women's Writing]. *Feminism and Korean Literature*, no. 48, 2019, pp. 60–86.

Ko, Changwŏn. "Hanguk SF wa yŏsŏng ŭi sisŏn: Chŏng So-yŏn sosŏljip yŏpjip ŭi yŏnghŭi ssi" [Korean SF and Women's Gaze: *Ms. Yŏnghŭi Next Door* by Chŏng So-yŏn]. *Ch'angbi ŏrini*, vol.52, Mar. 2016, pp. 231–34.

Lee, Ji-Eun. "(Dis)Embodiment of Memory." *The Routledge Companion to Korean Literature*, by Heekyoung Cho, 1st ed., New York, NY: Routledge, 2022, pp. 357–70.

Lee, Ji-Yong. "Introducing Korean Sci-Fi!," *K-Book Trends*, 8 Mar. 2021, https://www.kbook-eng.or.kr/sub/trend.php?ptype=view&idx=462&page=$page&code=trend.

———. (Yi, Chiyong). "Hanbando SF ŭi yuip kwa genre paljŏn yangsang." [Importation of SF to the Korean Peninsula and the Development of the Genre]. *Tonga inmunhak*, vol. 40. Sept. 2017, pp. 157–89.

———. "Han'guk SF ŭi genre-jŏk kaebyŏlsŏng kwa hyŏndae-jŏk chujae ŭisik." [Genre Individuality and Modern Theme Consciousness of Korean SF]. *Han'guk yŏn'gu*, no. 8, 2021, pp. 37–68.

Oh, Ŭn'gyo. "Tokcha order-made sosŏl, 'genre munhak' tamron kwa hanguk SF munhak i kŏrŏ on ŏnŭ kil" [Readers' Order-made Novel, Discourse on 'genre literature' and a Trajectory for Korean SF]. *Chaŭm kwa moŭm*, vol. 44, 2020, pp. 364–80.

Pak, Sangjun. "21-segi, hanguk, kŭrigo SF" [21st Century, Korea, and SF]. *Onŭl ŭi munye pip'yŏng*, vol. 59, 2005, pp. 44–58.

Pae, Sangmin. "Hanguk SF sosŏl ŭi ssiat tŭl" [Seeds of Korean SF]. *Chaŭm kwa moŭm*, vol. 34, 2017, pp. 294–305.

Park, Sunyoung. "Between Science and Politics: Science Fiction as a Critical Discourse in South Korea, 1960s–1990s." *Journal of Korean Studies*, vol. 23, no. 2, Oct. 2018, pp. 347–67.

———, editor. *Readymade Bodhisattva: The Kaya Anthology of South Korean Science Fiction*. Los Angeles, CA: Kaya Press, 2019.

———. "Afterword" in Kim, Bo-young, *On the Origin of Species and Other Stories*. Los Angeles, CA: Kaya Press, 2021. pp.298-300.

Russ, Joanna. "What Can a Heroine Do? Or Why Women Can't Write." In *To Write Like a Woman: Essays in Feminism and Science*, Bloomington, IN: Indiana University Press, 1995, pp. 79–93.

Ryu, Youngju. *Writers of the Winter Republic: Literature and Resistance in Park Chung Hee's Korea*. University of Hawai'i Press, 2016.

Seo, Bo. "The #MeToo Poem That Brought Down Korea's Most Revered Poet." *The Paris Review*, 30 Apr. 2018, https://www.theparisreview.org/blog/2018/04/30/the-metoo-poem-that-brought-down-koreas-most-revered-poet/.

Shin, Haerin. "The Curious Case of South Korean Science Fiction: A Hyper-Technological Society's Call for Speculative Imagination." *Azalea: Journal of Korean Literature & Culture*, vol. 6, no. 1, 2013, pp. 81–85.

Sim, Wansŏn. *Uri Nŭn SF rŭl Choahae: Onŭl ŭl Ssŭnŭn Han'guk ŭi SF Chakka Int'ŏbyujip* [We Like SF: Interviews of SF Writers]. Seoul: Minŭmsa, 2022.

Sin, Yŏnsŏn. "Kim Bo-young, SF man ssŭnŭn charkanŭn chŏkchiman SF sosŏl ŭn mugung mujin" *Channel YES24*. 2017, http://ch.yes24.com/Article/View/33852.

Yi, Sŏnok. "1960-nyŏndae kwahakchuŭi wa gender ŭi chaegusŏng: 'Sasanggye' rŭl chungsimŭro" [Research on Discourse of Scientism and Gender in 1960s Magazine 'Sasanggye']. *Yŏsŏng munhak yŏn'gu*, no. 39, 2016, pp. 261–302.

———. "1960-nyŏndae kwahakchuŭi tamron ŭi sinch'aehwa: 'Yŏhaksaeng' e nat'anan sonyŏ wa sach'ungi" [Research on the somatization of scientific discourse in the 1960s: Girls and puberty in the magazine 'yeohagsaeng']. *Yŏsŏng munhak yŏn'gu*, no. 42, 2017, pp. 225–54.

Yi, Yunghŭi. "Web sosŏl ŭi ch'angjakcha wa platform kujo" [Creators of Web-novels and the Structure of the Platform]. *Chaŭm kwa moŭm*, vol. 40, 2019, pp. 169–78.

Zur, Dafna. "Epilogue: The Turn to Science in Postwar North and South Korea." *Figuring Korean Futures: Children's Literature in Modern Korea*. Palo Alto, CA: Stanford University Press, 2017. pp. 191-214.

Two Can Play This *Squid Game:* The Japanese Entanglements of South Korean Speculative Fiction

Se Young Kim

T HE CINDERELLA STORY of South Korean media continued in 2021 with the astronomic success of *Squid Game*, the show becoming one of the country's most successful efforts to date. Produced with an initial $21 million investment, the show has returned an estimated $900 million for Netflix. In addition, *Squid Game* was the major driving force behind 4,380,000 new subscribers from July to September along with a record stock evaluation of $700 per share on November 19 of that year (Hayes, Shaw, Sherman). As part of *Hallyu* (the Korean Wave or Waves, as it were), *Squid Game* joins numerous other television series, films, video games, and music produced in South Korea and successfully exported since the late 1990s. As has consistently been the case over the last twenty-plus years, discussions around *Squid Game* attempt to understand why and how the show has been able to resonate with audiences to the degree that it has. Due to the fact that the series very clearly borrowed its central premise from *Battle Royale* (both Fukasaku Kinji's 2000 film and Takami Koushun's 1999 novel), much of the talk has centered around the familiar discussion on uniqueness and originality.[1] But even before it had become a full-blown phenomenon, South Korean commentators on YouTube and Twitter identified the striking similarities between *Squid Game* and another post-*Battle Royale* text, Miike Takashi's 2014 film *As the Gods Will*, based on Kaneshiro Muneyuki and Fujiomura Akeji's manga. More specifically, those critics focused on what would become one of the key viral images from the show, the Red Light, Green Light robot, noting that it shared striking similarities to the Daruma creature in Miike's film (General). The resemblance was strong enough that creator Hwang Dong-hyuk eventually addressed the accusations, acknowledging the influence of Japanese popular culture but denying any conscious malfeasance (Lee).

There are several things at stake in these discussions. One regards the nature of *Squid Game*'s success and whether it is merely an issue of sheer luck, or if Hwang Dong-hyuk deserves all the accolades that have been thrown his way. A relatively unknown filmmaker up until *Squid Game*, Hwang is at the time of writing in pre-production of the second season. In a broader sense, Hwang's tenuous status as a new and upcoming auteur fits into the ongoing discussion regarding the whole of contemporary South Korean media. One of the key reasons that the country has elicited such interest is because it is one of the few to successfully export the majority of its media, when global Hollywood domination is understood to be the natural way of things. To a certain degree, both internationally and domestically, there remains a certain amount of disbelief and skepticism regarding the popularity of South Korean media, with substantial focus on how the popularity can be prolonged. Much of the discussion on *Hallyu* both in and outside of scholarship has regarded its particularity, whether in terms of its regional specificity or its artistic uniqueness (a quick web search of "*Hallyu*" yields pages of results dedicated to that very topic).

Indeed, the charges of plagiarism against *Squid Game* belong in a longer history, seen for example in the way that the term "K-Pop" was derived from "J-Pop" (Lie 96). I bring up that example to signal yet another area where Japan reappears in consideration of South Korean media. Despite the many confluences in South Korean and Japanese media, the two countries of course share a much thornier history, from the end of the nineteenth century and into the twentieth, with Korea becoming a protectorate of Japan in 1905 before it was annexed in 1910. While the end of World War II marked the end of colonization, antipathy has persisted to this day, coalesced around, for example, Japan's response to the "comfort women" (meaning girls and women from Korea and other occupied countries forced into sexual slavery during World War II) and the sovereignty dispute over the Liancourt Rocks. Media has been another contested arena, with the Law for Punishing Anti-National Deeds enacted in 1945 outlawing Japanese culture in South Korea until 1998. In fact, it was the lifting of the ban and the importation of Japanese media that played a part in *Hallyu*, as Korean producers increased their efforts in anticipation of this "foreign invasion." And yet, well before the Korean Wave, and despite its ostensibly illegal status, Japanese culture was a mainstay in the country throughout the second half of the twentieth century, both semi-legally and illegally. To be more specific, Japanese comics and animation have maintained a heavy presence in South Korea, as the formats easily lent themselves to dubbing and editing. In particular, Japanese science fiction enjoyed a great deal of popularity because it allowed settings that were less distinctly Japanese and was thus more convenient for Korean importation (Sugawa-Shimada 177).

At the same time, those texts also make evident the dynamism of cultural flow that resists legal parameters and troubles strictly nationalist narratives. Against discussions centered on intellectual property and artistic merit, placing *Squid Game* in this broader historical context of cultural interchange between Japan and South Korean offers us an opportunity to consider how the two countries have interacted through science fiction. That opportunity, in turn, also allows us to tease out the particularity of the form in the South Korean context. In this article, I will use *Squid Game* as a starting point to trace the sustained engagement between South Korea and Japan through science fiction in order to begin considering a practice of East Asian speculative fiction. I begin with *Squid Game*'s main interlocutors, *Battle Royale* and *As the Gods Will,* as well as *Gantz,* the multimedia franchise that began as a manga (2000-2013) by Oku Hiroya. From these texts, *Squid Game* inherits the fundamental motif of apocalyptic imaginations of deadly games occupied by technology, extraterrestrials, and nonhuman entities. But well before *Squid Game* and in spite of the 1945 ban, manga and anime enjoyed a great deal of popularity in Korea, and series such as Nagai Go's *Mazinger Z* (1973-1974) led to Kim Cheong-gi's *Robot Taekwon V* (1976). Meanwhile, Honda Ishirô's *Godzilla* (1954) spawned the *tokusatsu* ("special filming") mode of speculative fiction in Japan, with Kim Ki-duk's 1967 film *Yonggary, Monster from the Deep* following suit. *Tokusatsu* superheroes came after *kaiju*, first in Japan and then in Korea, with the *Ureme* series of films following the blueprint of Japan's *Super Sentai* franchise (1975-ongoing).

On initial glance, this brief history seems to reinforce the notion that South Korea is always behind Japan. But what is critical in these texts is the frequency with which things are meshed, melded, and bonded. It is the persistence of hybridity, especially in the context of Japan, which emerges from the traumatic experience of World War II and the ways in which the atomic bombings of Hiroshima and Nagasaki in August of 1945 pushed the limits of what it meant to be human in the country. While South Korea did not experience the horror of the bombs, the country's sovereignty was also in flux, first because of colonization, and then due to the traumatic North-South split. Indeed, speculative fiction has time and time again proven itself to be particularly apt in tackling the intense processes of industrialization and modernization, and East Asia is no different in that regard.

Squid Game in fact becomes a nexus of a sort, following this trajectory, but also demonstrating how it becomes an intersection with the Korean Wave. After all, in terms of cinema, it was the violent work of filmmakers such as Park Chan-wook, Kim Jee-woon, and Bong Joon-ho that catapulted the country to the international forefront. Those filmmakers, in turn, had a critical precedent set by the success of directors such as Fukasaku, Miike, and Kitano Takeshi, especially on the international film festival circuit. And what is so critical about violent East Asian cinema is that it was a product of crises—the 1991 collapse of the Japanese bubble economy and the 1997 Asian Financial Crisis—that followed the two countries' so-called postwar miracles. This is why East Asian speculative fiction and violent cinema culminate in *Squid Game*, media forged in the crucible of industrial modernity, where the zero-sum-game of neoliberalism is imagined as a technological nightmare. The history that *Squid Game* so effectively puts to use, then, is one shared by both countries, a vicious circuit of collapse, rebirth, and collapse. And it is the resulting empathy generated through the persistent hybridity in South Korean speculative fiction that attempts to look past *ressentiment* and towards new ways of being and being with one another.

Squid Game and the Japanese Entanglements of South Korean Speculative Fiction

Squid Game is set in a fictional South Korea that, for the most part, mirrors the actual country. A mysterious international cabal sets up a game where contestants are solicited to compete on a remote island for a large sum of money. In the iteration shown in the series, the prize is 45.6 billion South Korean won, with each of the 456 contestants "contributing" ₩100 million to the pot. Those contestants are all in a massive amount of debt, which is why they desperately and willingly join the game. Netflix categorizes *Squid Game* under the genres of "Korean," "TV Thrillers," and "TV Dramas" and indeed on initial glance, it is arguable that the show is not technically a work of science fiction. But science fiction is a form that demands a great deal of scaffolding in the South Korean context. According to Min-Sung Park and Haerin Shin, one of the editors of this special issue that takes up this task, the genre has had a difficult time becoming established in Korea, partially because of the notion that speculation is a frivolous luxury, especially in a country where trauma characterizes its modern history. Park elaborates on the troubled status of science fiction, beginning with the most common term, *gongsanggwahak*. While *gwahak* refers to "science," *gongsang* or 空想, translates to "that which does not exist in reality." By definition, science fiction in South Korea has had to combat the notion that it is "fake" or "impossible" fiction (Park 163).

Similarly, Park also notes that science fiction has had to fight its Western roots. This is exacerbated by the fact that even *gongsanggwahak* as a term was borrowed from Japan (Park 164). As Roger Luckhurst suggests, researchers should perhaps not be too prescriptive (and judgmental) in discussing science fiction (9). For Luckhurst, consideration of science fiction requires elasticity and flexibility as hybridity has always been a fundamental component, beginning with the genre's codification in the 1880s (13). Indeed, *Squid Game,* and the genealogy in which it belongs, certainly fits Luckhurst's description, as it, *Battle Royale, As the Gods Will*, and *Gantz* incorporate elements from horror, fantasy, and comedy. That incorporation is so extensive that it is difficult to locate any of them purely in any single category. Thus, it is my contention that this is not an aberration, but a recurring pattern in both South Korean and Japanese science fiction. In charting the history of speculative fiction, Marek Oziewicz underscores how a lack of clearly defined borders (seen for example in its relationship to science fiction) is part and parcel of its modern use. More expansive than science fiction, speculative fiction has recently become a "fuzzy set super category that houses all non-mimetic genres" (Oziewicz). Beginning with what has since been established as postwar Japanese science fiction, tracing its proliferation in South Korea and into its influence on Korean science fiction, we thus reach a practice of speculative fiction that is invested in fuzzy borders, emblematized in *Squid Game*.

A clearer picture of that practice will emerge as we examine the ways that *Squid Game* engages the three texts mentioned above, from the specific elements to the broader, structural components. Let us begin with *As the Gods Will*, which follows a group of high school students as they are abruptly and mysteriously forced to play a series of games until only one of them remains. As previously mentioned, the main criticism against *Squid Game* and Hwang came from the fact that *As the Gods Will* also highlighted a Red Light, Green Light game, seven years earlier. It is important to note that it is not the presence of the game alone that was the source of criticism, but also the fact that it was one of many confluences between the film and the show, including the free-for-all metagame and the prevalence of graphic violence.

In terms of the game itself, the use of a visually striking robot (due to its size, bright and glossy primary colors, and the design itself) raised suspicions. Like the memorable costumes in the show, the robot's impact is heightened by its early appearance, hinting to both the contestants and the viewer that something is awry. The Red Light, Green Light robot thus operates in the same structural fashion as the Daruma doll in *As the Gods Will*. There, the Daruma doll shuttles the students and the viewer into the film's deadly game to shocking effect. The doll is even more uncanny than the robot, for the film suggests that it is a sentient, partially organic creature, as opposed to fully mechanical. In the same way that the *Squid Game*'s robot invokes a popular elementary school textbook character named Younghee for Korean viewers, *As the Gods Will* takes the familiar Daruma doll and sinisterly warps it, bringing it to eerie life, as it speaks and uncannily moves. As critics have noted, along with the Daruma doll, the Red Light, Green Light robot also shares similarities with the giant cat in the second *As the Gods Will* game (General). In addition to the irony of seemingly cute designs hiding deadly functionality, the robot and the supernatural entities all possess an oversized digital timer to mark the passage of game time. And although *As the Gods Will* unfolds in a supernatural setting, the digital clocks suggest a sort of machinic nature to its creatures that the Red Light, Green Light robot shares.

That same biomechanical nature proliferates throughout *Gantz*. Originally published from 2000 to 2013, *Gantz* was successful domestically and internationally, becoming a franchise that included anime, two live-action films and video games. Most recently, *Gantz* was adapted into a Netflix CGI animated film.[2] The series follows a group of people that are transported to a mysterious room after they have untimely deaths. In the room, they are given weapons and equipment in a game where they must hunt aliens. While *Gantz* has been mentioned in the broader discussion of texts like *Squid Game*, it was not directly invoked in terms of the show's alleged plagiarism. But *Gantz* may in fact be a direct influence on the series as Hwang said that he was inspired to write *Squid Game* after reading several comics, specifically citing *Liar Game* (2005-2015) and *Gambling Apocalypse: Kaiji* (1996-ongoing) (Kim). The unsettling way that the Red Light,

Green Light robot's eyes freely move invokes the "Tanaka" alien, one of the most popular antagonists in *Gantz*. Appearing in the second arc, the "Tanaka" alien is a small woodpecker-like creature that controls a glossy human-sized robot that moves in uncanny ways (its head, torso and limbs rotate 360 degrees). That the robot itself could be, in fact, organic connects to the indeterminate status of the "gods" in *As the Gods Will*. And by having a small creature pilot the robot from a cockpit in its head, *Gantz* directly references *Mazinger Z*, which we will discuss further.

Between *Gantz*, *As the Gods Will*, and even *Mazinger Z*, we begin to see the broader multi and intermedia context, from manga, anime, and video games, to film. As commentators have keenly noted, the Red Light, Green Light robot is where these various texts converge. If we expand the discussion further, it is not simply the presence of Younghee, the Tanaka robot, or the Daruma doll, but rather the fact that they are at the center of a game. Along these lines, it was *Squid Game*'s use of children's games that left an impression on many viewers. This is another place where the show overlaps with *As the Gods Will*. At the same time, *Squid Game* does not include any actual children, which is one of the key ways that it diverges from not only *As the Gods Will*, but the rest of its Japanese predecessors. On the other hand, this is exactly where *As the Gods Will* and *Gantz* intersect, as the core protagonists are high school and middle school students. And it is also where we reach *Battle Royale*.

The Historical Impact of *Battle Royale*

All the texts that we have discussed thus far lead back to *Battle Royale*. In a Japan devastated by recession, the government passes the BR (Battle Royale) Act as a last-ditch effort, which sees one class of third-year middle school students randomly selected to fight each other to the death at a remote location. This basic premise has proven to be emphatically powerful in the two decades since the releases of the novel and its adaptation, with numerous iterations across media around the world featuring their own desperate free-for-alls. The specific components that producers have borrowed from *Battle Royale* include the sense of scale generated by a large number of contestants; the basic rules of the game, the chief being that it must continue until only one competitor remains, the other being the constriction of time and space so as to constantly push contestants into conflict; and desperate, brutal violence. As mentioned above in the case of *As the Gods Will* and *Gantz*, *Battle Royale* remains as shocking today as it did twenty years ago, primarily due to the graphic violence committed by children against other children. While images of violence against children and teenagers have proliferated throughout popular media internationally, for example in the slasher genre, *Battle Royale* set a crucial and infamous precedent in having the children be the perpetrators.[3]

Battle Royale makes very clear that the game and its logic are absurd, and one of the film's most effective strategies is that it does not take away the responsibility of the children and their individual decisions to do harm to one another, while also holding the teachers, military, and government officials culpable for producing the conditions in which that violence is coercively enforced (children that refuse to participate are killed). But *Battle Royale* goes even further, carefully situating the students' experience in the broader conditions of its fictional Japan. The film opens with a dramatic legend explaining how the BR Act came to pass, namely a fifteen-percent unemployment rate, ten million people without work, and eight hundred thousand students boycotting school while juvenile crime rates soar. In that sense, the battle royales are merely brutal contests within an already inhospitable world, which is why Andrea G. Arai writes that the book and the film were fantastical situations meant to cope with the very real conditions of Japan in the ten years of recession following the 1991 collapse. The moral panic regarding failing homes, collapsing classrooms, and strange children was rerouted away from recession and into the vague problem of education, leading to the 2003 educational reforms, of which Arai reads *Battle Royale*'s BR Act as being a fictional anticipation. She writes:

> As the political atmosphere congealed around the current reforms, problems of school refusal (*tōkōkyohi*), bullying (*ijime*), inner-school violence (*kōnai bōryoku*), fatherless homes, and others—that had been dealt with through recourse to a top-down bureaucratization of school life during the previous decade—were now integrated into the new rationale of reform that called for a changed relationship between home, school and State. (371)

Arai continues, noting how the language of the reforms conspicuously glossed over the fact that they corresponded "closely with the view that a major shift in the requirements for a labour force has occurred as a result of the accelerated globalisation of markets" (371). What makes Arai's claim seem even more sound is not only the numerous texts that take up *Battle Royale*'s free-for all, but also the litany of Japanese speculative fiction texts in the twenty-first century that attempt to grapple with the so-called Lost Decades. *Lesson of the Evil* (dir. Miike Takashi, 2012), *Assassination Classroom* (2015-2016), *Alice in Borderland* (2020-ongoing) and countless others follow *Battle Royale*'s precedent, where "the new reality of survival is that not all will reach the top, but those who do, like the kids in the film, will have to engage desperately (*hisshi ni*) to become worthy competitors for Japan in the amorphous battlefield of the global economy" (Arai 374). Violent Japanese film and television so often articulate the country's moral panic, with the protagonists of *Battle Royale*, As *the Gods Will*, *Gantz*, and *Alice in Borderland* all hopeless young people with no future. In reality, this anxiety represents not merely a generation lost, but the particular conditions that young people have to face with a sustained recession.

While *Battle Royale* features a cast of schoolchildren, *Squid Game* follows *Gantz*'s lead of featuring a much more diverse cast. The latter derives a great deal of drama and comedy from the fact that the room seems to select participants at random, including schoolchildren, toddlers, senior citizens, and even a panda. Unlike the Japanese texts, *Squid Game* is limited to adults, which lends itself to certain thematic affordances, but like *Gantz*, the cast is diverse in terms of age, race, and nationality. In addition to contributing to its global popularity, the cast also provides further insight into *Squid Game*'s historical context. It is important to recognize that *Squid Game* debuted twenty years after not only *Battle Royale*, but also the Korean Wave, which is to say that it premiered to an international audience that was already familiar with both the battle royale genre as well as South Korean media (evident in the sizable number of works already on Netflix). If we move even further into the historical background of both the genre and Korean media, we also find the reason why the show resonated with viewers to a degree that its predecessors were unable to.

By 2021, the conditions that necessitate the fictional *Squid Game* were all too familiar to adult and young adult media consumers around the world. In the same way that schoolchildren at the turn of the century would have recognized the harsh conditions of *Battle Royale*, so too would adults see the disparate but analogously desperate lives of those in *Squid Game*. In fact, in many cases, it would be those very same children that lived through the Lost Decade, the IMF Crisis, and the 2008 Housing Crisis that watched *Squid Game* with an uncanny sense of recognition. In the year since the show's release, household debt accounted for 104.3% of South Korea's GDP, the highest of thirty-six major economies (S. Choi). The US fared no better, with the Federal Reserve Bank of New York reporting that total household debt surpassed $16 trillion in the second quarter of 2022 (Measy). In a recent *Guardian* interview, star Lee Jung-jae noted as much when he discussed the "bittersweet" success of the show. Lee commented, "The fact it [sic] resonated with so many around the world is worrying. You get a sense this is the reality for so many people globally. And that makes me feel hugely sad" (Segalov).

If *Battle Royale* was prescient for young viewers in 2000, by 2021, *Squid Game* was merely descriptive. And although it might not be immediately evident, *Hallyu* is entirely imbricated in this matrix. The Korean Wave, which arguably begins with music exported into Southeast Asia in the 1990s, truly takes off in the 2000s with the spread of television throughout Asia, the international success of South Korean cinema both with genre fans and on the film festival circuit, as well as its role in legitimizing esports. Venture capital played a key role in the Korean Wave, which in turn had to do with the loss of power of the *chaebeol* conglomerates, spurred by the economic restructuring attached to the IMF's $58 billion bailout fund following the 1997 Crisis (J. Choi 17; Paquet 72). In other words, the media that we are discussing here both in Japan and South Korea has its roots in socioeconomic collapse. As Joseph Jonghyun Jeon has argued, millennial South Korean cinema is simultaneously a product of and a rumination on financial turmoil (Jeon).

Much more explicitly than *Battle Royale*, *As the Gods Will*, and *Gantz*, *Squid Game* invokes this context. One effective way in which the show speaks to economic destitution is through Ali (Anupam Tripathi), a popular character who incorporates the broader geopolitical conditions of migrant labor and the systemic disenfranchisement that immigrant workers are submitted to. *Squid Game* thus more directly speaks to global economic conditions, but we would be remiss to think that it is alone in doing so. As mentioned above, *Battle Royale* is entirely interested in the effects of recession, and similarly, it engages those effects in an international framework, gesturing to the way that the longer history of geopolitics reverberates into the lived experience of the twentieth and twenty-first centuries. This occurs on a foundational level, beginning with the inspiration for its core concept: professional wrestling. The novel opens with a brief description of a battle royal match, which establishes some of the themes that the book will explore. But professional wrestling has a specific valence in the East Asian context (as opposed to, for example, North America), a valence that runs through Japanese speculative fiction.

More specifically, in addition to being central to the establishment of broadcast television in both Japan and Korea (a culture of gathering around a communal television), professional wrestling captured the imagination of the two countries through nationalist storytelling (Yoshimi, Hwang). In Japan, the ethnically Korean Rikidozan (Mitsuhiro Momota, born Kim Sin-rak), fended off "foreign invaders" such as "Classy" Freddie Blassie in the 1950s and early 60s. His May 24, 1963 WWA World Heavyweight title match against the Destroyer (Dick Beyer) exemplifies the enormous popularity of wrestling, drawing sixty-four-percent viewership, a record that remains the third highest television sports rating in the country's history (Wong et al. 248). As Shun'ya Yoshimi notes, pro wrestling was a "national symbolic drama" where Rikidozan "skillfully gave shape to Japanese people's complicate [sic] feelings toward America, an enemy country that had become both Japan's occupier and protector" (129).

Coupled with the advent of broadcast television, it was postwar ambivalence that created the conditions in which Rikidozan could so effectively harness a nationally symbolic drama. After all, Japan was still processing the catastrophic defeat of World War II and its denouncement of belligerency following the revised constitution and American occupation. Professional wrestling was an arena where those feelings could be worked through and nationalist aggression could be rerouted. Along these lines, World War II factors into *Battle Royale* not only through the novel's indebtedness to professional wrestling, but also in the film adaptation, as Fukasaku commented that he drew from his wartime experiences as a boy, articulating them through the bonds that the children develop (Arai 375-376). It is an understatement to say that Fukasaku was not the only producer of speculative fiction to use the genre in this regard.

Postwar Japanese Speculative Fiction in South Korea

The same process of rebuilding nationalism and redirecting bellicosity that catapulted Rikidozan to superstardom is evident in the country's comics and animation, specifically in the technonationalism that fueled its preoccupation with fictional robot weapons.[4] Those very same texts would very soon find their way into South Korea. And while importers introduced slight changes to eliminate the Japanese "odor," as Koichi Iwabuchi influentially phrased it, those same texts would appeal to Korean audiences for related reasons (Iwabuchi 27). Foundational series such as Tezuka Osamu's *Mighty Atom* (1952-1968) and Yokoyama Mitsuteru's *Tetsujin 28-go* (1956) were both imported in Korea as *Ujusonyeon Atomu* ("Spaceboy Atom") and *Cheorin 28-ho* ("Ironman Number 28"), and became household names. But more pointedly, *Mazinger Z*, which initially ran as a manga from 1972 to 1974 before becoming an anime, was also imported as *Majinga Jetteu*. A seminal series in establishing the "Super Robot" genre (as opposed to the "Real Robot" genre initiated by the *Mobile Suit Gundam* franchise), *Mazinger Z* follows the story of Kabuto Koji, a sixteen-year-old boy who pilots an eighteen-meter-tall robot developed to combat the monstrous creations of a mad scientist.

Whereas the child operator of *Tetsujin 28-go* controls the robot remotely, *Mazinger Z* changed the genre and Japanese speculative fiction by having a human pilot the mecha from within, entering its head via small aircraft.

Three years after the initial publication and television run of *Mazinger Z*, *Robot Taekwon V* was released in South Korea. The design of Taekwon V is nearly identical to Mazinger Z (the most substantial changes being the robot's head) with pilot Kim Hoon manning a small aircraft that fits into Taekwon V's head much in the same fashion as Mazinger Z. Likewise, the basic premise of the film follows *Mazinger Z*: a scientist develops the robot to combat the efforts of his morally bankrupt counterpart. Kim Cheong-gi later acknowledged the influence of the Japanese series. While this may seem to be a more straightforward instance of plagiarism, it is also important to remember that *Mazinger Z* followed *Tetsujin 28-go*, which was preceded by *Mighty Atom*. And the fact that Osamu based Atom's design on Mickey Mouse (and was still able to have a strong working relationship with Walt Disney) again demonstrates the way in which postwar East Asian speculative fiction was not contained within national borders, nor entirely preoccupied with questions of intellectual property.

In addition to its design and premise, *Taekwon V* also inherits the postwar influence of *Mazinger Z*, as a professional wrestling bout plays a large part in the narrative. More importantly, Kim and the titular robot both practice taekwondo, invoking the nationalist combat of both professional wrestling and karate, another martial art through which Japan's censored militancy was redirected (Allison 99-100).[5] And as was the case with both professional wrestling and anime, *Taekwon V* also maintains the same ambivalence towards recent history. As Dong-Yeon Koh notes, anime enjoyed a great deal of popularity in South Korea in the 1970s and 1980s. The dubbed broadcasts of *Atomu* and *Mazinger Z* were part of the processes of modernization and industrialization, and helped the country work through colonialism. The complicated feelings of South Korea's ambivalence stemmed from the residual trauma of its annexation; another part was the fact that Japan served as a role model for technonationalism and state-sponsored rebuilding (Koh 161). Koh reads *Taekwon V* in this fashion, again not as a straightforward aping, but rather a hybrid effort that meshed Japanese culture with Korean martial arts and the burgeoning steel industry, which was part and parcel of the country's transition from "light" (consumer products) to "heavy" industry (steel and electronics) (Koh 163, 168).

Just as speculative fiction manga and anime were beginning to pick up steam, so too was a new form of live action speculative fiction starting to emerge. Initiated by *Godzilla* in 1954, *tokusatsu* heavily relies on practical effects, primarily in the form of actors wearing elaborate suits (generally made of foam and latex), which is why the mode is also referred to as "suitmation." Arguably, the monster subgenre is the most recognizable in the *tokusatsu* catalogue, with the superhero subgenre being a close second. In recent years, *Kaiju* (怪獣) ("strange beast") has enjoyed popular English-language use, most likely because of its codification in Guillermo del Toro's blockbuster *Pacific Rim* (2013)[6] Released in October of 1954, *Godzilla* opens with a direct reference to the Bikini Atoll hydrogen bomb testing conducted by the US on March 1 that contaminated twenty-three Japanese fishermen (Godzilla sinks a Japanese vessel in the opening and it is also later revealed that it was American hydrogen bomb testing that awakened him).[7] That *Godzilla* evokes the horrors of nuclear warfare is common knowledge, but less discussed in the general discourse is how the film speaks to the specificity of Hiroshima and Nagasaki and the censorship during the American Occupation from 1945 to 1952 that prohibited public discussion of the bombings and effects

(Dower 116). After all, *Godzilla* was released just two years later, a high-profile mass culture text that used the distance afforded by speculative fiction to engage with still fresh traumatic history, an attempt to publicly understand what the country was still experiencing.

With *Godzilla* spawning a franchise in Japan, Kim Ki-duk produced *Yonggary, Monster from the Deep* in 1967. As the Chinese characters for *kaiju* are 怪獣, both Japanese and Korean monsters are referred to as *gwesu* in Korean.[8] The country's inaugural *gwesu*, *Yonggary* was also notable for the fact that Kim brought in six Toei technicians from Japan to work on the film. In that regard, *teukchwal gwesu* (*teukchwal* meaning "special filming," and thus analogous to *tokusatsu*) films were a transnational effort from the very beginning. Thirty-two years later, Shim Hyung-rae remade *Yonggary*, releasing the film just a year after Roland Emmerich's 1998 high-profile Hollywood remake of *Godzilla*. Shim returned to *gwesu* filmmaking in 2007 with *D-War*, which at the time was the most expensive South Korean film ever made. By that point, *Hallyu* was starting to expand beyond Asia, and *D-War* was released internationally to a revenue of $75 million. Part of that revenue could be attributed to the fact that just a year earlier, Bong Joon-ho's *The Host* had become the highest-grossing domestic film in Korean history, and had had a successful American release. Domestically, *The Host* is not referred to as a *teukchwal gwesu* film, for it does not feature the chief characteristics of the genre. And yet, it is often referred to as a *kaiju* film in English-language discussions. One may understandably bristle that Japanese words are being used to describe a South Korean film, for it does indicate the long-standing Orientalism that refuses to take into consideration the specificity of each region. At the same time, as we see in South

Korea, the interchangeability of *kaiju* and *gwesu* is also a key indicator of the slipperiness of East Asian speculative fiction.

The crossing of boundaries and borders is a focal point and critical concern in Japanese speculative fiction. We can see this in the way that *henshin* (怪獣), which translates to "transformation," is a keyword in *tokusatsu*. The latex and foam suits that litter the genre are used to express a spectrum of humanoid entities, whether they be monstrous, extraterrestrial, technological, or metahuman. Read in the aftermath of the atomic bombs, a moment when the country was to reconsider what it meant to be human (the most powerful example perhaps being the new category of the *hibakusha* or "bomb-affected people"), the Japanese appear to be using suitmation to negotiate questions of gender and identity as part of a broader discussion of humanism and posthumanism (Sugawa-Shimada; Dower 120). The bombs made a confrontation with the absolute limit point of humanity unavoidable, whether it be the extent of violence that could be perpetrated against the body, or a drastic reorientation of how beings could relate to one another. Hence, the mode of speculative fiction is rife with images of *kaiju, kaijin* ("strange humans"), aliens, androids, robots, and cyborgs, a full spectrum of possible iterations of humanity. And those images, across film, television, and print, were reproduced over and over, bleeding into the media of South Korea.

Second only to *kaiju* is the superhero subgenre of *tokusatsu*. Internationally, the most successful *tokusatsu* superhero franchise is the Super Sentai series, which rose to prominence with the American importation of the sixteenth series, *Kyōryū Sentai Zyuranger* ("Dinosaur Squad Zyuranger") (1992-1993) as the *Mighty Morphin Power Rangers* in 1993. Produced since 1972, Super Sentai features a group of young men and women in color-coded, themed costumes that use advanced technology to fend off alien invasions.[9] Well before Power Rangers became a household international name, Super Sentai was already enjoying popularity outside of Japan, especially in South America and South Korea. In 1989 Dae Young Panda, a Korean TV and film distribution company, imported, dubbed, and released the eighth series *Choushinsei Flashman* ("Supernova Flashman") (1986-1987) as *Jigubangwidae Huloesimaen* ("Earth Defense Force Flashman") on VHS, following it with five more series over the next eight years.[10] Other prominent series such as the well-known *Ultraman* franchise had also been distributed in South Korea, and Kim Cheong-gi began producing the *Ureme* series starting in 1986, drawing on *tokusatsu* hero series (*Super Sentai, Ultraman, Metal Hero, Kamen Rider*) and borrowing elements from the anime *Ninja Senshi Tobikage* ("Tobikage the Ninja Soldier") (1985-1986). Over the next seven years, Kim directed eight of the nine films in the series, with Shim Hyung-rae starring in seven of them. Revolving around an orphan raised by scientists, who discovers he has superpowers following an alien encounter, the themes of the films are just one way that *Ureme* fits into the *teukchwal* genre. More importantly, the films feature a litany of practical effects (sometimes mixing live action with animation), focusing on suit actors playing superheroes, monsters, and robots.

As Sugawa-Shimada contends, Super Sentai was a site in which Japan could negotiate questions of identity in the postwar period. Through its importation, South Korea did much of the same, tackling concerns that were not identical, but analogous, and in some cases, deeply entangled. Echoing Koh and his analysis of *Taekwon V*, Sugawa-Shimada discusses the Dae Young Panda imports and the *teukchwal* film *Byeonshinjeonsa Teuraenseutodi* ("Transforming Warriors Trans Toady") (1991, dir. Jo Myeong-hwa) thusly:

> In this sense, South Korean super-sentai works, which were influenced by their Japanese counterparts, serve as a site where it is possible to trace the impact of post-colonial status within South Korean media, as they oscillated between antagonism towards and admiration of Japanese source texts. (177)

Like Japan, South Korea had to meditate on how it would relate to the US. And in addition to relations to its former colonizer, the country also had the enormous task of orienting itself to the newly split North. Speculative fiction proved to be more than an apt forum in which to take up such questions, an arena where the country could consider how its people should move forward, past historical trauma, and into the coming century.

Conclusion

We have thus seen how South Korean speculative fiction is not merely a poor facsimile of Japanese science fiction. Much as Japan has used the genre to negotiate the twentieth and twenty-first centuries, so too has South Korea, which only makes sense considering the degree to which the two countries have been entangled with one another. Likewise, considering its historical aptitude in terms of such a task, it comes as no surprise that South Korea and Japan have turned so often to science fiction, generating together a more expansive practice of speculative fiction. Those with nationalist investments, both in South Korea and abroad, may read this essay and think that it compromises both *Squid Game* and South Korean speculative fiction. While I understand that position, I am less invested in questions of originality, be it in a nationalist sense or otherwise. To a certain degree, *Squid Game* articulates my reservations. As opposed to the more subdued critiques of the violent texts that it is indebted to, *Squid Game* is not shy about the untenable conditions of twenty-first-century capitalism and the way in which so many have been put in such dire situations. Asking questions such as whether Hwang plagiarized other filmmakers, if he deserves or does not deserve credit for the show, or if South Korean media warrants the success that it has gained, may seem to be harmless or even productive questions. But this is a discussion that is still motivated by capitalist ideology, of false promises of individualist meritocracy and as such, is still mired in the very framework that *Squid Game* critiques.

For this reason, we would be remiss to forget, at this point, another key thread of South Korean speculative fiction that *Squid Game* embodies—not only its indebtedness to Japan, but also the critical role of violent cinema around the turn of the century. Indeed, one of the most important scenes in the series, the final confrontation between Gi-hun (Lee Jung-jae) and Yeong-su (Oh Il-nam) proclaims as much, for when Gi-hun ascends the high-rise via elevator, we see and hear echoes of *Oldboy* (2003, dir. Park Chan-wook) and *A Bittersweet Life* (2005, dir. Kim Jee-woon). Indeed, the sequences where the protagonists of the three texts take elevators are so aesthetically aligned that they can be edited into one seamless clip. Films such as *Oldboy* and *A Bittersweet Life* were critical to the momentum of the Korean Wave, as well as invaluable opportunities to consider how South Korea grappled with financial crisis. In addition, they provide us, in the conclusion, one last moment to observe the history of Japanese-South Korean interchange. In the same way that filmmakers such as Kitano Takeshi aided the international success of Park Chan-wook, so too did Park's Vengeance Trilogy set a new standard for the simulation of brutality in media in South Korea, Japan, and beyond. Indeed, if anything has characterized manga in the twenty-first century, it may very well be the impact of violent Korean cinema.

In this article, I have attempted to articulate a practice of speculative fiction in South Korea and Japan that ultimately serves as a site for critique. Speculative fiction is germane to such efforts, partly of course due to the distance that the mode provides, the very same distance that was the source of the historical Korean dismissal of science fiction and lubricated Japanese importation. But what that dismissal can miss is that speculative fiction is so often not an evasion of reality, but rather a deep engagement. While encounters with alien life forms and the transcendence of human boundaries may suggest a drastic detachment, they simply make easier a commitment to what are, in some senses, even more radical ideas: looking past nationalist models deeply informed by colonial antipathy and the overbearing reality of neoliberalism. As a part of a genealogy of speculative fiction that weaves South Korean and Japanese media together, *Squid Game* continues the project of confronting life after socioeconomic collapse that necessitates an imagination that goes beyond what seems to be immediately probable, or even possible—not simply of technology and nonhuman life, but of something even perhaps more foreign, the idea of a currently inconceivable social arrangement.

Acknowledgements

I would like to thank Chang-Min Yu for pointing out how the depiction of violence intensified in Japanese comic books in the early 2000s, coinciding with the international popularity of violent South Korean cinema.

Notes

1. East Asian names are written with family name followed by given name. Korean is Romanized according to the Revised Romanization of Korean and Korean names are written accordingly with the exception of those with popularly used English spellings.
2. The two live action films are *Gantz* (2011, dir. Sato Shinsuke) and *Gantz: Perfect Answer* (2011, dir. Sato Shinsuke) while the Netflix

animated film is *Gantz: O* (2016, dirs. Sato Kei'ichi and Kawamura Yasushi.

3. In English-speaking contexts, William Golding's *Lord of the Flies* is frequently invoked in relation to *Battle Royale*. But what makes *Battle Royale* particular is the lack of emphasis on factions and their ideological grounding, as well as the extreme and graphic violence. That difference is evident in the fact that the film has not seen wide theatrical distribution in the US, as the film's initial release occurred while the country was still reeling from the Columbine massacre.

4. As Anne Allison points out, it also relates to Japan's status as the world's foremost producer of robotics (101).

5. Taekwondo is of course the national sport and a great source of nationalist pride. And yet, the martial art actually has its roots in Karate, which stems from Chinese martial arts, which in turn have their roots in India.

6. Relatedly, the original film has increasingly been referred to as *Gojira* in English-language discussions, as opposed to the more commonly-used *Godzilla*.

7. While the original 1954 film invoked the tests as a critique of US aggression and the very real effects of the atomic and hydrogen bombs, the 2014 American remake recontextualizes and reduces the tests by making Bikini Atoll a plot point where the US Navy used the bomb in an attempt to kill Godzilla. No mention is made of fishermen casualties.

8. In addition to *gwesu*, South Koreans also use *teukchwal*, and *jeondae* to refer to both domestic and Japanese productions. Similarly, while English-language discussions use *manga* and *manhwa* to differentiate between Japanese and Korean comics, Koreans simply use *manhwa* for both as the word is not a proper noun with regional specificity, but simply the word for "comic." I would argue that this is partly due to the fact that both countries share much through their common roots in Chinese culture. It also speaks to the ubiquity of Japanese comics in South Korea. Interestingly enough, Korean-language discussions tend to use *aeni* to refer to Japanese animation in the same way that English-language discussions use *anime*.

9. Whereas American superheroes generally feature one continued narrative for their publication and now, increasingly, cinematic history,

tokusatsu tend to have individually contained series in the same way that the vast majority of manga are not published in perpetuity.

10. The releases include *Choudenshi Bioman* ("Super Electron Bioman") (1984-1985) as *Uju teukgongdae baiomaen* ("Space Special Force Bioman") and *Hikari Sentai Maskman* 1987-1988) ("Light Squad Maskman") as *Biteui jeonsa maeseukeumaen* ("Warriors of Light Maskman") in 1990, *Choujuu Sentai Liveman* ("Super Beast Squad Liveman") (1988-1989) as *Pyeonghwaeui jeonsa raibeumaen* ("Warriors of Peace" Liveman) in 1994, *Dai Sentai Goggle-v* ("Great Squad Goggle-V") (1982-1983) as *Jiguteukgongdae gogeul paibeu* ("Earth Special Force Goggle Five") in 1995, and *Dengeki Sentai Changeman* ("Blitzkrieg Squad Changeman") (1985-1986) as *Jeongyeok jeondae cheinjeumaen* ("Lightning Squadron Changeman") in 1997.

Works Cited

Allison, Anne. *Millennial Monsters: Japanese Toys and the Global Imagination.* U of California P, 2006.

Arai, Andrea G. "Killing Kids: Recession and Survival in Twenty-First Century Japan." *Postcolonial Studies,* vol. 6, no. 3, 2003, pp. 367-379.

Choi, Jinhee. *The South Korean Film Renaissance: Local Hitmakers, Global Provocateurs.* Wesleyan UP, 2010.

Choi, Si-young. "Korea's Household Debt Highest among Major Economies: Report." *The Korea Herald,* 06 June 2022, https://www.koreaherald.com/view.phop?ud=20220606000172. Accessed 18 August 2022.

Dower, John W. "The Bombed: Hiroshimas and Nagasakis in Japanese Memory." *Hiroshima in History and Memory,* edited by Michael J. Hogan, Cambridge UP, 1996, pp. 116-142.

General, Ryan. "Netflix Series 'Squid Game' Accused of Plagiarizing Parts of Japanese Film 'As the Gods Will.'" *Yahoo!,* 22 September 2021, https://www.yahoo.com/video/netflix-series-squid-game-accused-175818640.html. Accessed 28 March 2023.

Hayes, Dade. "Netflix Beats Estimates in Third Quarter, Reaching 214 Million Subscribers." *Deadline,* 19 October 2021, https://deadline.com/2021/10/netflix-beats-estimates-third-quarter-streaming-1234858413/. Accessed 18 August 2022.

Hwang, Eun-ju. "민족의 한과 아픔을 달래주던 민족 스포츠: 프로 레슬링" [The People's Sport that Soothed the People's *Han* and Pain: Pro Wrestling]. *National Archives of Korea*, https://theme.archives.go.kr/next/koreaOfRecord/wrestling.do. Accessed 12 September 2022.

Iwabuchi, Koichi. *Recentering Globalization: Popular Culture and Japanese Transnationalism*. Duke UP, 2002.

Jeon, Joseph Jonghyun. *Vicious Circuits: Korea's IMF Cinema and the End of the American Century*. Stanford UP, 2019.

Kim, So-yeon. "[인터뷰+] 황동혁 감독 '"오징어게임' 10 년 전 거절 당한 아이템" [(Interview+) Director Hwang Dong-hyuk "'Squid Game'" An Item That Was Rejected 10 Years Ago"]. *Hankyung*, 01 Oct. 2021. https://www.hankyung.com/entertainment/article/202109281077H. Accessed 18 August 2022.

Koh, Dong-Yeon. "Growing Up with *Astro Boy* and *Mazinger Z*: Industrialization, 'High-Tech World,' and Japanese Animation in the Art and Culture of South Korea. *Japanese Animation: East Asian Perspectives*, edited by Masao Yokota and Tze-yue G. Hu, UP of Mississippi, 2013, pp. 155-182.

Lee, I-seul. "[인터뷰]'오징어게임' 감독 "표절·여성비하 의도無, 전화번호 노출은 죄송" [(Interview) "Squid Game" Director "No Intention of Plagiarism, Demeaning Women, Apologies for Exposing Phone Number"]. 28 September 2021, *Asia Gyeongje*, https://www.asiae.co.kr/article/2021092812152585452. Accessed 18 August 2022.

Lie, John. *K-Pop: Popular Music, Cultural Amnesia, and Economic Innovation in South Korea*. U of California P, 2015.

Luckhurst, Roger. *Science Fiction*. Polity Press, Cambridge, 2005.

Measy, Mariah. "Total Household Debt Surpasses $16 Trillion in Q2 2022; Mortgage, Auto Loan, and Credit Card Balances Increase." *Federal Reserve Bank of New York*, 02 August 2022, https://www.newyorkfed.org/newsevents/news/research/2022/202 20802. Accessed 18 August 2022.

Oziewicz, Marek. "Speculative Fiction." *Oxford Research Encyclopedia*, 29 March 2017, https://doi.org/10.1093/acrefore/9780190201098.013.78. Accessed 29 March 2023.

Paquet, Darcy. *New Korean Cinema: Breaking the Waves*. Wallflower Press, 2009.

Park, Min-Sung. "Korea's Force Is Not Strong – Exploring the Definitions of Science Fiction." *Plaridel*, vol. 14, no. 2, 2017, pp. 163-168.

Shaw, Lucas. "Netflix Estimates 'Squid Game' Will Be Worth Almost $900 Million." *Bloomberg*, 16 October 2021, https://www.bloomberg.com/news/articles/2021-10-17/squid-game-season-2-series-worth-900-million-to-netflix-so-far. Accessed 18 August 2022.

Sherman, Alex. "For Netflix Stock, It's Like the Pandemic Never Happened." *CNBC*, 24 January 2022, https://www.cnbc.com/2022/01/24/netflix-shares-fall-to-lowest-since-april-2020-on-subscriber-concern.html. Accessed 18 August 2022.

Shin, Haerin. "The Curious Case of South Korean Science Fiction: A Hyper-Technological Society's Call for Speculative Imagination." *Azalea: Journal of Korean Literature & Culture*, vol. 6, 2013, pp. 81-85.

Segalov, Michael. "Lee Jung-jae: 'Squid Game Made Me Rethink How I Look at the World," *The Guardian*, 4 November 2022, https://www.theguardian.com/film/2022/nov/04/lee-jung-jae-squid-game-hunt-south-korea. Accessed 29 March 2023.

Song, Hyeon-seo. "'조금 억울할지도...' 일본 언론, '오징어게임' 수상에 보인 솔직 반응" ["They Might Feel a Little Resentful..." Japanese Media, Honest Response to "Squid Game" Awards] *Now News*, 14 September 2022, https://nownews.seoul.co.kr/news/newsView.php?id=20220914601017. Accessed 28 March 2023.

Sugawa-Shimada, Akiko. "Japanese Superhero Teams at Home and Abroad: Super-Sentai in Japan and Their Adaptation in South Korean Cinema." *Journal of Japanese and Korean Cinema*, vol. 6, no. 2, 2014, pp. 167-183.

Wong, Donna, et al. "Sports, Broadcasting, and Cultural Citizenship in Japan." *Sport, Public Broadcasting, and Cultural Citizenship: Signal Lost?*, edited by David Rowe and Jay Scherer, Taylor and Francis, 2013, pp. 243-262.

Yoshimi, Shun'ya. "From Street Corner to Living Room: Domestication of TV Culture and National Time/Narrative." Translated by Jodie Beck. *Mechademia*, vol. 9, 2014, pp. 126-142.

Becoming a Ghost: Newtrospective Representation of Historical Violence through Virtual Reality Media in Gina Kim's *Bloodless*

Sang-Keun Yoo

Trigger Warning: This article contains descriptions of sexual assault.

Introduction

IS VIRTUAL REALITY (VR) STILL THE FUTURE awaiting fruition or a present-day reality that has already popularized? In their seminal work, *New Media: A Critical Introduction* (2009), Martin Lister et al. contend that virtual reality "was once as absorbing and hyped as the internet but [...] unlike the internet and WWW, seems not to have delivered" (106). Undeniably, VR proponents and investors have anticipated the imminent surge in popularity for VR technology and equipment time and again over the past three decades, asserting that "by 2025, the market for AR and VR will grow to $80 billion, reaching a size comparable to that of today's PC market" (Herz and Rauschnabel 229). Likewise, Goldman Sachs projected VR to emerge as the most substantial market by 2025, boasting an estimated user base of 3.4 million (Koenig et al.), while the Forbes Agency Council relayed interviews with industry leaders who declared, "The virtual reality phenomenon is more than just a trend," "Virtual reality is the future," and "VR is 'communications' blossoming" (Forbes Agency

Council). Concurrently, the U.S. Department of Education and the European Commission, in 2017 and 2018 respectively, initiated "the large-scale implementation of digital technologies in the classroom" (Meyer et al. 1) and the Consortium for School Networking (CoSN) posited in 2017 that VR would soon become "vital to schools around the world" (46). In a similar vein, Meta CEO Mark Zuckerberg allocated $10 billion toward VR advancements (Kastrenakes and Heath), with the company's rebranding from Facebook to Meta signifying a strategic shift toward VR hardware and metaverse software development.

Particularly during the COVID-19 lockdown, when the majority of the global population was compelled to remain indoors, and to seek alternative methods of socialization in the digital realm, proponents of VR anticipated the emergence and establishment of novel forms of social interaction within virtual environments. Although the pandemic has since receded and life has resumed normalcy, the much-anticipated future of VR has yet to materialize. VR has not become "vital to schools," nor has it been implemented on a "large-scale" basis in any educational institution across the globe. Contrarily, Meta experienced a 21% decline in the stock market, following an unprecedented 26% single-day crash in February 2022 (Marcos). The adoption of more conventional online platforms such as Zoom, Google Meet, and Microsoft Teams has persisted and become normalized in daily life, rather than customers utilizing VR equipment for the aforementioned socialization purposes. It appears that since its inception, with the term's coinage by Antonin Artaud in 1958 (Cogburn and Silcox 561), VR technology has continually permeated the discourse among industry leaders, investors, and academics alike as a harbinger of an imminent future. Yet, this potential has not been actualized in the present.

Nonetheless, the authors of *New Media: A Critical Introduction* assert that "throughout the 1990s, little can have exercised the minds and imagination of technologists, journalists, artists, film directors, or academics as much as 'VR'" (106). While debates persist regarding the true origins of the first VR device— be it Sir Charles Wheatstone's 1870s stereoscope (Cook 140; Champion 4), Morton Heilig's 1962 Sensorama (Robertson and Zelenko), or Jaron Lanier's 1989 head-mounted display (HMD) VR gear (Zwiebach et al. 66)—it is indisputable that cultural interest and academic scholarship in VR technology experienced a renaissance in the 1980s and 90s.[1]

Following this, there is currently a notable surge of interest in novels and films that depict futures immersed in virtual reality, not only in academic circles but also in the broader cultural domain and the contemporary mediascape. The body of scholarship on VR has since expanded to encompass a wide array of disciplines, ranging from engineering and media studies to psychology, education, medical studies, sociology, and beyond.[2] Although William Gibson's groundbreaking novel *Neuromancer* (1984), which introduced the term "cyberspace," and Philip K. Dick's 1981 work *Valis*, which imagined VR-like technology even before Gibson, were initially directed toward a specialized audience of science fiction aficionados, the notion of virtual reality and cyberpunk's imaginative forays into mind-machine integration have garnered mainstream cultural attention since the 2000s. A few notable examples include Hollywood blockbuster films such as *The Matrix* (1999) and its three sequels (May 2003, November 2003, 2021), Steven Spielberg's *Ready Player One* (2018), James Cameron's *Avatar* (2009) and its sequel (2022), as well as television dramas like *Peripheral* (2023), *Westworld* (2016–2022), and *Black Mirror* (2016–present). Furthermore, a new genre has emerged, characterized not by VR subject matter but by its utilization of VR as a medium. VR refugee documentaries or what Steven Anderson terms "social issue VR" such as Chris Milk and Gabo Arora's *Clouds Over Sidra* (2015),

Nonny de la Peña's *One Dark Night* (2015), and Alejandro Iñárritu's *Carne y Arena* (2017), exemplify this new approach to storytelling (365).

As elaborated further below in this article, these Hollywood blockbuster films and mainstream TV dramas, which explore VR or related technologies as subject matter, often exhibit problems associated with what Lisa Nakamura terms the "ideology of liberation" (*Cybertypes* 4). This concept presents cyberspace as a race-free environment, yet defaults to whiteness. On the other hand, social issue VR films expose different but related problems associated with "toxic re-embodiment" of racial minorities' bodies and "identity tourism," wherein automated experiences of racial trauma are designed or commercialized to enhance white audiences' empathy ("Feeling Good about Feeling Bad" 54, 60). As Nakamura's incisive critique aptly illustrates the emerging interdisciplinary nexus between Science and Technology Studies (STS) and Critical Race Studies (CRT), this area of research has experienced significant growth in parallel with the expanding influence of VR technologies in our daily lives. It has been led by trailblazing scholars such as Wendy Hui Kyung Chun, Ruha Benjamin, Safiya Umoja Noble, Simone Browne, and Cathy O'Neil, who are predominantly female scholars of color. Although these academics adopt different approaches to various new technologies, they share a common goal: to critically examine the current landscape of science and technology in relation to the ways in which new technologies perpetuate, and sometimes exacerbate, societal issues such as racism, sexism, and class inequalities.

In this regard, this article engages with this burgeoning interdisciplinary research by examining Gina Kim's speculative VR film *Bloodless* (2017) and its potential for utilizing VR media as an ethical means of representing others' past trauma. The challenge of depicting the past trauma of others has been contemplated within the fields of trauma studies and memory studies by historians, philosophers, and media scholars for many decades. Often, these discussions have led to conclusions about the impossibility of representation, as exemplified by notions such as the "impossibility of seeing" (Agamben 54), "inaccessibility" (Caruth 19, 45), Emmanuel Levinas' "ethics of incalculable responsibility" (qtd. in Ward 156), or Theodor Adorno's impossibility of writing poetry after Auschwitz (26). Gina Kim, a South Korea-born diasporic film director and professor at the University of California-Los Angeles, has also been grappling with this issue for over 25 years. Rather than relegating historical trauma to an inaccessible and incalculable experience or guiding the audience to merely observe the faces of others, Kim has discovered a means through VR media to immerse her audience in the historically traumatic event of Yun Kûm Yi's death, the scandalous murder perpetrated by a U.S. army private in 1992.

In examining Kim's engagement with this traumatic historical event, this article focuses on her utilization of VR media as a means to challenge the pitfalls of VR-related media content that Nakamura and others have criticized, namely both the ideology of liberation and the toxic embodiment of marginalized others' virtual bodies for the purpose of enhancing empathy. In this vein, this article argues Kim employs three innovative strategies to address these concerns. Firstly, Kim employs VR film as a medium that neither replicates reality nor generates an entirely virtual and simulated fantasy. By depicting victims of past violence as ghostly figures, she visualizes their liminal status within the (360-degree) screen. Secondly, Kim eliminates the hierarchical distinction between the audience and the victim through VR media, thus challenging the problematic voyeurism prevalent in other social issue VR documentaries. As discussed later in this article, her film's audience experiences a transformation into ghostly figures themselves, shedding their comfortable status as epistemophilic and exploitative voyeurs. Thirdly, rather than concentrating solely on the visual aspect of VR films, Kim utilizes sound to guide the audience's field of vision. A conventional issue with earlier VR films is that audiences have full control over their viewing location unless guidance is provided. This unguided freedom may result in audiences choosing to watch whatever they decide, such as focusing on an empty corner of a room for the entire screening time. To overcome this common problem in VR experiences, Kim creatively employs sound to direct audiences' attention in accordance with her intentions while still preserving their freedom of choice.

In this context, this article contends that Kim's VR film, while revisiting and representing a past trauma, can be characterized as not merely retrospective, but rather as *new*-trospective. To explicate, her VR film offers a response to the question of how to ethically represent the seemingly unrepresentable historical trauma by utilizing emerging technology. Through the potential of VR film, the artistic portrayal of a past event discovers a novel approach for its ethical reproduction and re-experiencing in the present. Consequently, this paper highlights the significance of Kim's approach to employing VR media as an exemplar of the medium's potential by crafting a novel dimension of empathy—first, by manifesting the "ghostly" status of camptown women, and second, by guiding the audience to assume the role of these speculative figures.

Ideology of Liberation, Toxic Re-Embodiment, and Identity Tourism

No inventor sets out to create new technology with the intent to harm its users and society; newly invented technologies are supposed to benefit their users and society—at least that has been the claim made by Silicon Valley companies regarding their new products. However, Ruha Benjamin, in her book *Race After*

Technology (2019), highlights that this is not always the case; in fact, it often results in the opposite outcome. She asserts, "tech fixes often hide, speed up, and even deepen discrimination, while appearing to be neutral or benevolent when compared to the racism of a previous era" (8). Wendy Hui Kyung Chun, in her book *Discriminating Data* (2021), echoes a similar sentiment, while focusing her arguments on the internet and artificial intelligence. She contends, "The Internet has become a nightmare, the source–it is claimed–of almost everything bad in this world. [...] The irony is that the Internet and artificial intelligence were promised to be and do the opposite" (1). These scholars concur that the internet, online spaces, video games, social media, and other recent technologies pledge to provide solutions to social issues such as racism and sexism. However, in reality, these technologies often exacerbate social discrimination and other problems, or even give rise to entirely new dilemmas.

The same pattern of incongruity between the initial promises and the actual outcomes can be observed in the realm of VR technologies. For instance, in 2017, Mark Zuckerberg, while promoting the Oculus Quest 2 against the backdrop of hurricane-ravaged Puerto Rico, remarked, "One of the things that's really magical about virtual reality is you can get the feeling that you're really in a place [...] we're looking around and it feels like we're really here in Puerto Rico where it's obviously a tough place to get to now and a lot of people are really suffering with the aftermath of the hurricanes" (qtd. in Anderson 361). In his article "New (Old) Ontologies of Documentary," Anderson critically examines this promotional video, taking issue with Zuckerberg's insensitivity towards the disaster's victims and his exploitation of their experience to market his new commercial product. He further argues that VR companies are leveraging social issues and empathy as marketing tools for their VR products, thereby exhibiting "appropriative tendencies" (365). Consequently, he concludes that VR content does not serve as "an antidote to Western voyeurism but rather an extension of it" (365).

A distinct yet related issue emerges in films that engage with VR technology as their central theme. For instance, the protagonist in Steven Spielberg's *Ready Player One* epitomizes this issue during his introductory description of OASIS, the film's fictional virtual space. Primarily, the film's narrator emphasizes the enhanced—in fact, unlimited—mobility within the virtual realm: "You can do anything, go anywhere, like the vacation planet, [...] you can ski down the pyramid, you can climb Mount Everest with Batman" (4:00-4:20). The narrator further underscores the notion of race-blindness and liberation from discrimination, stating, "People come to the OASIS for all the things they can do, but they stay because of all the things they can be. Tall, beautiful, scary, a different sex, a different species, live-action, cartoon. It's all your call" (4:20-4:40). Indeed, in this VR game-like virtual environment, users can select any avatar they desire, illustrating what Lisa Nakamura refers to as "an ideology of liberation from marginalized and devalued bodies" (*Cybertypes* 4).

Strangely, however, there is a conspicuous absence of African American individuals, particularly African American women, within the purportedly "liberated" and "race-free" virtual environment. To emphasize the so-called "liberation from marginalized bodies," both the film and the original novel portray African American woman Helen Harris (played by Lena Waithe) selecting a Caucasian male avatar, Aech. This representation demonstrates how the imagination of a future VR-saturated world perpetuates the problems associated with what Bonilla-Silva terms "color-blind racism" or the "ideology of liberation" that Nakamura identified in relation to the early stages of online spaces and their avatars two decades ago—as she contends, "when users are free to choose their own race, all were assumed to be white" (*Racism without Racists; Cybertypes* 5).

It is not only the absence of African American women that is problematic, but also the virtual presence of the Asian American population, as they are depicted solely in traditionally stereotypical ways, taking the forms of cartoonish Japanese Samurais—Daito (played by Burmese actor Win Morisaki) and Shoto (played by Chinese American actor Philip Zhao). While the space claims to be "liberated" and "race-free," African Americans simply remain absent and Asian Americans continue to be confined to stereotypes. This highlights the problems with the ideology of liberation, as it fosters a false perception of liberation whereby "liberation" involves becoming either a White male or conforming to problematic stereotypes, instead of normalizing the presence of racial minorities and women in cyberspace.

The same problem of the ideology of liberation is perpetuated by numerous films exemplified above. For instance, the film *Avatar* portrays Jake Sully (played by Sam Worthington), a man with paraplegia due to his military service, obtaining a new able-bodied and thus "liberated" form through his artificial alien body. This transformation into an able-bodied form and the abandonment of his disabled body allow him to indulge in the White male's sexual fantasy of interacting with and marrying an "exotic" Indigenous woman. Similarly, the Amazon Video's recent drama *Peripheral* features African American war veteran Conner Penske (played by Eli Goree), who, having lost both legs and an arm, regains mobility in cyberspace by adopting the body of a White person. All these examples reinforce the notion of the White abled body as the default and perpetuate White Supremacy and ableist ideology, rather than normalizing the presence of racial minorities and disabled bodies.

Rather than emphasizing the benefits of VR technology as a means to become "liberated" into able-bodied White male forms, several scholars and artists have employed VR technology for the opposite purpose. Numerous researchers have sought to create VR content wherein users embody the virtual forms of racial minorities, women, disabled people, patients, or even animals. The objective is for users to vicariously experience life in socially marginalized and disabled bodies of others, thereby fostering empathy for these marginalized groups. For instance, Hasler et al., in their article "Virtual Race Transformation Reverses Racial In-Group Bias," experimented with users' experiences of assuming another person's identity with a different skin color. Steptoe et al. explored the psychological effects of becoming a human with a tail. Ahn et al. crafted an experience of assuming the form of a cow, rather than a human. Mado and Bailenson conducted experiments involving non-autistic research participants virtually embodying autistic people, healthcare workers embodying patients, or mothers embodying four-year-old children (176).

This body of research—mostly in the fields of psychology and education—has revealed that users of these virtual avatars experience a sense of ownership over the virtual personas, even though they do not correspond to their real bodies or selves. Owing to this ownership and virtual identification, these studies have found that this sense of ownership influences empathy levels to the target marginalized groups. Particularly, Mado and Bailenson, in their article, "The Psychology of Virtual Reality," conclude that VR has been employed to reduce racial stereotyping and increase empathy toward disabled individuals, victims of domestic violence, and even the natural environment because it fosters a "greater [sense of] self-other merging with people with disabilities and promote[s] more helping behavior" compared to when users simply imagine themselves as the targeted subjects of empathy (163, 173). Furthermore, they discovered that the positive attitude toward the embodied avatar, such as that of a homeless person or a member of a marginalized group, diminished "more slowly over time" for those educated through VR when contrasted with individuals educated through traditionally "narrative-based perspective-taking tasks" (176).[3]

While research involving participants embodying avatars of socially marginalized groups or other oppressed species is undoubtedly well-intentioned, critics caution that such experiences might inadvertently harm the socially marginalized group rather than fostering empathy toward them. For instance, Charles P. Linscott contends that utilizing VR as an empathy tool carries the risk of identity commodification and essentialism, especially when employed to simulate the experiences of other races. He cites a VR simulation program of Blackness as an example and identifies two primary issues with it. First, in order to virtually simulate the experience of being Black (thus allowing the user to develop empathy toward Black individuals), the program must first define the quintessential Black experience. Linscott argues that this essentialization of Blackness could exacerbate racial stereotypes. Second, he highlights the potential for appropriating the trauma of a racial minority group, as if it were a mere accessory that a White user could casually don and remove for entertainment purposes.

Nakamura offers a similar critique of social issue VR films that allow users to adopt avatars, citing examples such as Milk's *Clouds over Sidra* and de la Peña's *One Dark Night*. For instance, she contends that de la Peña's film is problematic as it reproduces "the murder of Trayvon Martin, a 17-year-old African-American teenager [...] in the name of reducing it" while simultaneously perpetuating "toxic re-embodiment" and "identity tourism" (51). In these films, Nakamura argues that users strive to feel "good about feeling bad," deriving a unique form of toxic pleasure from the VR experience (54, 60). As a result, she disputes the notion of VR as the ultimate empathy machine. Nakamura maintains that the hyperbolic claims made by VR enterprises regarding their technology's capacity for social good and the investments in this idea are predominantly marketing strategies. According to her, given that video games and pornography are currently the most popular applications of VR, these enterprises need to promote the technology as capable of fostering utopian social connections through the use of social issue and refugee VR documentaries.

Historical Background of Gina Kim's *Bloodless*

Kim's *Bloodless* adeptly sidesteps the ideology of liberation, identity tourism, and voyeuristic epistemophilia, successfully navigating the challenges outlined by Linscott, Nakamura, and Anderson. Prior to delving into a comprehensive analysis of her film, it may prove beneficial to provide a brief background of the historical event she revisits, particularly for readers who may be unfamiliar with this occurrence, which transpired in South Korea three decades ago.

Kim's initial interest in South Korean camptown sex workers emerged during her college years. Camptown, known as Kijichon in Korean, refers to the towns located in the vicinity of United States Forces Korea (USFK) military bases, with its origins dating back to the 1940s and 1950s. On October 28, 1992, a U.S. Army private named Kenneth Markle, stationed in South Korea, brutally murdered a young South Korean female sex worker, Yun Kûm Yi (also anglicized as Yoon Geum Yi, Yun Keum Yi, or Yun Geum-I, depending on the writer of the articles). Korean scholars and historians concur that this incident served as "a case in point" in reference to the "ignit[ion]" of a nationwide anti-American movement (Moon, "Resurrecting" 133; Lee 395), primarily due to the appalling nature of the murder. The injuries and abuse inflicted upon Yun's body were shockingly severe. She was "found naked, bloody, and covered with bruises and contusions—with laundry detergent sprinkled over the crime site. In addition, a Coke bottle was embedded in Yun's uterus and the trunk of an umbrella driven 27 cm into her rectum" (qtd. in Moon, "Resurrecting" 129).

Although Yun's murder incited the Korean public to engage in widespread anti-American protests, her death was not an isolated incident but rather a component of the ongoing systemic violence perpetrated by both the Korean government and the U.S. military. For example, Na-Young Lee contends that "military prostitution in U.S. camptowns has remained tacitly condoned by the Korean government because of national security and economic growth" (386). This is due to the fact that U.S. troops' spending in Korea accounted for 25% of South Korea's Gross National Product during the 1960s, and the U.S. military served as a powerful ally to South Korea's military regime throughout the 1960s and 70s, continuing to be a formidable economic and military partner to this day (Lee 386).

Katharine H. S. Moon also asserts that the camptown system "is highly regulated and sustained by official policies and practices of the U.S. military and the Korean government" ("South Korean Movements" 316). All camptown businesses were required to be licensed by the Korea Special Tourist Association and the Korean Ministry of Transportation. The Korean government not only regulated the businesses and female sex workers in camptowns but also even actively encouraged them by referring to them as a group of "patriots" and "diplomatic corps" (Hong 55). Furthermore, she states, "The U.S. military also keeps extensive files on [camptown] bar workers as a way to 'track' the 'source' of STDs that their men may contract" (316). Under the systematic regulation of the Korean military regime and due to the U.S. army's tacit agreement with the complicit government, numerous cases of rape, economic and sexual exploitation, forced drug use, and physical violence inflicted upon workers in camptowns went unreported and were consequently forgotten.

The abhorrent predicament of camptown sex workers in South Korea was further exacerbated by the pervasive societal ostracization and discrimination they faced, even from their fellow Korean citizens. It was only following the tragic murder of Yun Kûm Yi, which incited public outrage against this violence, that the plight of these individuals garnered attention. Despite this, the derogatory labels of "yanggongju" (Western princess) and the even more contemptuous "yanggalbo" (Western whore) persisted, casting millions of camptown workers as a source of national disgrace (Jodi Kim 101). Stigmatization these workers experienced remained entrenched within Korean society; even after Yun's case altered public sentiment, their testimonies were continuously silenced, depriving them of their legal rights. As evidenced in accounts from other trauma survivors, witnesses to these heinous acts frequently encountered skepticism and mistrust, both within legal proceedings and amongst the general public. In this regards, Grace Kyungwon Hong, in her thought-provoking article "Ghosts of Camptown," posits that camptown workers epitomize spectral beings. This characterization is not merely due to the numerous concealed fatalities within camptowns, but primarily because these individuals occupy a liminal state, straddling the domains of life and death, without fully belonging to either. This condition encapsulates the intricate juridical status of camptown residents (Hong 51). Moreover, their "unrememberable past" further contributes to their ghostly nature (52).[4]

The sheer brutality of Yun's demise, however, was not the sole aspect that profoundly disturbed filmmaker Kim; activist groups' exploitation of the crime scene imagery further exacerbated her unease. In an attempt to disseminate the truth and provoke anti-American sentiments, these activist groups chose to print, reproduce, and distribute photographs depicting Yun's naked and violated body. Consequently, this imagery was disseminated nationwide through thousands of pamphlets. As a college student at the time, Kim perceived this tactic as perpetuating violence.

Reflecting upon the incident, she recalls, "Every time I saw (the victim's) brutally mutilated body being endlessly reproduced in posters and flyers, I saw her dignity being once again destroyed" ("Empathy without exploitation").

Later, as a film director, Kim sought to revisit the harrowing event through her visual work, but confronted the inherent limitations of cinema in ethically representing the violated body. She notes, "every time, I had to abandon the project because of cinema's limitations in ethical representation" ("Interview with Gina Kim").[5] Kim grappled with the ethical dilemma of portraying the victim's image without inadvertently perpetuating the original violence. It was only a quarter of a century later that Kim discovered the potential of VR filmmaking as an alternative medium. She realized, "with VR, it's possible to experience another's story without emotionally distancing yourself from the subject of the piece" ("Interview with Gina Kim"). Harnessing the capabilities of VR, Kim was able to revisit the traumatic past in a more ethical manner through her artistic expression. The outcome was her groundbreaking VR film, *Bloodless*, which serves as the focal point of this article's analysis and is the first installment of her planned camptown VR film trilogy. Kim's second VR film, *Tearless* (2021) and her third, *Comfortless* (2023) have recently been released and are currently being showcased at numerous international venues.

Is Virtual Reality a Reality Duplicator or Reality Transformer?

In examining how Kim devised an ethically sound approach to portraying historical suffering through the medium of VR, it is imperative to engage with the ongoing discourse surrounding the quintessence of VR technology. The perspectives of various scholars and artists employing VR technology as a creative tool evince a striking divergence of opinions regarding the fundamental nature of VR technology.[6] Contemporary virtual reality experiences predominantly hinge on computer-generated imagery as a means of crafting entirely fictive environments conducive to user immersion. However, it is noteworthy that the initial aspirations of VR visionaries centered upon replicating the extant world with remarkable verisimilitude. This ambition continues to be pursued by VR documentarians such as de la Peña, Milk, and Iñárritu, who leverage virtual reality to create more accurate duplications of reality for their audiences.

These artists underscore the capacity of the medium to recreate external reality, particularly in addressing pressing societal concerns. For instance, de la Peña posits that VR technology serves as a remedy for the public's skepticism and apathy towards news media in the era of fake news. She contends that virtual reality constitutes "a much more faithful *duplication of real events*" thereby offering "a profoundly different way to experience the news, and therefore ultimately to understand it in a way that is otherwise impossible, without really being there" (emphasis added; 299–300). In a TED talk, Milk also refers to VR technology as the "ultimate empathy machine," emphasizing its capacity to facilitate users' vicarious exploration of the realities habitually confronted by marginalized communities ("How Virtual Reality"). Moreover, video game designer and researcher Brenda Laurel postulates that VR technology even harbors the potential to ameliorate ecological crises. She elucidates, "It can raise consciousness about the natural world by giving people remote first-person access to places on the earth. [...] If any significant percentage of the population ends up telecommuting through personal VR systems, the result will be fewer cars on the road and cleaner air" (14).

In contrast, pessimistic perspectives contend that the essence of VR technology does not lie in the reproduction of reality, but rather in the generation of fantastical realms. For instance, Jon Cogburn and Mark Silcox encapsulate the trepidations of numerous scholars vis-à-vis VR technology. They expound on the apprehensions of critics and philosophers with regard to the technology engendering a phenomenon of "brain-in-a-vatism," a renowned thought experiment which postulates the possibility of our existence being solely a brain submerged in life-sustaining fluid, connected to a supercomputer that supplies a simulated reality. Thus, they assert that immersion in VR's simulated environment could potentially constitute "a real threat to human well-being" as VR fabricates illusory realities (562). Timothy J. Beck also accentuates that some individuals harbor skepticism towards VR technology, dismissing it as merely a means of producing audiences who passively absorb non-existent realities. Citing Baudrillard, he states, "Now the media are no longer a stage where something is played, they are a strip, a track, a perforated map of which we are no longer even spectators: receiver" (qtd. in Beck 31).

In light of these conflicting responses to the same technology, the question of VR media's relationship to external reality becomes unavoidable. A VR documentary presents 360-degree visuals devoid of filmmaker intervention through framing, thus reproducing reality with enhanced accuracy. Simultaneously, a substantial proportion of VR content generates computer-simulated environments, such as extraterrestrial worlds or three-dimensional renditions of "ancient Pompeii" (Gutiérrez 180). This inquiry leads to an intricate philosophical conundrum: how should we interpret the concepts of "virtual" and "reality," two notoriously elusive philosophical terms?

The hardship of defining what "virtual" and "reality" mean in their aesthetic, technological, and philosophical senses makes it also challenging to define the first VR gear. For some, the essence of virtual reality should come from realistic virtuality, which comes from computer simulated environment (Zwiebach et al. 66), whereas for others the essence of virtual reality comes from how realistic a user feels subjectively, which necessitates multisensory experiences (Gutiérrez et al. 4). With regard to this, Erik Malcolm Champion, in his article "A Potted History of Virtual Reality," presents the contradictory ways in which the term VR has been defined in diverse scholarly books.[7] Noticing this incongruence, he found that the definitions of VR technology from different sources have differed drastically. He points out that some writers "tended to base VR on notions of technology rather than experience," while others focus more on users' subjective experience. He also states some definitions are mostly "vision based," while others highlight its multisensory representation of reality (10). Some writers define VR technology as "just the use of computer technology to create a simulated environment," while others highlight its role in reproducing reality (12).

Embodying the Ghostly Presence of Yun: Passing-Through the Camera

In the context of these dichotomous arguments concerning the essence of VR, Gina Kim's film astutely demonstrates a judicious employment of VR technology—neither solely as a duplicator of reality nor as a fabricator of fantasy. The film commences with a view of a desolate street adjacent to an unidentified railway line. It permits users to acclimate to the novel 360-degree screen experience for several minutes before the screen fades to black and a brief description of the film's historical context materializes. The description elucidates, "US servicemen have been stationed in South Korea since the 1900s. US military bases have occupied as much as 17.7 percent of the country's habitable land. They have also produced 96 camptowns offering prostitutions for servicemen, involving one million women. This space exists between two countries, and outside the protection of laws" (00:46).

Subsequently, the film transports the audience to the threshold of a dilapidated street bearing the sign "Dongducheon Special Tourism Zone for Foreigners." The audience then discerns their virtual location—one of the Korean camptowns initially alluded to as a lawless domain. As day transitions to night, the audience observes genuine U.S. soldiers, who are seemingly not actors but actual passersby, thereby indicating that the film constitutes a realistic documentary rather than a fictitious or computer-generated cyberspace. The soldiers traverse the foreboding street, firearms secured to their belts. As the film guides the audience further into the zone and the street becomes increasingly darker, a woman (presumably portraying Yun Kûm Yi's character; played by actresses Boryeong Kim) adorned with heavy makeup and revealing attire strolls by, oblivious to the camera and providing no indication to the audience of her role as an actress.

Certain audience members may even overlook her presence if their attention is diverted by other elements in the 360-degree film. As the sequence unfolds, the film redirects the audience's focus towards her by employing the sound of her high heels. Consequently, the audience endeavors to locate the woman, yet she remains visually elusive, existing solely as the ambient sound of her footsteps. The film deftly transitions from what Bazin referred to as "a total simulacrum of reality," characterized by a faithful reproduction of the camptown's milieu, to a seemingly fantastical space imbued with transformed reality. The audience experiences the sensation that the woman, who manifests solely through the auditory cues she generates without an observable form, is akin to a specter. Thus, her *invisible* yet *hyperaural* presence accentuates that she is not a real inhabitant of the documentary, but rather the ghost of Yun. This notion corroborates Hong's characterization of the ghostly status of camptown sex workers: "[the] state of in-betweenness, characterized by both life and death" (52). In addition, the workers belong neither to Korea nor the United States; they occupy an intermediary status betwixt life and death, as well as between serving as diplomatic patriots and being labeled as "Western whores."

In the ensuing scene, the woman abruptly strides towards the camera, gazing intently at the lens. Subsequently, she traverses the camera's field of view. The audience experiences this as if she passes through their very beings. Upon turning around, they find her stationed behind them, scrutinizing the camera once more. It is worth noting that this scene was captured and produced without resorting to computer-generated imagery; it in fact employs a live actress. In this respect, the film speculatively resurrects the silenced (deceased) victim of the past within the VR domain in the guise of a ghost, eschewing both a strict reproduction of reality and the creation of an entirely fantastical space. Moreover, this passage intensifies the audience's perception of her as a spectral figure because she passes through the audience's virtual bodies, and increases empathy between the character and the audience by rendering the users' virtual bodies temporarily overlapping with Yun's spectral form.

In what I term the *passing-through scene*, Kim propels the potential of VR media further. The scene amplifies what Matt Burdette terms the "Swayze effect" rather than diminishing it. Originating from the 1990s Hollywood film *Ghost*, which featured Patrick Swayze as the ghost of Sam Wheat, Burdette's concept encapsulates "the sensation of having no tangible relationship with your surroundings despite feeling present in the world." Indeed, in a VR environment, the audience lacks a physical body, precluding their physical interaction with the film's characters; users can virtually explore, for example, the depths of the ocean, seemingly swimming alongside sea turtles and whales, but at a certain point, the audience experiences detachment instead of deepening connection to the objects when they discover they cannot touch or interact with the marine creatures. Thus, the audience feels akin to Swayze's character in *Ghost*—a spectral entity who can sense his lover's presence yet remains physically disconnected. Thus, to augment the sense of reality within virtual environments, the prevailing objective of VR media has been to mitigate the Swayze effect rather than intensify it.

Kim, however, transcends the issue of detachment and lack of empathy in VR media not by attempting to mitigate the Swayze effect but by maximizing it to its utmost extent.[8] By facilitating the woman's passage through the audience's virtual body, the viewers can no longer avoid recognizing the absence of their virtual bodies while simultaneously reminding themselves of the actual presence of their physical bodies. The chasm between the heightened sensation of their virtual body's absence and their physical body's presence prompts the audience to assume a spectral form akin to Yun's character in the film. Up until the moment the woman fixates on the camera lens, the audience undergoes an intensified sense of detachment from her and experiences a relative sense of safety, as they are aware of being invisible voyeurs within this virtual realm. Her passage through the audience's virtual bodies paradoxically reminds them of their presence in the virtual world by highlighting the absence of their virtual bodies. This unique attribute distinguishes Kim's VR film from other social issue VR documentaries as she effectively overcomes the problem of exploitative voyeurism.

This distinctive aspect of her VR film reaffirms the director's persistent inquiry into making VR a genuine empathy machine that avoids the pitfalls of identity tourism, voyeuristic epistemophilia, and toxic re-embodiment. In an interview, she stated, "I've been asked repeatedly the same question 'Is VR an empathy machine?' My answer is yes" ("Sex Crimes and Virtual Reality"). However, she immediately followed with another question: "And what can we do with it?" ("Sex Crimes"). In addressing this question—What can we do with it as an empathy machine?—she contends, "When VR is used for exploitation, especially in depicting violence, it can only create further violence against the viewer [...][;] if VR is an empathy machine, toward what end do we want to create empathy?" ("Sex Crimes"). In another interview, she says, "To put it very succinctly and bluntly, any representation of anything is exploitation. But the question is, to what end? Where do you compromise?" ("Empathy"). Her answer is to establish "empathy without exploitation," resulting in a VR film that abstains from voyeuristically reproducing past incidents associated with the historical mistreatment of socially marginalized groups ("Empathy").

From Identity Tourism to Embodying a Ghostly Status

It is also crucial to highlight that *Bloodless* does not endeavor to have the audience assume the role of the historical victim in order to vicariously experience Yun's life. Rather than unethically re-embodying or commodifying Yun's body, Kim allows her audience to grapple with the ontological uncertainty of their presence either by witnessing Yun passing through the camera or by being in a liminal status between witness and victim. For example, in the concluding scene of the film, Kim transports the audience to a cramped, dilapidated motel room, meticulously recreated by Kim and her team to resemble the actual room where Yun Kûm Yi's murder transpired. A mirror on the wall features a six-digit phone number, evoking a sense of nostalgia for Korean audiences who recall the nationwide change from six to seven-digit phone numbers in the 1990s. Through the mirror and the room's dated furnishings, even those unfamiliar with Korean culture can perceive a palpable sense of time-travel to the past.

Within this claustrophobic, fluorescent-lit, buzzing, and disquieting space, blood slowly oozes from an old blanket, pooling on the floor without any visible body nearby. In this scene, Kim once again obscures the boundaries between observer and observed, witness and victim, reality and fantasy. As there is no physical body within the observed space, except for the spectral presence of the audience, they may feel as though the blood is emanating from their own semi-corporeal form. Consequently, the audience is not merely a passive, ghostly witness but is immersed in an ambiguous state, straddling the roles of both witness and victim. Furthermore, despite the absence of a visible body, the audience vividly recalls and senses the woman's gaze and her eerie presence somewhere within the room. The film dismantles the audience's position as secure observers, propelling them into an uncertain space between observer and observed.

Ultimately, as the blood seeps from the blanket and pools on the floor, a new image materializes through a dissolve effect solely within the mirror, revealing the lower half of a woman's body beneath the blanket. The dissonance between what the audience perceives in the room and the reflection in the mirror calls into question their epistemological understanding, fostering doubt about whether they inhabit a realm of reality or fantasy. This blurred demarcation between documentary realism and the fantastical construction of spectral entities precludes the audience from comfortably assuming the role of passive voyeurs. Through her innovative employment of VR media as a means to retrospect historical trauma, Kim unveils the untapped potential of VR as a true instrument of empathy. Rather than merely replicating reality or generating computer-rendered imagery, she challenges the audience's epistemological grasp of reality and ontological certainty. It is only by interrogating the audience's conventional perception of reality that an alternative reality emerges, wherein the deceased Yun can reclaim her voice and secure an ethically grounded representation, notwithstanding her spectral status.

Conclusion

South Korean director Gina Kim's *Bloodless* endeavors to revisit a past traumatic event in Korea—the brutal murder of Yun Kûm Yi—which she initially deemed impossible to retrospectively represent in non-VR cinema without perpetuating the violence inflicted upon the victim. Given that the victims of this systematic and institutional violence are either deceased or relegated to a juridical limbo, resurrecting their voices presents a formidable challenge as it necessitates invoking their spectral status. Nevertheless, Kim innovatively reconceptualizes past trauma by harnessing the capabilities of VR media. Utilizing VR as an emerging technology, Kim seeks neither to replicate the past event nor to convert reality into fantasy, but instead transcends the boundaries between the real and the fantastical. In doing so, she identifies a direction in which VR media should be steered if it is to truly function as an empathy machine without exploitation. Rather than employing VR media to commodify the identities of marginalized groups or indulge in voyeuristic epistemophilia, Kim uses it as an instrument enabling audiences to embody the ghostly status of past victims. This approach blurs the hierarchical distinctions between observer and observed, as well as between victim and witness, fostering a deeper sense of empathy and understanding.

Notes

1. See, for example, Heim, Michael. *The Metaphysics of Virtual Reality.* Oxford University Press, 1993; Morse, Margaret. *Virtualities: Television, Media Art, and Cyberculture.* Indiana University Press, 1998; Hayward, Philip, and Tana Wollen, editors. *Future Visions: New Technologies of*

the Screen. BFI Publications, 1993, pp. 148-165; Mirzoeff, Nicholas. *An Introduction to Visual Culture*. Routledge, 1999; Holmes, David, editor. *Virtual Politics: Identity and Community in Cyberspace*. SAGE Publications, 1997; Rheingold, Howard. *Virtual Reality: The Revolutionary Technology of Computer-Generated Artificial Worlds—and How It Promises to Transform Society*. A Touchstone Book, 1991; Lippit, Akira Mizuta. "Virtual Annihilation: Optics, VR, and the Discourse of Subjectivity." *Criticism*, vol. 36, no. 4, 1994, pp. 595-610; Laurel, Brenda. "Art and Activism in VR." *Wide Angle*, vol. 15, no. 4, 1993, pp. 13-21; Grau, Oliver. "Into the Belly of the Image: Historical Aspects of Virtual Reality." *Leonardo*, vol. 32, no. 5, 1999, pp. 365-371.

2. Diverse forms of VR technologies are expanding into various fields of research and industry. As Marc Herz and Philipp A. Rauschnabel summarize, numerous academic fields such as marketing, tourism, medicine, and education have proliferated during the last 10 years (229). Another article by Mahfud Sholihin et al. effectively summarizes recent research on various topics within VR in education, including student motivation enhancement, behavior skills training, learning effectiveness, biology study, health care, fire safety behavioral skills, ethical efficacy, and students' imagination (1-2). VR technologies are also widely used in the medical field, as demonstrated by Koenig, et al., for applications such as motor rehabilitation, neuropsychological assessment, treatment of phobias and PTSD, chronic pain management, and more (521).

3. Furthermore, Hu-Au, E., and Lee, J. J. in their article "Virtual Reality in Education: A Tool for Learning in the Experience Age" present their research on VR as a pedagogical tool that can provide new perspectives and create empathy (qtd. in Kim, So, and Park 120). Jamie McRoberts, in the article "Are We There Yet? Media Content and Sense of Presence in Non-Fiction Virtual Reality," argues that VR, due to its effect of virtual presence, enhances empathy and further motivates users to engage in social transformation. The philosopher Michael Heim also echoes this in his book *The Metaphysics of Virtual Reality* when he argues the essence of VR lies in its power to "shift the Western philosophy of presence" and "enhanc[ing] the power of art to transform reality" by overcoming the previous art forms' limits of making the audience passive spectators (127). He further writes that VR's function of transforming reality and not

duplicating it "can reduce apathy and the couch-potato syndrome simply by requiring creative decisions"; VR can "become a training tool to enhance receptivity" (126). One notable point is that there is also a case showing VR decreases empathy rather than increases it. Mado and Bailenson include an example that when there is not enough background information about the educational goal and "when empathizing with the social target becomes inconvenient in the social setting," the education could not only be ineffective but even counterproductive (175).

4. This spectral representation of comfort women and other historically marginalized groups in South Korea is also evident in various Korean fantasy novels and visual media, including Nora Okja Keller's *Fox Girl* and the Netflix series *The School Nurse Files*. Scholar Stephen Hong Sohn refers to this phenomenon as "Korean American ethnoformalism" (224–25).

5. Although Kim's comment may suggest a binary distinction between cinema as "old media" and VR film as "new media," she does not use these terms in her interviews. Instead, she refers to VR film as a "new technology." This choice of words is thoughtful, as media scholars have critiqued the problematic nature of the term "new media," which suggests an ideology of innovation from "old" to "new" media. Bolter and Grusin argue that the attempt to distinguish virtual reality from all other media anchors it more firmly in the history of representation (162–63). Similarly, Wendy Chun suggests that the moment of "newness" for the term "new media" was less about its invention or usage and more about a political move to deregulate it and increase its coverage in mass media ("Did Somebody Say New Media" 3). Therefore, Kim's deliberate choice of words indicates that VR is not the only medium capable of ethnic representation, but rather an alternative medium that offers different possibilities and capabilities from non-VR cinema.

6. The debate surrounding VR often revolves around two questions: what constitutes "reality" in VR, and how can we determine if a user's experience is real? Critics such as Meyer et al. argue that even rudimentary devices like a traditional computer can be considered a VR machine if a user feels its medium is "real" enough. For instance, Gutiérrez et al. categorize VR into non-immersive (desktop-based VR), semi-immersive (large projection screens), and fully immersive (head-mounted display) and suggest distinguishing "presence" from

"immersion" (3–4). This way of defining VR highlights the importance of individual subjective and psychological experiences. Mado and Bailenson further report that different demographics can have vastly different experiences of presence in VR, which implies that what defines VR depends on the user's subjective experience rather than the machine's capability (165, 180). Therefore, scholars have yet to reach a consensus on the essence of VR, whether it is about the users' feeling of "realness" or the machine's capability of creating a computer-simulated image.

7. For example, he compares the books such as *The Oxford Handbook of Virtual Reality*, *The Metaphysics of Virtual Reality*, and *The Oxford Handbook of Virtuality* as well as definitions from *Oxford English Dictionary*, *Encyclopedia Britannica*, *Online Cambridge Dictionary*, and *Merriam-Webster*.

8. See also Kim, Seon-ah. "The Point of View and Frame in The VR Movie-Focusing on <Bloodless>." *The Journal of the Korea Contents Association*, vol. 20, no. 4, 2020, pp. 518-529. In this paper, Seon-ah Kim argues that *Bloodless* "destroys the Swayze effect in a rough and radical way" (522). Although I agree with this argument, I aim to analyze it more in detail, positing that *Bloodless* actually manages to mitigate the Swayze effect by *maximizing* it, rather than "destroy[ing]" it.

Works Cited

Adorno, Theodor. "Kulturkritik und Gesellschaft," *Prismen*. Kulturkritik und Gesellschaft, 1963, pp. 7–26.

Agamben, Giorgio. *Remnants of Auschwitz: The Witness and the Archive.* Zone Books, 2002.

Ahn, S. J., Bostick, J., Ogle, E., Nowak, K., McGillicuddy, K., and Bailenson, J. N. "Experiencing Nature: Embodying Animals in Immersive Virtual Environments Increases Inclusion of Nature in Self and Involvement with Nature." *Journal of Computer-Mediated Communication*, vol. 21, no. 6, 2016, pp. 399–419.

Anderson, Steve. F. "New (Old) Ontologies of Documentary." *Reclaiming Popular Documentary*, edited by Christie Milliken and Steve F. Anderson, Indiana UP, 2021, pp. 356–370.

Avatar. Directed by James Cameron, 20th Century Studios, 2009.

Beck, Timothy J. "Actualization of the Virtual through an Aesthetic Encounter with Virtual Reality Technology." *Art as Revolt: Thinking Politics through Immanent Aesthetics*, edited by David Fancy and Hans Skott-Myhre, McGill-Queen's UP, 2019, pp. 29–52.

Benjamin, Ruha. *Race After Technology*, Polity, 2019.

Bloodless. Directed by Gina Kim, performances by Boryeong Kim, Cyan Films, 2017.

Bolter, Jay David and Richard Grusin. *Remediation: Understanding New Media*. MIT Press, 2000.

Bonilla-Silva, Eduardo. *Racism without Racists: Color-Blind Racism and the Persistence of Racial Inequality in America*. Rowman and Littlefield, 2014.

Burdette, Matt. "Swayze Effect." *Meta Quest*, 18 November 2015, https://www.oculus.com/story-studio/blog/the-swayze-effect/. Accessed 5 October 2022.

Caruth, Cathy. *Unclaimed Experience: Trauma, Narrative and History*. The Johns Hopkins UP, 1996.

Champion, Erik Malcolm. "A Potted History of Virtual Reality." *Rethinking Virtual Places*. Indiana UP, 2021, pp. 4–26.

Chun, Wendy Hui Kyong. "Did Somebody Say New Media." *New Media Old Media*, edited by Wendy Hui Kyong Chun, Anna Watkins Fisher, and Thomas Keenan, Routledge, 2005.

———. *Discriminating Data*. MIT Press, 2021.

Cline, Ernest. *Ready Player One: A Novel*. Random House Publishing Group, 2011.

Cogburn, Jon and Mark Silcox. "Against Brain-in-a-vatism: On the Value of Virtual Reality." *Philosophy & Technology*, vol. 27, no. 4, 2014, pp. 561–579.

Cook, David A. *A History of Three-Dimensional Cinema*. Anthem Press, 2021.

de la Peña, Nonny, Peggy Weil, Joan Llobera, Elias Giannopoulos, Ausiàs Pomés, Bernhard Spanlang, Doron Friedman, Maria V. Sanchez-Vives, and Mel Slater. "Immersive Journalism: Immersive Virtual Reality for the First Person Experience of News." *Presence: Teleoperators and Virtual Environments*, vol. 19, no. 4, 2010, pp. 291–301.

Forbes Agency Council. "Virtual Reality—The Future Of Media Or Just A Passing Trend?." *Forbes*, 30 May 2017, https://www.forbes.com/sites/forbesagencycouncil/2017/05/30/virtual-reality-the-future-of-media-or-just-a-passing-trend/?sh=282fea777d8f. Accessed 5 Oct 2022.

Gibson, William. *Neuromancer*. Ace Books, 1984.

Grau, Oliver. "Into the Belly of the Image: Historical Aspects of Virtual Reality." *Leonardo*, vol. 32, no. 5, 1999, pp. 365-371.

Gutiérrez A., Mario A., Frédéric Vexo and Daniel Thalmann. *Stepping into Virtual Reality*. Springer, 2008.

Hasler, Beatrice S., Bernhard Spanlang and Mel Slater. "Virtual Race Transformation Reverses Racial In-group Bias." *PLOS ONE*, vol. 12, no. 4, 2017. https://journals.plos.org/plosone/article?id=10.1371/journal.pone.0174965. Accessed 5 October 2022.

Hayward, Philip and Tana Wollen, editors. *Future Visions: New Technologies of the Screen*. BFI Publications, 1993, pp. 148-165.

Heim, Michael. *The Metaphysics of Virtual Reality*. Oxford UP, 1993.

Herz, Marc and Philipp A. Rauschnabel. "Understanding the Diffusion of Virtual Reality Glasses: The Role of Media, Fashion and Technology." *Technological Forecasting & Social Change*, vol. 138, 2019, pp. 228–242.

Holmes, David, editor. *Virtual Politics: Identity and Community in Cyberspace*. SAGE Publications, 1997.

Hong, Grace Kyungwon. "Ghosts of Camptown." *MELUS: Multi-Ethnic Literature of the U.S.*, vol. 39, no. 3, 2014, pp. 49–67.

Kastrenakes, Jacob and Alex Heath. "Facebook is Spending at Least $10 Billion this Year on its Metaverse Division." *The Verge*, 25 October 2022. https://www.theverge.com/2021/10/25/22745381/facebook-reality-labs-10-billion-metaverse. Accessed 5 October 2022.

Kim, Gina and Jay Kim. "Interview with Gina Kim on BLOODLESS and TEARLESS." *XRMust*, 2 September 2021, https://www.xrmust.com/xrmagazine/case-study-gina-kim-bloodless-tearless/. Accessed 5 October 2022.

Kim, Gina and Lauren Wissot. "Sex Crimes and Virtual Reality: Best VR Storytelling of 2017, Gina Kim's Bloodless." *Filmmaker Magazine*,

22 Dec. 2017, https://filmmakermagazine.com/104182-sex-crimes-and-virtual-reality-best-vr-storytelling-of-2017-gina-kims-bloodless/#.Yz4DPuzMKvA. Accessed 5 October 2022.

Kim, Gina and Rumy Doo. "Empathy Without Exploitation." *The Korea Herald*, 4 October 2017, https://m.koreaherald.com/view.php?ud=20170915000677. Accessed 5 October 2022.

Kim, Hyojung, Hyo-Jeong So and Ju-Yeon Park. "Examining the Effect of Socially Engaged Art Education with Virtual Reality on Creative Problem Solving." *Educational Technology & Society*, vol. 25, no. 2, 2022, pp. 117–129.

Kim, Jodi. *Settler Garrison: Debt Imperialism, Militarism, and Transpacific Imaginaries*. Duke UP, 2022.

Kim, Seon-ah. "The Point of View and Frame in The VR Movie-Focusing on <Bloodless>." *The Journal of the Korea Contents Association*, vol. 20, no. 4, 2020, pp. 518-529.

Koenig, Sebastian T., Denise Krch, Belinda S. Lange and Albert "Skip" Rizzo. "Virtual Reality and Rehabilitation." *Handbook of Rehabilitation Psychology*, edited by Lisa A. Brenner, Stephanie A. Reid-Arndt, Timothy R. Elliott, Robert G. Frank, Bruce Caplan. American Psychological Association, 2019, pp. 521–539.

Laurel, Brenda. "Art and Activism in VR." *Wide Angle*, vol. 15, no. 4, 1993, pp. 13–21.

Lee, Na-Young. "Beyond the Boundaries of Nationalism, Christianity and Feminism: South Korean Women's Movement against U.S. Military Prostitution." *Routledge Handbook of East Asian Gender Studies*, edited by Jieyu Liu and Junko Yamashita. Routledge, 2020, pp. 385–402.

Linscott, Charles P. "Virtually and Actually Black: On VR and Racial Empathy." *ASAP/Journal*, vol. 4, no. 2, 2019, pp. 303–306.

Lippit, Akira Mizuta. "Virtual Annihilation: Optics, VR, and the Discourse of Subjectivity." *Criticism*, vol. 36, no. 4, 1994, pp. 595–610.

Lister, Martin, Jon Dovey, Seth Giddings, Iain Grant, and Kieran Kelly. *New Media: A Critical Introduction*. Routledge, 2009.

Mado, Marijn and Jeremy Bailenson. "The Psychology of Virtual Reality." *The Psychology of Technology*, edited by Sandra C. Matz. American Psychological Association, 2022, pp. 155–193.

McRoberts, Jamie. "Are We There Yet?. Media Content and Sense of Presence in Non-fiction Virtual Reality." *Studies in Documentary Film*, vol. 12, no. 2, 2018, pp. 101–118.

Meyer, Oliver, Magnus K. Omdahl, and Guido Makransky. "Investigating the Effect of Pre-training When Learning Through Immersive Virtual Reality and Video: A Media and Methods Experiment." *Computers & Education*, vol. 140, 2019, pp. 1–17.

Milk, Chris. "How Virtual Reality Can Create the Ultimate Empathy Machine." *TED*, April 2015, https://www.ted.com/talks/chris_milk_how_virtual_reality_can_c reate_the_ultimate_empathy_machine?language=en. Accessed 5 October 2022.

Mirzoeff, Nicholas. *An Introduction to Visual Culture*. Routledge, 1999.

Moon, Katharine H. S. "Resurrecting Prostitutes and Overturning Treaties: Gender Politics in the 'Anti-American' Movement in South Korea." *The Journal of Asian Studies*, vol. 66, no. 1, 2007, pp. 129–157.

———. "South Korean Movements against Militarized Sexual Labor." *Asian Survey*, vol. 39, no. 2, 1999, pp. 310–327.

Morse, Margaret. *Virtualities: Television, Media Art, and Cyberculture*. Indiana University Press, 1998.

Nakamura, Lisa. "Feeling Good About Feeling Bad: Virtuous Virtual Reality and the Automation of Racial Empathy." *Journal of Visual Culture*, vol. 19, no. 1, 2020, pp. 47–64.

———. *Cybertypes: Race, Ethnicity, and Identity on the Internet*. Routledge, 2002.

Peripheral. Created by Scott B. Smith, Amazon Video, 2023.

Ready Player One. Directed by Steven Spielberg, Warner Bros. Pictures, 2018.

Rheingold, Howard. *Virtual Reality: The Revolutionary Technology of Computer-Generated Artificial Worlds–and How It Promises to Transform Society*. A Touchstone Book, 1991.

Robertson, Adi and Michael Zelenko. "Voices from a Virtual Past: An Oral History of a Technology Whose Time Has Come Again." *The Verge*, https://www.theverge.com/a/virtual-reality/oral_history. Accessed 5 October 2022.

Sholihin, Mahfud, Ratna Candra Sari, Nurhening Yuniarti, and Sariyatul Ilyana. "A New Way of Teaching Business Ethics: The Evaluation of Virtual Reality-based Learning Media." *The International Journal of Management Education*, vol. 18, 2020, pp. 1–13.

Sohn, Stephen Hong. "Toward Korean American Ethnoformalisms: The Historian-Archivist and Speculative Gendered Empowerments in Minsoo Kang's Of Tales and Enigmas," *Journal of the Fantastic in the Arts*, vol. 31, no. 2, 2020, pp. 223-245.

Steptoe, William, Anthony Steed, and Mel Slater. "Human Tails: Ownership and Control of Extended Humanoid Avatars." *IEEE Transactions on Visualization and Computer Graphics*, vol. 19, no. 4, 2013, pp. 583–90.

Ward, Graham. "On Time and Salvation: The Eschatology of Emmanuel Levinas." *Facing the Other: The Ethics of Emmanuel Levinas*, edited by Seán Hand, Routledge, 1996, pp. 153-172.

Zwiebach, Liza C., Laura Loucks, Devika Fiorillo and Marat V. Zanov. "Virtual Reality Psychotherapy." *Using Technology in Mental Health Practice*, edited by Jeffrey J. Magnavita, American Psychological Association, 2018, pp. 65–83.

Life Reset: Resisting Gamified Life in South Korean Speculative Webtoons

Sang Eun Eunice Lee

A SEMI-TRANSPARENT PURPLE DIALOGUE BOX appears mid-air. "Linguistics [Frank]/ language abilities have increased." Next to an icon of a man with a talk bubble, a yellow experience bar—about a fifth filled in—informs the progress to the next language ability rank. Juhŏn, a thirty-something-year-old grave robber in search of enchanted artifacts in the South Korean webtoon *Tomb Raider King* (2019-2023), sees many of these purple dialogue boxes. Suspended mid-air, they tell him, in no uncertain terms, just how much progress he has made in honing his various grave robbing skills, and how his rapidly changing surroundings have transformed.

On one hand, these dialogue boxes mimic those that appear in various video games, especially role-playing games (RPGs), in which the player plays through a protagonist they may design in the likeness they want or who may be preset for them. Playing through the avatar, the player completes a series of quests in increasing difficulty as they travel through fictional lands towards a main goal. Their progress through quests adds numeric value to their abilities and skill levels, often expressed through leveling up or ranking up, allowing the player to tackle larger and stronger enemies, eventually making their way to a final boss or challenge.

Much of Juhŏn's graverobbing journey through various magical tombs is similarly structured. His "quests" begin with a simple tomb with a familiar story—Aesop's tale of the Honest Woodcutter—as the requisite for "clearing" the grave and acquiring its artifacts, the golden axe and the silver axe. Once he clears them, he "levels up" his skills and utilizes the artifacts as items that can aid his journey into achieving his final goal of becoming the "tomb raider king." In one striking deviation, though, Juhŏn, unlike a character in an RPG game, but much like the player holding the console controller, has completed these quests before. He was brought back to life after meeting an untimely and woeful death, and he re-plays his life stories to change his fate.

Set in a world where "artifacts" can grant special abilities and powers to the wielder, the immensely popular *Tomb Raider King* (*Togurwang*) tells the story of a 38-year-old grave robber Sŏ Juhŏn. In his first life, he is an exploited low-level employee, working for a large artifact-collection corporation, only to meet an untimely death as a sacrifice in one of its excavations. When he dies, however, an unknown figure called Crow revives him, and turns back the clock by fifteen years to the year 2025 when the artifacts and tombs are yet to appear in the world. With a new life and the foresight of the events to come, Juhŏn begins to raid tombs before anyone else understands their significance, and builds his own artifact empire.

If *Tomb Raider King* revolves around a speculative world of legendary artifacts and their mystical powers, *Again My Life* (*Ŏgein Mai Raip'ŭ*) tells a legal drama of a passionate prosecutor, Kim Hŭiu, bringing down a formidable corrupt politician, Cho T'aesŏp. Like the opening of *Tomb Raider King* in which Juhŏn meets an untimely death working for an exploitative owner, *Again My Life* begins with a hired gun pushing Hŭiu into the Han River and stating that his noble attempts will be remembered as the lonesome suicide of a drug-addicted corrupt prosecutor. Much like the Crow in *Tomb Raider King*, the Grim Reaper in Korean folklore (Chŏsŭngsaja) brings Hŭiu back to life to relive his life from the year 1997 when he was only a high school student. Hŭiu promises her that he will meticulously plan his investigation of Cho and will bring him to justice.

A growing subset of South Korean webtoons, or serial comics produced for digital platforms, interweave cyclical temporality of rebirth narratives with the gamification of the everyday to provide an alternate model of future worldmaking. Focusing on two such webtoons centering on protagonists who are brought back to life, *Tomb Raider King* and *Again My Life*, this article explores the ways in which the overt gamification of life in webtoons attempts to critique and resist the covert yet pervasive pointification of "real" life. This "pointification" consistently keeps certain populations fungible and marginal by enforcing an overt hierarchical social order. At the same time, by highlighting the ways in which the webtoons pose technoliberal conceptions of the human as protagonist-player in their climb through the social hierarchy, this article explores the stakes of dismantling existing structures of social inequality.

Gamification of the Everyday

In their attempts to define an expansive and diffusive use of "gamification," ranging from marketing and branding to tourism and education, Sebastian Deterding et al. provide the following expansive definition for the term as "the use of game design elements in non-game contexts" (9). With this deceptively simple definition of gamification, the term brings to question the difficulty of defining the key referent, games, and its ludic qualities and logic. In an early discussion of game studies, Johan Huizinga provides an expansive characterization of play as a voluntary activity contained within a set of laws that engages the players. Building on the scholarship, Brian Sutton-Smith outlines varying rhetorics regarding play ranging from animal progress and child play to fate, power and identity, to highlight the very ambiguity of play. In these efforts to understand games, they highlight games' ludic qualities, yet game and play overflow a single definition. Encapsulating this ambiguity and difficulty of defining what makes games indeed games, video game designer and researcher Ian Bogost highlights the effects of games, stating that "'games' seem both trivial and powerful all at once" (141). Despite the prevalence of games and their association with triviality and fantasy, he writes, "even condemnations of video games acknowledge that they contain special power, power to captivate us and draw us in, power to encourage us to repeat things we've seemingly done before, power to get us to spend money on things that seem not to exist, and so forth" (140-141).

Similarly recognizing the difficulty of defining gamification, interaction and user experience computing researchers Katie Seaborn and Deborah Fels, in their survey of literature on gamification, expand the definition to "those features of an interactive system that aim to motivate and engage end-users through the use of game elements and mechanics" (15). Seaborn and Fels' inclusion of motivation and engagement speak to the central position that consumer psychology takes in discussions of gamification in a variety of industries, in particular in their attempts to ensure brand loyalty and consumer spending. Detailing specifics of consumer psychology, businessman and speaker on gamification Gabe Zichermann and journalist Joselin Linder write that gamification functions by providing "substantial psychological rewards simply by tapping into users' intrinsic motivations" and that "Funware and game-based marketing readily excite today's consumers" (199). Such perspectives on gamification and its perceived motivational impact on its users have resulted in the implementation of game design elements in wide-ranging fields, from local bakery loyalty points systems and visit incentives in tourism bureaus to the Nike+ running app.

Against the backdrop of industry-based and consumer-focused usages of gamification, critics highlight gamification's fundamental misunderstanding of the key concepts of games and play, and the misappropriation and misrepresentation of ludic logic and qualities. Bogost, for instance, presents the following strongly worded argument that criticizes gamification as capital-driven exploitationware:

> Exploitationware captures gamifiers' real intentions: a grifter's game, pursued to capitalize on a cultural moment, through services about which they have questionable expertise, to bring about results meant to last only long enough to pad their bank accounts before the next bullshit trend comes along. ("Gamification is Bullshit")

Calling Zichermann "the gamification movement's Dark Lord," Bogost notes the misrepresentation of ludic qualities in Zichermann's understanding of gamification. Quoting Zichermann, who states that "The presence of key game mechanics, such as points, badges, levels, challenges, leader boards, rewards and onboarding, are signals that a game is taking place," Bogost emphasizes the emotional investment of games as its central ludic quality ("The purpose of gamification"). He writes:

> Note how deftly Zichermann makes his readers believe that points, badges, levels, leaderboards, and rewards are "key game mechanics." This is wrong, of course—key game mechanics are the operational parts of games that produce an experience of interest, enlightenment, terror, fascination, hope, or any number of other sensations. Points and levels and the like are mere gestures that provide structure and measure progress within such a system. ("Exploitationware")

Similarly intervening into proponents of gamification's simplistic approach to the ludic qualities of games, Margaret Robertson writes:

> What we're currently terming gamification is in fact the process of taking *the thing that is least essential to games* and representing it as the core of the experience. Points and badges have no closer a relationship to games than they do to websites and fitness apps and loyalty cards. [...] They are the least important bit of a game, the bit that has the least to do with all of the rich cognitive, emotional and social drivers which gamifiers are intending to connect with. (Emphasis original; Robertson "Can't Play, Won't Play")

She instead proposes pointification as a term to refer to existing efforts towards gamifying industries, and argues that imbuing ludic qualities should replace gimmicks like points and badges as markers of progress.

Technoliberalism of Gamification

Understanding the historical contexts through which gamification took root similarly demonstrates the distinctive lack of ludic quality in the gamification of industries. Computer scientist Mark Nelson, for instance, locates earlier gamification movements in the Cold War moment, in which the Soviet Union and the United States employed video game mechanics to incentivize and motivate workers. He outlines that the Soviet Union highlighted competitive games to stimulate production "to replace capitalist competition with something that would be simultaneously more engaging and humane," while the US focused on elements of childhood play "aiming to weaken the work/play split, but often with games and competition integrated into the framework" (23).

Similarly, game and media studies scholars Jennifer deWinter, Carly Kocurek, and Randall Nichols locate gamification as an expansion of Taylorism, or Frederick Winslow Taylor's methods of scientific management spanning "division of labour, the structure of control over task performance, and the implicit minimum interaction employment relationship" (Littler 185). They write:

> [G]ames under a Taylorist model shift the competitions from how well you sell to the specific mechanics of selling—micromanaging producers and consumers on an unprecedented scale. Indeed, what we find most disturbing here is not just that Taylorism as gamification extends micromanagement to incorporate the practices of leisure time, attempting to make work seem like fun (even when it's not inherently, like counting the number of olives allowed on a Subway sandwich), but also that it opens the potential to force leisure time to become productive, whether in relation to one's own work or as an extension of some outside agent's need for production. (deWinter 3)

Understanding gamification as an extension of Taylorism and its principles of fragmented and separated laborers in their relationship to work presents a stark separation between the management's attempt to recreate ludic qualities of games and the shortcomings of pointification in that very attempt. It demonstrates the exploitative intent of gamification in its goal of intrinsic and extrinsic motivation as blurring the division between leisure and work, overrepresenting work in the worker and the consumption in consumers, and complicating the boundaries of what counts as entertainment. Reduced to work in both work and leisure, the worker functions as an embodiment of productivity— mere hands without the rest of the body—much like technological and even artificial intelligence inventions that are manufactured specifically for a single purpose of work, like ticketing kiosks or robot vacuums. Stating that "technoliberalism is the present-day racial capitalism" (3), Kalindi Vora and Neda Atanososki highlight the ways in which technology builds on the existing relations of labor and power as mediated through race and gender. They write:

> Technological futures tied to capitalist development iterate a fantasy that as machines, algorithms, and artificial intelligence take over the dull, dirty, repetitive, and even reproductive labor performed by racialized, gendered, and colonized workers in the past, the full humanity of the (already) human subject will be freed for creative capacities. [...] Engineering imaginaries, even as they claim revolutionary status for the techno-objects and platforms they produce to better human life, thus tend to be limited by prior racial and gendered imaginaries of what kinds of tasks separate the human from the less-than or not-quite human other. (3-4)

As a technology of scientific management, gamification similarly invokes promises of technoliberalism for the "(already) human subject," not by creating artificial intelligence and machines to perform rote tasks and tiresome labor, but as a technology that overrepresents work in both work and labor and reduces the worker solely to work. Zicherman's public speaking and consulting sessions promote methods of gamification that envision workers whose work and leisure both exist in service of the "(already) human subject," "a subject whose freedom is possible only through the racial unfreedom of the surrogate" (4).

Citing his earlier work on the "technonormative matrix," or "the matrix of power and discursive relations that effectively produce and regulate the intelligibility of [sex, gender, or sexuality] for us," video game scholar Edmond Y. Chang describes the "technonormative" subject as "adolescent, straight, white, cisgender, masculine, able, male, and 'hardcore' bodies and desires" (15). The throughline between the technoliberal subject and the technonormative subject locates the normative subject as a racial and gendered dominant figure, whose presence in video games presents a paternalistic evolution from an adolescent player into a gamifier. The normative adolescent subject imagined and forcefully figured in dominant narratives of video games then, grows into the heteronormative technoliberal subject for whom present-day racial capitalism is built.

Situated in the gamification of the everyday, *Again My Life* and *Tomb Raider King* similarly echo the technoliberal and technonormative subject in contemporary racial capitalism in which the hierarchy of life subjugates those in the margins and defines them as "less than" the fully human subject to define the few at the top as the "(already) human subject" who claim the full range of rights and access bestowed on the normative visions of the human. Not only do ludic qualities permeate the everyday within the text, but reader responses also further highlight ludic digestion of the texts. If *Again My Life* presents the reset, or the replay through life, as an aesthetic consumption of the harmless past and technologies of the future, *Tomb Raider King* further presents the magical technology of artifacts to highlight the technoliberal subject within racial capitalism, as the matured technonormative subject for whose benefit the gamified everyday is built.

Rebirth, Reset and Another Playthrough in *Tomb Raider King* and *Again My Life*

Time travel meets good defeats evil; these narratives center on the injustice of social structures and their nebulous inner workings for those made fungible by the system. As a powerless employee, Juhŏn uses his meager abilities from an artifact for the benefit of the owner of the company, Kwŏn T'aejun, while struggling against constant poverty and illness from artifact poisoning. Hŭiu, similarly, exemplifies a character who did everything "right." In the brief reminiscence while he sinks to the bottom of the river, he remembers his hard work as one who came from stifling poverty without the safety of a home to rise to the position of a prosecutor. The motif of unrewarded effort and injustice in starting points in life paves the foundations for these narratives as they criticize the inner workings of a society built for maintaining class differences. These narratives depict South Korean society as a "rigged game," in which only the select few can reap the benefits of the majority.

Intervening into this rigged game is the concept of rebirth, an opportunity to level the playing field. Like Buddhist notions of reincarnation or a fantastical device of space and/or time travel, rebirth in this instance disrupts the present (often riddled with injustice) and provides an alternate way out. For instance, reincarnation, as a foundational Buddhist concept, entails inter-species or inter-subjective movements that elongate the temporality of a single life, and gestures towards an ecologically entangled sense of being. Space and/or time travel on the other hand, often maintain the body and mind intact and highlight the incongruity of the traveling body and its changing surroundings, even as the travel often attempts to provide guidance through the past. Bringing reincarnation and time/space travel together, the plot device of spiritual possession offers a similar ownership of different subjectivities and worldmaking, and introduces a protagonist who seeks to solve conflict in a fantasy world.

Rebirth, in this sense, focuses on a return to a specific moment in the past before the point of no return, restoring agency to the traveler who has met an untimely and otherwise unfair death. Several studies have examined the rebirth/return narratives—largely categorized as an amalgamation of three concepts: return to past, spiritual possession of a different body, and reincarnation—in web-based novels (web-novels) to note their appeal in the readers' latent desires to live vicariously through the characters, in order to ease their dissatisfaction with the unjust world they live in. For instance, Ahn Sang-Won asserts that the protagonist's ability to know the future and help oneself accordingly befits readers' desires to take control of their situations (279-307). Similarly, Koh Kyungeun and Cho Hyejung analyze reader responses, keywords and taglines to argue that these rebirth narratives highlight the narratives' focus on righting past wrongs and finding success, and resonate with readers' desires to overcome the hardships in their own lives, be it the prevalence of sexism and misogyny in contemporary society or cutthroat societal pressure to meet external markers of success (2551-2564).

Alongside the significance of vicarious justice, rebirth in the two webtoons proposes the concept of reset, a foundational method of progression in video games that allows the player to repeat the stage—as in the case of Nintendo's original *Mario* games—or the entire game, as in the case of FromSoftware's *Dark Souls* series. The possibility of repetition allows the game designer to make a game out-of-reach for most players, and at times even stake their fame based on their sheer difficulty (in the case of games like the *Dark Souls* series and *Sekiro: Shadows Die Twice*), as players can "git gud": either play better, or depend on the future potential of learning through repeated failure to play better.[1] Repeating the same content in a video game, after all, allows the player to learn the structures of various obstacles that construct the game, from the landscape and moving platforms to enemy positions and their projectiles, and train the timing of the jump or hone the perfect technique and select the perfect weapon to beat the enemy and ultimately the game. At the same time, this potential of bettering one's techniques creates a culture of shame towards players who cannot "git gud" and beat the game, and justifies gatekeeping efforts to demarcate the lines of those good enough to be a serious "gamer" and those who are not.[2] In this sense, repetition supports what Brian Sutton-Smith calls "the rhetoric of play as progress," in which play, in particular children and animals' play, have the function of learning to adapt to the larger world through imitations and trying (9–10). In this theorization, play has a function of learning and adapting through repetition, ultimately supporting a hierarchical structure that encourages and often demands conformity to its standards of "good."

Another Chance to Play the Game in *Again My Life* and *Tomb Raider King*

Just as the rhetoric of play as repetition and improvement focuses on finding one's place within the fabric of society, the pseudo-bildungsroman narrative of *Again My Life* highlights protagonist Hŭiu's initial run at life as a play from which he learns to progress in life. While *Again My Life* does not conform to the traditional childhood-to-adulthood conception of a bildungsroman, the webtoon sets key concerns of bildungsromans in its focus. Through the narrative device of reset, it highlights personal growth and character-forming dynamic changes, as Hŭiu is given another chance to restart and excel at a game he had just learned to play when he died.

When he is sent back in time for his second run at life, Hŭiu finds himself as a high school student living within a classroom as a microcosm of the larger unjust society. He wakes up, seemingly from a nap, rudely awakened with a smack to the back of the head by his high school bully. When he runs to the bathroom to find a mirror, he similarly runs into another group of bullies cornering another student. The high school he returns to is as he remembers; as a microcosm, it is a tightly wound violent hierarchy in which students at the top exploit those beneath them. Hŭiu's initial run through life before the reset, then, functions as an initial run through which to learn the lay of the ground and, as he tells himself, an opportunity to become stronger and to "change everything one by one to protect [his] family as well as [him]self" (*Again My Life* ep. 2).

His return to his formative years creates a division between the self, revived with the knowledge of events to come, and his body, which is missing the lived experiences that provided the foundation for the knowledge he possesses in his rebirth. On his second day of school since the reset, Hŭiu begins a paternalistic relationship with his body, chastising his old teenage body as a man in his mid-thirties. He thinks to himself, "My god, how am I already tired when all I did was wake up and come to school? Just how little did my high school self work out? I need to train this body as soon as possible" (*Again My Life* ep. 2). Through his reset, Hŭiu begins to treat his body like a digital avatar in a video game, that players can choose and train to optimize for the gameworld to come. With the knowledge that his body needs to achieve a certain level of dexterity and agility, his relationship to his body changes: his body shifts from a part of his selfhood to a tool to hone and wield, and he experiences his second playthrough as pseudo-hyperrealistic virtual reality.

Tomb Raider King further presents a clear-cut example of gamification through user interface (UI) design elements, the pointification of abilities and relationships, and battle arenas and item rankings. Imitating a video game interface, floating dialogue boxes quantify, confirm, and visually establish changes in Juhŏn's self, surroundings and possessions. After the reset, Juhŏn finds himself in a holding cell after an altercation with a high school student and his mother. While he is sitting on the ground, the webtoon provides Juhŏn's first-person view of purple letters, "Tomb Raider Sŏ Juhŏn," floating mid-air. As he doubts what he sees, the perspective shifts to a disembodied third person depicting him in a medium shot with the letters in mirror image. The floating words expand into a dialogue box informing Juhŏn of the "Tomb Raider Base Skills" including "Snooping (rank F)/investigate surroundings within 1 meter diameter," which he identifies as a "video game skill window." A subsequent dialogue box further provides him with a "quest," asking Juhŏn to uncover all four base skills for a tomb raider. Such clear-cut instances of gamification in Juhŏn's second play through life share gamified narrative devices with other popular webtoons that use video game UI dialogue boxes, such as *Leveling Up from Max Level* (*Mallepput'ŏ reberŏp*) from Kakao webtoon and *Army Cook Becomes a Legend* (*Ch'wisabyŏng chŏnsŏri toeda*) from Naver webtoon. In his second play through life, Juhŏn experiences his surroundings as though through a video game; his goals are clearly stated as quests, and his personal abilities are coded as quantifiable stats.

Following the stage and difficulty progression for video games, Hŭiu begins in what can be likened to a "tutorial stage," or his high school classroom. Rather than returning to his life as a prosecutor with the authority to collect evidence and punish Taesup, he returns as he wakes up from a nap at his school desk, facing the microcosm of the larger injustice of the society through schoolyard bullying. His "clearing" the stage requires the skill sets he needs to hone to take down the final boss, namely physical dexterity and strength and the ability to build shrewd strategies. Recognizing these progression-based game elements, readers remark on Hŭiu's need for "clearing" the high school level before the final boss and identify the similarities between the schoolyard and the larger society. Similarly, when Hŭiu meets other characters at school or in the law academy, readers often register the relationships not simply as a high school student or a law student befriending another, but rather, as an inclusion of a "party member" to Hŭiu's larger "quest" of defeating Cho Taesup, and as a potential "romancing partner."[3] Terms such as "party member," "quest," and "romancing partner" stem from RPGs in which a protagonist collects other team members to command throughout the storyline and complete individual quests to increase stats, while romancing in-game characters as a secondary storyline. Reader reception of *Again My Life* further highlights the ways in which the webtoon uses video game elements even without overt dialogue boxes and the pointification of individual and object stats.

The Rules of the (Technoliberal and Technonormative) Game

As protagonists in gamified narratives, Hŭiu and Juhŏn embody technoliberal and technonomative subjects who evolve to command racial capitalism, and who rule the world in their own terms. Hŭiu, as the player-protagonist who already knows the stages of the game, alters his route by playing the money game and accumulating astronomical wealth through the knowledge of the coming real estate boom and the subsequent precipitous fall in the 1997 Asian financial crisis. Specifically, he takes on the role of the magnanimous landlord with a front company run by one of his assistants, Pak Sangman. After clearing the tutorial stage of schoolyard bullies, he begins to accumulate wealth by investing in the stock market and finding foreclosed homes and businesses in promising locations in preparation for the real estate boom before the fall. Hŭiu, like his real estate teacher and his nemesis and final boss, Taesup, easily navigates the real estate and stock market spaces as a racially dominant cisgender, overtly masculine male person. The narrative portrays him as the one with the brain and the brawn, thriving in both law and fights, while various non-technonoliberal subjects appear in subjugated roles, be it paradoxically racialized Korean-Chinese mercenaries who make clandestine crossings into South Korea to do Cho Taesup's bidding, or Kim Hanmi, Hŭiu's highschool classmate and the extramarital child of one of Cho Taesup's cronies, whose gender limits her and her mother to her biological father's violent and exploitative influences until Hŭiu "rescues" her.

Similarly, *Tomb Raider King* presents Juhŏn as a technoliberal subject who commands the use of technology in a rapidly changing world. The webtoon presents a world in flux with the introduction of a new technology that literally and figuratively changes its landscape. Tombs in varying sizes appear randomly in the world, each presenting a contained stage where whoever clears its final boss will earn the artifact. For instance, the first tomb Juhŏn clears, the tomb of the Honest Woodcutter, presents a contained tomb with a pond in the middle, from which a dragon offers a riddle. Juhŏn, rather than answering that the iron axe is his, and thus clearing the tomb in the "set" way, presents his own solution by killing the dragon. Just as Hŭiu snowballs his wealth by playing the game of the stock and real estate markets, Juhŏn uses his knowledge of artifacts to collect useful ones and exert his dominance over a world still learning to grapple with the new technology. Collecting wealth-related artifacts and strategically helping those in need for their use value, Juhŏn rises through the ranks towards the title "tomb raider king," who commands the tomb-ridden world. He, as a technoliberal subject whose humanity is ensured in his second playthrough of life, commands an overwhelming power over artifacts, which curiously resemble "smart" gadgets with specific abilities that can make the lives of the "(already) human" easier. On objects like "Roomba self-directing vacuum cleaner" and "prescription pill bottles that automatically order refills when their volume gets low," Atanososki and Vora write, "The desire for technological enchantment, that is, for animate and 'intelligent' technological objects that perform degraded and devalued tasks to uphold the freedom of the liberal subject, perpetuates the surrogate effect of technoliberalism, erasing the ongoing ways in which the colonial structures of racialized and gendered exploitation that enable the feeling of being human produce the desire for enchanting technology" (17).

The webtoon, in its depiction of the world on a global scale, curiously presents Juhŏn as a post-racial subject. As a South Korean with rapidly improving language abilities and vast wealth at his disposal, he travels across national boundaries with little awareness of his race. Similarly, the pointification of Juhŏn's artifact-strengthened abilities presents a technonormative subject who can frictionlessly own narratives of nationhood and cultural specificity and rank the value of each system under one neoliberal conception of the world. Here, folklore and nation-making legends are reduced to referent objects, or artifacts, ranked from SS to F.[4]

For instance, the South Korean folklore of *Pyŏn'gangsoewa ongnyŏ* (the stud and the resilient woman) is reduced to two artifacts, a traditional sock (*Pŏsŏn*) and a traditional wooden ward (*Changsŭng*), which Juhŏn dismisses as low-rank artifacts. The Chosŏn-era folklore, told in *p'ansori*, or musical storytelling, tells of the difficulties of peasant life unable to take root in a strictly hierarchical society through the story of a couple with vast misfortunes. The webtoon frames this grassroots snapshot into Chosŏn life as a low-ranking, insignificant folktale, while celebrating large-scale and often Western European myths and legends as highly ranked artifacts, as is the case with the Roman emperor Caesar. By casting folklore in this way, the webtoon maintains the top-down historical value hierarchy that places (often) Western imperial historical figures at the top of the value hierarchy. Juhŏn's frictionless travel across borders and racialized spaces like the auction room, then, posits South Korean racialization as a part of the global post-racial class of the already human, while, at the same time, it accepts imperial and colonial value structures that place certain narratives like Western European and Chinese tales above Korean national folklore. In the post-racial world of enchanted technology in *Tomb Raider King*,

Juhŏn travels frictionlessly as a technoliberal subject, whose humanness depends on those he subjugates. Correcting the injustice of the world, for both Juhŏn and Hŭiu, then, depends not on the restructuring of the world that produces injustice, but on the magnanimity of those at the top.

Conclusion: Imagining a Nonnormative Future

The two webtoons, *Tomb Raider King* and *Again My Life*, tell tales of a racially dominant male protagonist's return to the past and his rise through the ranks based on his previous playthrough of life. This narrative of learning based on a previous experience depicts the world through linear progression with a starting point and an endpoint. The narrative is a heteronormative recapitulation that prioritizes individual progression instead of advancing a queer future that reimagines the structures that reproduce injustice. Queer studies scholar Jack Halberstam writes, "I argue that success in a heteronormative, capitalist society equates too easily to specific forms of reproductive maturity combined with wealth accumulation" (2). Both Juhŏn and Hŭiu have intimate knowledge of the violent injustice of the world through their initial play-through of life, in which their strivings towards success inevitably followed a linear life trajectory. As a prosecutor, arguably one of the most powerful positions in the legal-carceral system in South Korea, Hŭiu embodies the idealized life trajectory: he begins with an elite university before moving to a law academy, then to the prosecutor's office, in both plays through life. Supplementing his career trajectory in his second run at life, Hŭiu further accumulates covert capital by playing the real estate market through the tumultuous times of the late 1990s East Asian economy. Similarly, Juhŏn quickly accumulates his wealth and power by raiding newly discovered tombs, overpowering the artifacts instead of building kinship ties with them.

Both Hŭiu and Juhŏn consolidate their reach through the hierarchical wielding of power, with several subordinates following their every order. Their replays at life, as such, reproduce specific forms of progression that the game of life recognizes as a winning condition, and uphold the structures of injustice that try to reproduce a specific heteronormative power structure. As heteronormative male protagonist figures, Hŭiu and Juhŏn replay the game without reimagining or queering the structures of injustice; instead, their reset changes those in power from past evil to those who are (questionably) good for now. In her assertion that "gamification" is different from "pointification," Margaret Roberson argues that "a world of badges and points only offers upwards escalation." As those in power and at the end of their gamified life, protagonists like Hŭiu and Juhŏn reach the very tip of this "upwards escalation," as those to whom the rules of the game no longer apply. In order for the future to maintain justice, the readers must imagine a future in which they maintain their dedication to justice. Should they succumb to allures of power at their fingertips in their second play through life, just as their enemies did, the heteronormative capitalist society will reproduce the same injustices that resulted in Hŭiu's and Juhŏn's wrongful deaths in the first place, just with different victims. The webtoons offer a future where the king changes but the monarchy remains.

Queer studies scholar José Esteban Muñoz argues that "Queerness is essentially about the rejection of a here and now and an insistence on potentiality or concrete possibility for another world" (1). A key quality that games and webtoons share is not only their devotion to "fun," but also the possibility of imagining and even (vicariously) living in a world vastly different from our own. Queering the imaginary worlds of *Again My Life* and *Tomb Raider King* that currently build on the foundation of "upward escalation" would open up the possibility of "really [...] gamify[ing] them," and offer a chance to explore the "fascinating, exciting and troubling" question of gamification and future worldmaking (Robertson).

Notes

1. The first *Demon Souls* game from FromSoftware, the predecessor to the *Dark Soul* series, built the game mechanic in service of the cyclical worldview as a curse for humanity. The mechanic served as an embodiment of the cycle of death and revival to tell the story of a world trapped in a cycle of death, and communicate the feeling of entrapment in its players. In later iterations, however, much of the game's reception turned into the "git gud" narrative.

2. For instance, *Sekiro: Shadows Die Twice* stirred a heated discussion on whether video games should have difficulty settings that allow players to control how they enjoy—or suffer through—the game, and whether the punishing difficulty is a foundational aspect of the game's artistic goal. As a snapshot into this debate, Forbes published an article titled "'Sekiro: Shadows Dies Twice' Needs To Respect Its Players And Add An Easy Mode" in which the writer calls for the ability to customize game difficulties, amidst hundreds of articles in other platforms and countless more online discussions in various capacities.

3. This particular video game language is frequently used in readers' comments throughout the series.

4. This ranking system draws from Japanese and Japanese-inspired game makers that use SSS-D instead of A-F as the rating criteria. One such video game that popularized the use is gamemaker Hideki Kamiya's *Devil May Cry* that rated players' performances in a given fight as a way to emulate arcade games' scoring systems for a single-player video game.

Works Cited

Ahn, Sang-Won. "A Study on Characteristics of Regression Motifs in Korean Web Novels." *Korean Literary Theory and Criticism* vol. 22, no. 3, 2018, pp. 279-307.

Atanososki, Neda and Kalindi Vora. *Surrogate Humanity: Race, Robots, and the Politics of Technological Futures*. Duke University Press, 2019.

Bogost, Ian. "Exploitationware." *Rhetoric/Composition/Play though Video Games: Reshaping Theory and Practice of Writing*, edited by Richard Colby, Matthew Johnson and Rebekah Shultz Colby, Palgrave Macmillan, 2013, pp. 139-148.

———. "Gamification is Bullshit." *bogost.com*, 8 August 2011, http://bogost.com/writing/blog/gamification_is_bullshit/. Accessed July 17, 2022.

Chang, Edmond Y. "Queergaming." *Queer Game Studies*, edited by Bonnie Rubert and Adreinne Shaw, University of Minnesota Press, 2017, pp. 15-23.

Deterding, Sebastian, Dan Dixon, Rilla Khaled, and Lennart Nacke. "From Game Design Elements to Gamefulness: Defining 'gamification.'" *MindTrek '11: Proceedings of the 15th International Academic MindTrek Conference: Envisioning Future Media*, 2011, pp. 9-15.

deWinter, Jennifer, Carly A.Kocurek, and Randall Nichols. "Taylorism 2.0: Gamification, Scientific Management and the Capitalist Appropriation of Play." *SIAS Faculty Publications*, vol. 531, 2014. https://digitalcommons.tacoma.uw.edu/ias_pub/531.

Halberstam, Jack. *Queer Art of Failure.* Duke University Press, 2011.

Huizinga, Johan. *Homo Ludens: A Study of the Play-Element in Culture.* Routledge, 2014.

Koh, Kyungeun and Hyejung Cho. "A Study on Narrative Motif Types and 'AI User Response' of Korean Web Novels: Focus on Kakao Page." *The Journal of Humanities and Social Science (HSS21)*, vol. 13, no. 4, 2022, pp. 2551-2564.

Littler, Craig R. "Understanding Taylorism." *British Journal of Sociology*, vol. 29, no. 2, 1978, pp. 185-202.

Muñoz, José Esteban. *Cruising Utopia: The Then and There of Queer Futurity.* New York University Press, 2009.

Nelson, Mark J. "Soviet and American Precursors to the Gamification of Work." *Proceedings of the 16th International Academic MindTrek Conference*, 2012, pp. 23-26.

Robertson, Margaret. "Can't Play, Won't Play." *Kotaku.com*. Nov 10, 2010. https://kotaku.com/cant-play-wont-play-5686393. Accessed July 17, 2022.

Seaborn, Katie and Deborah Fels. "Gamification in Theory and Action: A Survey." *International Journal of Human-Computer Studies*, vol. 74, 2015, pp. 14-31.

Thier, Dave. "'Sekiro: Shadows Dies Twice' Needs To Respect Its Players And Add An Easy Mode." *Forbes*. March 28, 2019. https://www.forbes.com/sites/davidthier/2019/03/28/sekiro-shadows-dies-twice-needs-to-respect-its-players-and-add-an-easy-mode/?sh=461725b16393

Sutton-Smith, Brian. *The Ambiguity of Play*. Harvard University Press, 1997.

Zichermann, Gabe and Joselin Linder. *Game-Based Marketing: Inspire Customer Loyalty through Rewards, Challenges, and Contests*. Wile, 2010.

Design Fiction

Excerpts from an Anti-Standardized "수능": A Design-Fictional Approach to Korea

Seo-Young Chu

THIS PIECE USES DESIGN FICTION to disrupt overly rehearsed ways of thinking about Korea's past, present, and future(s).

Design fiction is an interdisciplinary practice that emerged in the early 21st century. Prominent theorists and practitioners of design fiction include Bruce Sterling and Julian Bleecker. No single definition of "design fiction" exists, though there seems to be a consensus that design-fictioneers are storytellers who invent experimental artifacts—for instance, a fictional grocery store receipt from the year 2050—and use these prototypical artifacts as storytelling props to spark, enact, mobilize, make haptically available, and meaningfully choreograph speculative dialogue about a specific topic.

Like all works of design fiction, the preliminary models below are unfinished conversation pieces. They are not polished "final versions." Their purpose is to encourage playful brainstorming and generate mind-opening guesswork and speculative discussion. I have formatted them explicitly as prompts in a "수능"/"suneung"

(a standardized exam in South Korea also known as
"대학수학능력시험" or "College Scholastic Ability Test") to encourage
interactivity—and to disrupt routine ways of thinking about
standardized tests in Korea and beyond. Each prompt below, then,
is a design-fictional invitation to think in anti-standardized ways
about Korea within the larger framework of a design-fictional
examination (itself a prototypical artifact).

Excerpts from an Anti-Standardized "수능":
A Design-Fictional Approach to Korea

1. Write the instructions for this exam. Then follow your own
instructions.

2. You are an extraterrestrial alien visiting Earth for the first time.
For reasons unknown to you, the planet is deserted. Buildings are
in ruins. Debris abounds. The only intact relic you can find is a
copy of the questions from a 수능/suneung exam from the early
21st century. With the help of your super-advanced translation
technology, you are able to read the document. What does this
relic tell you about the world in which it originated? Record your
findings in a brief report.

3. Math problem: Calculate how many Koreas exist by imagining
the square root of minus Korea. What equals the square root of
one negative Korea?

4. Sketch an outfit engineered to make its wearer feel palpably and
entirely Korean. Some questions you may wish to consider: What
does it mean to feel palpably and entirely Korean—and what
would it take for an outfit to make this experience possible? Would

the outfit be comfortable? Uncomfortable? High-tech? Low-tech? All of the above? Does the outfit need to take the form of hanbok? What textures, odors, colors, and shapes might you incorporate? How would you design the shoes, jewelry, and accessories that accompany the outfit?

5. Draft a blueprint for renovating a 독서실 (study room) into a playground geared towards enhancing the physical and mental health of high school students.

6. Create a nutrition facts label and ingredient list for a typical Korean breakfast item from the early 22nd century.

7. Outline a map of the Korean Peninsula in an alternate universe where Charles Bonesteel and Dean Rusk decided to use not the 38th parallel (line of latitude) but the 127th meridian east (line of longitude) to divide Korea into "East Korea" and "West Korea" (rather than "North" and "South"). Write a short essay contextualizing your map and explaining its historical significance. Some questions you might wish to consider: In your version of this alternate Korea, is there a Demilitarized Zone (DMZ)? How do the two Koreas differ ideologically? At what point—if any—does reunification take place?

8. Write an image description of a robot-generated 책거리 screen from the year 2099. Be as neutral and succinct as possible in describing the 책거리's content and form. What objects are included in the still life? How are the objects arranged? What are the artwork's exact dimensions? Is the still life two-dimensional, three-dimensional, and/or even four-dimensional?

9. What will Hangul look and sound like 100 years from now? To what extent and in what ways will technology (e.g., A.I.) and globalization (e.g., loan words) have reshaped the Korean alphabet? Explain the futuristic Korean alphabet as you imagine it. Give concrete examples of re-spellings of familiar names (including your own name!). Finally, write an original poem in futuristic Hangul.

10. Un-redact the following erasure poem (inspired by a question from a recent 수능). xxxxxxxx xxxxxxxxxxx xxxxxxxxx machine-like xxxxxxxxxxxxxx xxxxx xxxxxx xxxxxxxxxxxxxxxx xxxxxxxx people xxxxxx   xxxxxx   xxxxx   xxx   xxxxxxxxxxx   xxxx   xxxxxxxx xxxxxxxxxxxxxxx xxxxxxxx xxxx xxxxxxxxxxxx xxxxxxxxx are xxxxxxxxx xx people xxxxxxxx.

11. Compose a Korean anthem from the 22nd century. Some elements you may wish to incorporate: 판소리, K-pop, gayageum, piri, buk, the sounds made by animals native to the Korean Peninsula.

12. Multiple choice question: Hwabyung is
    a. a medical condition
    b. a culture-specific syndrome
    c. a fictional malady that does not really exist
    d. a tool of colonial oppression
    e. a cathartic way of experiencing political agency and creative power
    f. a term that some Korean Americans are trying to reclaim
    g. _____
    h. all of the above
    i. none of the above
    j. other

13. If the Republic of Korea and the Democratic People's Republic of Korea become one Korea, what should the Korean flag look like?

14. Design a recipe for a type of kimchi incorporating the petals of kimjongilia, kimilsungia, mugunghwa, azalea. Questions you may wish to consider: How would such flavors taste (individually and together)? For whom might such kimchi be allergenic? For whom would it be appealing? Distasteful? Appetizing? Nauseating? How might such a product be marketed (if at all)? What would be the correct ratio of one ingredient to another?

15. Compose a short story set in a 1990s Korea in an alternate universe where the International Monetary Fund (IMF) has never existed.

16. Create a brochure advertising a South Korean rehabilitation facility for patients diagnosed with late-stage capitalism.

17. You are a historian living in the 23rd century. Write a short biography of a significant figure in Korean history born in 2022.

18. Design a contest (similar to the contest in *Squid Game*) where contestants play to win forgiveness not of financial debt but of emotional debt accumulated through generations of inherited trauma (a kind of psychic/spiritual deficit) and unresolved han. What would it mean to experience the opposite of han, and how far would someone go to achieve that spiritual "surplus"?

19. Compose the lyrics to a viral DPRK-Pop song.

20. Imagine a future where most of Korea is underwater due to climate change. Thus the peninsula is now an archipelago. Write a brief overview addressing the following kinds of questions. Is

Korea still divided into South and North? Are Seoul and Pyongyang still major cities? What are Korea's natural resources? Where do most Koreans live? How has Korea's new landscape/waterscape shaped—and been shaped by—Korean culture and traditions?

21. Post a dispatch from a utopian futurescape where the Korean DMZ has been granted personhood and human rights and responsibilities (much as the Whanganui River has legal personhood and rights and responsibilities in real life today).

22. Fail this exam on purpose. Make the failure meaningful.

23. Grade your own exam.

"Genre Narratives Are Powerful Tools to Illustrate the Beauty of an Unfamiliar World": Haerin Shin's Interview with SF novelist Bo-Young Kim

Translated by Sang-Keun Yoo

BO-YOUNG KIM is a leading South Korean science fiction writer whose works have significantly influenced numerous emerging authors since the early 2000s. Kim made her debut with "The Experience of Touch," which won the inaugural Science Technology Creative Fiction Novella Award of Korea in 2004. Kim's literary accomplishments include numerous accolades, such as the Grand Prize at the first Annual Korean SF Novel Award for "The Seven Executioners" and the fifth Grand Prize at the first Annual Korean SF Novella Award for "How Alike Are We."

Kim's short story "An Evolutionary Myth" was featured in the American science fiction magazine *Clarkesworld*, while her short story collection *I'm Waiting For You and Other Stories* was published in English by HarperCollins in the US and UK. Additionally, Kim's translated short story collection *On the Origin of Species and Other Stories*, published by Kaya Press, was nominated for a National Book Award, and her work "Whale Snows Down" was nominated for the SFF Rosetta Award. Prior to her literary debut, Kim worked as a video game scenario writer and producer for the game developer team Garam and Baram.

* * *

Vol. 34, No. 2, *Journal of the Fantastic in the Arts*
Copyright © 2023, International Association for the Fantastic in the Arts

JFA: Greetings, Bo-young. It's a pleasure to host this interview with you for the *Journal of the Fantastic in the Arts* (*JFA*) special issue focused on Korean SF and Fantasy. First of all, would you kindly introduce yourself to our readers?

Kim: Delighted to make your acquaintance. I am Bo Young Kim, a science fiction novelist hailing from South Korea. I'm deeply honored by your invitation.

JFA: Your writing first captivated me when I encountered your 2004 Science and Technology Creative Writing Mid-Length Prize-winning story, "The Experience of Touch" (2002). The innovative approach and refreshing impact it had on me as a reader is unforgettable. You artfully elucidated the ontological nuances of the senses, elements that prelude consciousness, through your solid narrative structure and realistic character development. Even with the clone character, you adeptly used irony to highlight the absence of senses. You transformed the epitome of alienation into a vibrant celebration of life, a feat that I found to be groundbreaking. Your writing challenges the prevalent anthropocentric worldview and goes a step further to deconstruct binaries. You also portrayed the concept of "otherness" as inherent within us, creating and sustaining its own significance in a relationship dynamic that transcends mere conflict.

As this was your debut piece, your writing prowess and wisdom leave me in admiration. This theme of affirming and recontextualizing "otherness" through the lens of enjoyment seems to be a recurring motif in your works, from "The Fifth Sense" and "An Evolutionary Myth" to "That Prophet." I interpret this as a form of hope for humanity, a progressive step beyond mere criticism and marginalization. What intrigues me is what motivates you to confront and critique various forms of discrimination in your works, such as sexism, ableism, speciesism, and racism, which arise from a rationalistic anthropocentric perspective. Thus, I wonder, how do you manage to keep this thread of hope consistently alive in your narratives?

Kim: It's heartening to know you've read my debut work! I appreciate your kind words. I believe that each day I evolve into a different version of myself from who I was yesterday, and tomorrow, I'll again transform into a different person. This constant change applies to everyone else, to the world around us, and has been a consistent part of my lived experience. Sometimes, change brings improvement, other times it can lead to regressions, but the crucial part is to continuously strive to move in the right direction. Without this belief, I don't think I could pen a novel, let alone do anything else.

JFA: As we navigate into the Hallyu (Korean Wave) 5.0 era, the recurring question of "what is Korean" or "why is Korean culture appealing to the world" seems to be resurfacing. While there are concerns that such queries are products of a modernity that imposes hierarchical and absolute national or systemic divisions, I believe we can uncover alternative answers in your work. Your work not only bends genres, merging fantasy and science fiction, but also stands out due to its hybridity—it incorporates lyrical stylistics with scientific rigor, East Asian mythological archetypes with Western science fiction motifs, and blends the expanse of cosmic history with the immediate sensations of our senses. The vast spectrum of your work is also notable, with the narrative voice oscillating between an omniscient/retrospective distance and maximizing the emotional immersion of a first-person perspective, depending on the narrative. Given such an extensive range of themes, materials, and methods, I'm curious if there's a unifying theme across your work. If not, could you shed light on the process or triggers that inspire you when you write?

Kim: I appreciate your continued kindness. It's not that I find myself intrigued by a different subject each time, but rather I feel as though I craft a distinct novel every time due to the ever-changing issues in contemporary society. As I frequently mention, my novel invariably embeds a part of me, and my identity inherently contains a part of the world. I believe this is an inescapable truth, even with one's best efforts to avoid it.

The concept of "now" has always been, and will continue to be, a world unknown to humankind. We've never before experienced a world so interconnected and communicative, nor have we witnessed such massive extinction and environmental devastation.

The excessive influx of (mis-)information from the internet, which I would not have imagined just a few years ago, is now a topic I frequently contemplate. Simply living my ordinary life, carrying out my daily routines, presents a unique narrative each time. I'm constantly observing how the commonplace and the familiar teem with mystery. In one of my novels, I penned a line, "Even with a single seed, it bears a hundredfold in a few months." When asked about the enigmatic future crop I was alluding to, I was about to respond, "corn..." Likewise, I take pleasure in reflecting on the everyday mysteries that permeate reality.

JFA: In 2015, your short story "An Evolutionary Myth" was featured in *Clarkesworld*, one of the most prominent SF webzines in the United States. Moreover, HarperCollins, a titan in the Anglo-American SF publishing scene, launched an anthology of your work titled *I'm Waiting for You and Other Stories*. Your work also made an appearance in the 9th issue of *Future Science Fiction Digest*, and your short stories were part of the first Korean SF anthology translated into English, *Readymade Bodhisattva*. Based on responses from book discussion platforms such as Goodreads, it seems you've already amassed a considerable international fanbase. Naturally, exceptional literature transcends temporal and cultural boundaries, but what do you think contributes to the strong resonance your work has found among readers in the somewhat exclusive realm of the Anglo-American publishing world?

Kim: I wasn't aware that my work was making such an impact. Readers on Goodreads have always been generous to authors, not just me! However, I was astounded to discover that only 3% of books in the US are translations from foreign languages. In Korea, the proportion of published books that are translations sits at around 30%, and some estimate it's closer to 50% if you exclude academic books. Like many Koreans, my reading list since childhood has been an equal mix of foreign and domestic books, so the idea that cultural differences could pose a barrier to reading never occurred to me. To foreign readers, both classic and modern Korean novels are similarly unfamiliar, rendering them indistinguishable.

Yet, I've always viewed science fiction as a genre that transcends national boundaries. SF readers are perpetually in search of new worlds, so shouldn't different cultures be seen as a delight rather than an obstacle? In Korea, realism may currently be all the rage, but the most successful foreign films at the box office have consistently been SF or fantasy. I believe that genre narratives are powerful tools to illustrate the beauty of an unfamiliar world.

JFA: Your work spans a remarkable range of subjects, including outer space, genetic engineering, robotics and artificial intelligence, mythology, the medium of video games, and even tarot cards. Is there a particular subject or genre to which you feel especially drawn?

Kim: As mentioned earlier, when I become consumed by a particular thought, it often takes writing a novel about it for me to move beyond it. I also view novel-writing as a means of breaking free from cyclical thoughts. After investing ample time in writing one novel, I typically arrive at a conclusion in my mind, allowing me to cease dwelling on that idea. If I don't reach a resolution within one novel, the idea tends to resurface.

JFA: Contrary to a common misconception, Korean culture has a longstanding tradition of scientific imagination. However, it seems there has been a misunderstanding, viewing Korea as a barren land for science fiction prior to the 2000s. Especially in literature, this can likely be attributed to critical realism that dominated during Korea's turbulent modern history. Nevertheless, I believe this tradition of intensity has evolved into a kind of strength that underpins the lineage of Korean science fiction today. In the realm of films and streaming content, works such as *Train to Busan*, *Squid Game*, *All of Us Are Dead*, and *Kingdom* have gained recognition for their adept use of genre tropes while critiquing and satirizing societal issues. Are there any works or writers in the Korean literary and cultural scene that have inspired you, and if so, how have they influenced you—be it thematically, materially, or stylistically?

Kim: Whenever I'm asked about the influences on my novels, I find myself at a loss for words. Growing up, most of my time was spent crafting stories and playing within those narratives, given the lack of other diversions. During these formative years, I often composed two kinds of stories: conventional fiction that I would show to adults when they asked, "What on earth are you doing?" and a different type of fiction I kept solely for my own enjoyment, never intended for anyone else's eyes.

The novels I'm writing now are an extension of these "for-my-eyes-only" narratives. Hence, in my novels, I feel a limitless freedom, and virtually anything can transpire, because these were originally stories I crafted solely for myself. Thus, I could say my science fiction novels carry influences from all sorts of children's films and media I was exposed to back then, but it's difficult to identify specific sources.

At some point, I realized I was immensely bored with writing fiction that was "for others to read," and found myself investing all my time and energy into narratives that were "for-my-eyes-only." The notion that I could actually publish these private narratives and even build a professional career around them didn't dawn on me until much later in life.

Honestly, even after my debut as a science fiction writer, I was skeptical about the potential of sustaining a professional career with this genre of novels. I kept thinking, "No one's going to buy and read these anyway." Therefore, I continued to write novels that I, personally, found enjoyable and contemplated part-time jobs that would afford me the time to keep doing so. I was uncertain how long I could sustain this, always anticipating that the novel I was working on might be my last. The literary contests that gave me my debut were soon discontinued, and there weren't many science fiction magazines or awards where I could publish my work.

While it's hard for me to pin down specific influences, I can certainly share who my favorite author is. That would be Korean cartoonist Ko Yu-Sung. Purely by chance, when I was very young, the only children's book in my home was a chapter titled "Princess of the Star Kingdom" from his comic series *Robot King* (1977–1981). I hadn't even learned to read at that point, but I pored over that comic hundreds of times, eventually memorizing the whole thing. Later on, I fully immersed myself in his comics, drawn to the vivacious energy he poured into his storytelling and his sense of humor. His utilization of science fiction themes was innovative and pioneering, even by today's standards.

As a teenager, I was also deeply engrossed in the comics of Kim Jin. Her work was grounded in science fiction, but she also had a knack for reinterpreting mythology in contemporary contexts. Even as a female author, she dared to imagine expansive worlds with bold narratives, allowing her stories to unfold from the inside out, driven more by characters' internal emotions than by strict control of the plot. Her work was also replete with intricate symbolism that often required multiple readings to fully appreciate. Kim's series, *Blue Phoenix* (1988-), was published in fits and starts due to the limited space available for science fiction in Korea at the time. I know that even though the series remains unfinished, it's still held dear by many veteran Korean science fiction fans.

JFA: Reading your work, it carries the rigorous theoretical accuracy and realistic extrapolations of hard science fiction, a style that was fairly uncommon in Korea at the time of your debut. Yet, your writing also possesses the lyricism and thematic resonance associated with the New Wave movement of the 1960s. I'm intrigued if there were any foreign authors or works that significantly inspired you in terms of themes, subjects, or stylistic approach, and if so, how?

Kim: As I said, it's difficult for me to point to specific science fiction novelists who have influenced me, whether they're Korean or from elsewhere. That said, there are definitely authors whose work I've treasured. As a child, I was captivated by Osamu Tezuka's work *Astro Boy*, which I watched on television. Later in life, I discovered and came to appreciate his other works that carried humanistic and Buddhist themes, such as *The Fire Bird* and *Buddha*. I was also a big fan of Hayao Miyazaki's *Future Boy Conan*. Agatha Christie's detective stories have been a long-time favorite of mine, not for their physical tricks but for their psychological ones, and for the way Christie cleverly obscures parts of her narrative world using words alone.

Hermann Hesse's fantasy novels, which center heavily on introspection, have also been a great source of inspiration for me. After becoming a writer, I stumbled upon Roger Zelazny's mythological science fiction and was enthralled by his audacious combination of folklore and science fiction, as well as by his invocation of mythological heroes.

Margaret Atwood once remarked that she didn't realize she was writing science fiction until it was pointed out to her. She suggested that fantasy is a fundamental form of human storytelling and argued that modern people, finding it difficult to root their stories in mythology, instead create worlds based on science. I find myself in agreement with Atwood's perspective and tend to believe that, for modern people, science fiction can serve as a form of storytelling that arises naturally, much like ancient folklore.

JFA: I understand you were involved in the initial screenplay for the movie *Snowpiercer*, directed by the Oscar-winning Bong Joon-ho. I imagine there's a significant difference between expressing your thoughts in the written form and crafting narratives for audiovisual media. Could you share your experience with us?

Kim: Director Bong Joon-ho entirely penned the screenplay. However, after he read one of my novellas in my first anthology, he approached me and offered me the role. He gave me the freedom to "do whatever I want," promising to incorporate what he could from my contributions.

Reflecting back, it's incredible that he allowed me such latitude. He told me at the time that "Movies are the language of images," a concept I don't think I fully grasped. A novel represents the artistry of written words, and the majority of events occur in the writer's mind. It wasn't until I read his script and watched the actual movie that I was struck by the profound meaning behind "the language of images." In a novel, you inhabit a world where nothing is visually seen, while a movie portrays a world where nothing exists but what is seen. If I were to truly learn the language of movies, I'd need to dedicate as much time as I did to writing novels. Recognizing that I couldn't commit to both, I chose to focus my energies on novel-writing.

JFA: A few years ago at the International Women's Film Festival, you mentioned in response to a question about gender, if I remember correctly, that you don't write with any particular gender theory in mind. Instead, you said your focus is on exploring existence, rather than differentiating between men and women. However, as per my earlier question, I'm interested in your thoughts on the various mechanisms of social marginalization you've explored in your work. In the English-speaking world of science fiction and fantasy, there is a pronounced male dominance, despite recent efforts to counterbalance this. In contrast, women writers and creators currently lead the way in Korean science fiction, particularly in literature. This seems a unique phenomenon, especially considering Korea's strong tradition of patriarchal social structures. Could you share your thoughts on why this might be the case and what significance it holds?

Kim: As you've noted, science fiction in Korea was a marginalized genre, largely dismissed by mainstream culture. This actually allowed it to become a genre of choice for marginalized writers within Korea. It's an irony of history that women, who've been marginalized in every era and culture, found a voice in this genre. One blind spot of tradition and history is that they often contain outdated values. While we're expected to respect and carry on these traditions, there's also a contradictory need to overthrow them. In the case of Korean SF, there isn't much in terms of traditions to inherit or overthrow, which I believe has made it a space where younger writers can freely express their progressive values.

JFA: You have a dedicated fan base composed of both men and women, but I've noticed that your work particularly appeals to young female readers in Korea. Why do you think young women are drawn to your SF and fantasy narratives?

Kim: The answer to this question is connected to what I've previously mentioned. Interestingly, SF began gaining traction in Korea around 2015 or 2016, when the publishing industry revisited feminist literature, largely due to the growing influence of the feminist movement. Novels like Mary Shelley's *Frankenstein*, Ursula K. Le Guin's *The Left Hand of Darkness*, Gerd Brantenberg's *Egalia's Daughters*, and Margaret Atwood's *The Handmaid's Tale* were all gaining attention—most of these are in the SF genre. Since feminist utopian/dystopian fiction falls under SF, it naturally attracted many female readers who couldn't find narratives they could relate to in mainstream Korean literature. Additionally, the majority of the Korean reading population is female.

Around the same time, there was a significant influx of young female creators, which led to a greater public recognition of the fact that many established Korean SF writers were women. Frankly, it was only then that I felt my identity as a woman writer was acknowledged by the broader public. SF was so marginalized that my gender never seemed to matter to readers.

Of course, it wasn't just women who were creating during this period. Writer Lee Sanhwa, who originally wrote light novels geared towards males, made a shift to writing science fiction when his works were cancelled and boycotted within a day. This came about after he voiced his support for a worker whose work was unfairly removed during the Nexon Censorship Incident[1] in 2016— a move interpreted as a feminist statement at the time.

Sherryl Vint once made a statement that resonated deeply with me. She said, "People who can't find their stories in mainstream literature often have no choice but to venture to another world. That world is science fiction." I was thrilled by that quote because it resonated with my own journey as a writer. I had always created my own stories since I couldn't find narratives that I could truly identify with, and it was heartening to see that journey reflected and validated as a path to science fiction.

I was also delighted when Sun-Young Park, a professor at USC, identified elements of science fiction in Jo Sehui's novel *The Dwarf* (1978). This novel, an iconic work in the Korean labor movement, follows the urban poor who, dispossessed by rampant overdevelopment, dream of relocating to the moon. They talk of astronauts and the Klein bottle cosmology. This suggests a persistent tendency among the marginalized to seek refuge in worlds beyond the here and now.

The most prolific science fiction writer in South Korea today, Djuna, identifies as gender non-conforming. Kim Choyup, who enjoys the status of being the best-selling SF novelist in Korea, has a hearing disability. Booker Prize finalist Bora Chung is a social activist. Choi Eui-taek, who recently won the SF Literary Award, is living with muscular dystrophy. He shares that it was reading the works of Bora Chung and Kim Choyup that inspired him to write science fiction and gave him hope that disability could be explored through this genre.

In an ironic twist, the rejection of science fiction by the mainstream has allowed us to reforge narratives in light of modern values. It's heartening to think that this will form part of our history in the years to come. Thank you again for this interview and your thought-provoking questions.

Notes

1. The 2016 Nexon Censorship Incident refers to an event in which the South Korean game development company Nexon terminated voice actress Jayeon Kim's contract after a group of male users lodged complaints regarding her feminist tweet. This action led to a strong response from feminist groups, subsequently resulting in a boycott of Nexon's games (Translator).

Original Korean text follows.

"장르 서사는 낯선 세계가 얼마나 아름다운지 보여주는 서사": 김보영 작가와의 대화

(인터뷰: 신혜린, 번역: 유상근)

김보영 작가

한국을 대표하는 SF 작가 중 한 사람으로, 2000년대 이후의 신진 SF 작가들에게 여러 영향을 끼쳤다. 2004년 「촉각의 경험」으로 제 1 회 과학기술 창작문예 중편 부문에서 수상하며 작가 활동을 시작했다. 『7 인의 집행관』으로 제 1 회 SF 어워드 장편 부문 대상, 「얼마나 닮았는가」로 제 5 회 SF 어워드 중단편 부문 대상을 수상했다.

한국 SF 작가로서는 처음으로 미국의 『클락스월드(*Clarkesworld*)』에 단편소설 「진화신화」를 발표했고, 미국 하퍼콜린스(HarperCollins), 영국 하퍼콜린스에서 「당신을 기다리고 있어」, 「저 이승의 선지자」 등을 포함한 선집 『*I'm Waiting for You and Other Stories*』가 출간되었다.

2021년 개인 영문 단편집 『*On the Origin of Species and Other Stories* (종의 기원과 그 외의 이야기들)』(Kaya press)로 전미도서상(National Book Award) 번역서 부문 후보에, 「Whale Snows Down (고래 눈이 내리다)」으로 로제타상(SFF Rosetta Award)후보에 올랐다. 소설가가 되기 전에는 게임 개발팀 '가람과바람 (Garam&Baram)'에서 시나리오 작가/기획자로 활동했다.

* * *

JFA: 안녕하세요 작가님, 세계적으로 한국의 문화 컨텐츠에 대한 관심이 높아지고 있는 상황에서 <Journal of the Fantastic In the

Arts>(JFA)의 한국 SF/판타지 특집호를 통해 작가님을 인터뷰 할 수 있게 되어 영광입니다. 한국 독자들에게는 다양한 매체에 실린 인터뷰와 여러 책에 써 주신 작가의 말, 그리고 행사 등을 통해 작가님의 생각을 여러 차례 공유해 주신 만큼, 아래 드릴 질문들 중 그와 중복되는 내용이 있을 수 밖에 없기에 미리 양해를 구하고자 합니다. JFA 는 세계 최대규모의 환상예술 학술단체 <International Association for the Fantastic in the Arts>(세계환상문학학회)에서 발간하는 학술 계간지로서, 영미권에서 SF 및 판타지 관련 예술작품들에 관한 연구를 지난 30 년간 선도해 왔습니다. JFA 의 독자분들께 간단한 인사 말씀 부탁드립니다.

김보영: 만나서 반갑습니다. 한국의 SF 소설가 김보영입니다. 초대해주셔서 저도 영광입니다.

JFA: 처음 작가님의 글을 접하게 된 건 2004 과학기술 창작문예 중편 수상작 「촉각의 경험」을 통해서였는데요. 독자로서, 당시 이 작품을 읽고 신선한 충격을 받았던 기억이 아직도 생생합니다. 탄탄한 구성과 실감나는 인물상 (내지는 클론의 경우, 그 아이러니한 부재)의 구축을 통해 의식에 선행하는 감각의 존재론적 의미를 유려한 문장력으로 풀어내셨는데요. 궁극적인 소외의 경험을 생의 찬미로 승화시키셨다는 점이 감명깊었습니다. 기존의 인간지상주의적인 세계관에 정면으로 도전장을 던지면서도, 이분법적 가치론의 전복에서 한 걸음 더 나아가 우리 안에 내재한, 그리고 단순한 대치 이상의 관계 역학 속에서 자체적으로 의미를 생성하고 영위하는 타자성을 표현한 수작이라는 점에서 파격적이기 그지없다는 느낌이었습니다. 심지어 이 작품이 작가님의 데뷔작이었다는 점에서, 그 필력과 혜안에 새삼 감탄하지 않을 수 없습니다. 향유의 경험을 통한 타자성의 긍정과 재전유라는 주제 의식은 이후 「다섯번째 감각」과 「진화 신화」를 위시해 「저 이승의 선지자」에 이르기까지 작품 전반에 걸쳐 지속적으로 드러나고 있는 것 같은데요, 이를 "(비판과 소외에서 한 걸음 더 나아간, 인간이라는 종에 대한 일종의) 희망으로서의 경이"라고 감히 표현해 봐도 될지요? 성차별, 장애인 차별, 종차별, 인종차별 등 합리론에 기반한 인간지상주의에서 연원하는 각종 차별의 담론을 다양한 작품에 걸쳐 비판적으로 다루고 계시면서도 계속 "희망"의 끈을 놓지 않으시도록 해 주는 원동력은 무엇인지요?

김보영: 제 데뷔작부터 보아주셨군요! 과분한 찬사에 감사드립니다. 희망 없이 어떻게 소설을 쓰겠어요. 저도 매일 오늘은 어제와 다르고, 내일은 오늘과 다른 사람으로 변해간다고 생각합니다. 그러니 다른 사람도 당연히 그럴 수 있고, 세상도 그럴 수 있다고 생각합니다. 제 체험에서도 언제나 그러했습니다. 변화는 좋은 방향일 때도 있고 나쁜 방향일 때도 있으니, 한 걸음이라도 좋은 방향으로 가기 위해 계속 노력해야겠지요. 그런 믿음이 없다면 소설을 쓸 수 없고, 사실 아무것도 하지 못할 것만 같습니다.

JFA: 한류 5.0 의 시대에 접어들면서 "무엇이 한국적인가" 내지는 "왜 한국적인 것이 세계에 어필하는가"라는 화두가 다시 뜨는 것 같은데요, 그런 질문들 자체가 국가/체제적 구분을 위계화하고 절대시하는 근대론의 산물이라는 우려가 큰 와중에 작가님의 작품 세계에서 대안적 해법을 찾아 볼 수 있을 것 같습니다. 판타지와 SF 의 경계를 자유로이 오가는 장르적 파격은 물론이고 서정적 문체와 과학적인 핍진성, 동아시아 신화의 원형과 서구 SF/판타지의 주요 모티브, 그리고 우주적 역사의 광대함과 피부로 다가오는 감각의 지근성을 아우르는 그 혼종성이 인상깊기 그지 없는데요. 또, 작품에 따라 서술자의 목소리가 전지적/회고적 거리감을 유지하기도 하고 1 인칭 시점에서의 정동적인 몰입감을 극대화하기도 하는 등 매번 새로운 작품을 접할 때마다 작가님의 광활한 스펙트럼에 감탄을 금할 수 없습니다. 이렇듯 다양한 주제와 소재, 접근 방식을 다루고 또 구사해 오셨기에 여쭙지 않을 수 없는데요, 작품 세계 전반을 관통하는 그 어떤 대주제가 혹시 있는지, 또 딱히 그렇지는 않다면 작품을 집필하실 때 어떤 과정이나 계기를 통해 영감을 얻으시는지 궁금합니다.

김보영: 다시금 좋은 말씀 감사합니다. 제가 매번 다른 소재에 관심을 둔다기보다는, 현대사회의 화두가 매년 격변하기에 매번 다른 소설을 쓰게 된다고 느낍니다. 자주 말하지만, 소설에는 어쩔 수 없이 내가 담기고, 내게는 어쩔 수 없이 세상이 담기니까요. 그건 온 힘을 다해 피하려 애써도 어쩔 수 없이 담아지는 것이라 생각합니다.

과거에도 그랬겠지만, '현재'는 언제나 인류가 지금까지 접해본 적이 없는 세계입니다. 앞으로는 더욱 그러겠지요. 전 세계가 이처럼 서로 연결되고 소통했던 적도 없고, 이만한 대량멸종과 자연 파괴를 경험한 적도 없지요. 인터넷의 대량 정보오염은 몇 년 전만 해도 상상하지 못했던 소재지만 지금은 자주 생각합니다. 평범한 한 사람이 일상을 사는 것만으로도 매번 다른 소재가 찾아온다고 느낍니다.

단지 우리에게 익숙한 일상이 가만 들여다보면 얼마나 기이하고 신비로 가득한가에 대해서는 늘 생각하는 듯합니다. 예전에 소설에, "씨앗 한 알을 갖고 타도 몇 달 뒤에는 수백 배의 열매를 맺어"라는 문장을 썼는데, 어떤 분이 무슨 신비의 미래의 작물이냐고 묻더군요. 저는 "옥수수……."라고 답하려다 말았지요. 저는 현실을 둘러싼 평이한 신비에 대해 생각하기를 좋아합니다.

JFA: 2015 년 미국 최고의 SF 웹진 중 하나인 『클락스월드』 (*Clarkesworld*)에 단편 「진화신화」를 내셨고, 영미 SF 출판계의 강자인 하퍼콜린스에서는 작가님의 작품 선집 *I'm Waiting for You and Other Stories* 이 나왔구요. *Future Science Fiction Digest* 9 호에서도 작가님의 작품을 볼 수 있었고, 최초의 한국 SF 영문 번역 앤솔로지 『레디메이드 보살』에도 단편을 실으시는 등 한국 밖에서도 작가님의 활약이 눈부신데요. Goodreads 같은 독서 토론 사이트에 뜬 반응만 보더라도 해외에서 이미 두터운 팬층을 확보하고 계신 것 같습니다. 물론 훌륭한 문학작품은 시대와 문화권을 초월해서 어필하게 마련이지만, 특히 작가남의 작품 세계가 나름 배타적인 측면을 지니고 있는 영미권 출판계와 독자들 사이에서 이렇듯 큰 반향을 일으키고 있는 이유는 무엇이라고 생각하시는지요?

김보영: 제 작품이 반향을 일으키는지 몰랐습니다! Goodreads 독자님들은 다른 작품도 다 열렬히 칭찬해주시던데요!

단지 작품을 해외에 판 뒤에야 미국의 번역서 비중이 3%에 불과하다는 말을 듣고 깜짝 놀랐습니다. 한국은 번역서 비중이 30%고, 학술서를 제외하면 실상 50%에 가깝다고도 합니다. 저도 다른 한국인처럼 어릴 때부터 외서와 국내서를 반반씩 보아왔기 때문에, 문화 차이가 독서에 방해가 될 수 있다고 생각해보지 못했어요. 낯선 문화라는 점은 한국 고전소설이나 근대소설도 마찬가지입니다!

그래도 저는 SF 가 세계적인 장르라고 늘 생각해왔습니다. SF 독자는 늘 새로운 세계를 찾는 독자니까요. 그러면 다른 문화는 장벽이라기보다는 즐거움이 되지 않을까요? 한국만 해도 사실주의가 대세라지만 극장에서 흥행하는 해외 작품은 늘 판타지가 아니면 SF 였습니다. 장르 서사는 낯선 세계가 얼마나 아름다운지 보여주는 서사라고 생각합니다.

JFA: 작품에서 우주, 유전공학, 로봇/인공지능, 신화, 비디오게임 매체, 심지어 타로카드까지 그야말로 다양한 소재를 섭렵하셨는데요, 이 중에서도 특히 애착을 지니고 계신 소재/장르가 있는지요?

김보영: 앞에서 답을 했네요. 어떤 생각에 빠지면 결국 그에 대한 소설을 써야 겨우 그 생각에서 벗어날 수 있는 듯합니다. 반복되는 생각에서 벗어나고자 소설을 쓴다는 생각도 합니다. 충분히 시간을 들여 하나의 소설을 쓰고 나면 제 안에서 하나의 결론이 나고, 이후로는 더 생각나지 않는 편입니다. 하나의 소설로 결론을 내지 못했으면 또 떠오르겠지요.

JFA: 일반적인 통념과 달리 한국 문화계에도 유구한 과학적 상상력의 전통이 존재하지만, 아무래도 2000년대 이전까지는 한국이 SF의 불모지라는 인식이 있었던 것 같습니다. 특히 문학의 경우 굴곡 많은 근현대 역사 속에서 비판적 리얼리즘이 주도권을 잡고 있었기 때문이라고 할 수 있지 않을까 싶은데요. 하지만 그런 치열함의 전통이 한편으로는 오늘날 한국 SF의 계보로 이어지는 일종의 강점으로 승화되지 않았나 싶기도 하구요. 영화나 스트리밍 컨텐츠 부문에서는 장르물의 클리셰를 효과적으로 활용하면서도 사회상을 비판/풍자한다는 면에서 <부산행>이나 <오징어게임>, <지금 우리 학교는>, <킹덤> 등이 주목을 받은 것 같습니다. 혹시 한국 문학계에서, 나아가 문화계 전반에 작가님께 영감을 준 작품이나 작가가 있을지요? 있다면, 어떠한 면 (주제, 소재, 문체)에서 그러했는지요?

김보영: 제 소설이 어디에서 영향을 받았는가 하는 질문을 받으면 늘 머리를 싸매지 않을 수 없습니다.

저는 어릴 때부터 이야기를 만들며 노는 것으로 시간을 다 보냈는데, 그랬던 이유는 그땐 즐길 것이 별로 없어서였습니다. 저는 그때 이야기를 두 종류로 만들었어요. 어른들이 '대체 뭘 하는 거냐.' 하고 들여다볼 때 내밀 평범한 소설과, 절대로 아무에게도 보여주지 않고 오직 저 혼자만 볼 용도의 소설이었습니다.

제가 지금 쓰는 소설은 그 '절대로 아무에게도 보여주지 않을' 소설의 연장선에 있습니다. 그 안에는 무한한 자유가 있었고 일어날 수 있는 거의 모든 일이 다 일어났는데, 왜냐하면 누구에게도 보여줄 필요가 없어서였기 때문입니다. 그때 제가 접한 모든 어린이 매체가 담겼겠지만 특정하기가 어렵습니다.

하지만 어느 순간부터 저는 '남에게 보일 용도'의 소설 쓰기를 극단적으로 지루해하고, '아무에게도 보여줄 수 없는' 소설에 시간을 다 바치며 열광하고 있다는 것을 깨달았지요. 그것을 세상에 내보일 수 있고, 하다못해 직업으로 가질 수 있다는 생각은 아주 뒤늦게 생겨났습니다.

솔직히 말하면 데뷔한 뒤에도 오랫동안 못했다고 생각합니다. '어차피 보아줄 사람은 없을 테니' 계속 나 혼자만 좋아할 소설을 쓸 생각이었고, 그럴 시간을 확보할 수 있는 부업이나 궁리했지요. 얼마나 갈지 모를 일이고 매번 지금 쓰는 소설이 마지막이 될 수도 있다고 생각했어요. 제가 데뷔한 공모전은 금방 사라졌고, 지면은 여전히 많지 않았으니까요.

단지 좋아한 '작가'를 말하자면 고유성 화백을 언급하지 않을 수 없겠습니다. 순전히 우연이었겠습니다만 제 유아 시절에, 집에 있던 유일한 아동용 책이 만화 〈로보트 킹(1977~1981)〉의 〈별나라 왕녀〉 편이었어요. 아직 글을 익히기 전이었다고 생각하는데, 수백 번은 보았고 내용을 전부 암기했어요. 나중에 고유성 화백의 만화를 닥치는 대로 보았는데, 포복절도하는 웃음 속에 힘이 넘치는 이야기를 하셨지요. 지금 보아도 선구적인 SF 장치를 많이 쓰신 분이었습니다.

10대에는 김진 화백의 작품에 빠져 지냈습니다. 김진은 SF도 썼지만, 신화를 현대적으로 재해석하는 데 능한 작가였습니다. 여성 작가면서 선이 굵고 스케일이 큰 작품을 쓰면서, 플롯을 통제하기보다는 내면과 감정의 흐름에 전개를 맡기는 이야기를 쓰셨지요. 여러 번 다시 보아야 찾아낼 수 있는 복잡한 상징을 많이 쓰기도 했어요. 김진의 〈푸른 포에닉스(1988~)〉는 당시 한국에서 SF 지면을 잘 주지 않는 환경 때문에 이곳저곳에 뚝뚝 끊겨 소개되었고, 지금까지도 완결이 나지 않았는데도, 여전히 많은 옛 한국 SF 팬들이 사랑하는 작품으로 압니다.

JFA: 작가님 글을 읽노라면 이론적으로 충실하고 사실적인 외삽법을 구사하시고 계산다는 점에서 (특히 작가님 데뷔 시점에는 한국 내에서 상대적으로 드물었던) 하드 SF의 느낌이 나면서도, 그 서정성이나 주제 면에서는 60년대 뉴웨이브의 느낌이 나기도 하더라구요. 주제나 소재, 내지는 문체 면에서 많은 영감을 받으신 외국작가 또는 작품도 있는지, 어떠한 면에서 그러했는지 궁금합니다.

김보영: 한국 작가와 마찬가지로 SF '소설가'를 말하기는 어렵습니다만 당연히 사랑한 작가들이 있지요.

어릴 때 TV 에서 본 데즈카 오사무의 만화 <우주소년 아톰>을 많이 사랑했고, 나중에 보게 된 <불새>와 <붓다>를 포함하여, 그의 휴머니즘적이고 불교적인 색채의 이야기들을 좋아합니다. 미야자키 하야오의 <미래소년 코난>도 좋아했지요. 애거서 크리스티의 추리소설을 늘 좋아했습니다. 이분은 물리적인 트릭이 아니라 심리 트릭을 쓰시는데, 문자로 세계의 일부를 감추는 방식에 늘 열광했지요. 헤르만 헤세가 쓴 자아 성찰의 메시지가 뚜렷한 환상소설들도 늘 좋아했습니다. 그리고 제가 작가가 된 뒤에야 접했습니다만 로저 젤라즈니의 신화적인 SF 도 많이 좋아했습니다. 과감하게 민담과 SF 를 결합하면서 신화 속의 영웅을 불러내는 뻔뻔한 전개를 사랑했지요.

마거릿 애트우드는 자신이 SF 를 쓰는 줄 몰랐다가 뒤늦게 깨달았다고 해요. 그리고 말하기를, 환상소설은 본래 사람이 만드는 원초적인 이야기의 형태인데, 현대인은 신화에서 이야기의 근거를 찾기 어려워 과학을 기반으로 세계를 만든다고 해요. 저도 그 말에 동의하며, 현대인에게 SF 는 고대의 민담처럼 자연스럽게 발생하는 이야기일 수 있다고 믿는 편입니다.

JFA: 영화 <설국열차>의 1 차 시나리오 작업에 참여하신 걸로 알고 있는데요, 생각을 오롯이 글의 형태로 풀어내는 것과 시청각적 재매개를 염두에 둔 집필 과정에는 차이가 있을 것 같아요. 그 경험이 어떠셨는지 말씀해 주실 수 있을까요?

김보영: 그 시나리오는 당연한 말입니다만 봉준호 감독님이 다 쓰셨어요. 한국에서는 거의 언급하지 않는 이력인데, 외국인은 아무래도 저를 모르다 보니 송구하게도 이름을 빌려 썼네요.

봉준호 감독님께서 제가 첫 앤솔러지를 냈을 때, 제 중편 딱 한 편 읽고 전화하셔서 일을 맡기셨어요. 감독님께서는 '아무것이나 해도 좋고, 거기서 내가 얻어갈 것을 얻어갈 테니 하고 싶은 것을 해라.'고 하시며 긴 시간을 기다려주셨어요. 지금 생각해도 정말로 놀라운 분입니다.

감독님께서 그때 '영화는 이미지의 언어다'라고 하셨는데, 저는 끝까지 감을 못 잡았다고 생각합니다. 소설은 글자의 예술이고, 실은 사건 대부분이 화자의 머릿속에서 일어나지요. 감독님의 대본을 읽고 실제 영화를 본 뒤에야, '이미지의 언어'라는 말이 무슨 뜻인지 충격적으로 깨달았어요. 소설은 실상 아무것도 보이지 않는 세계고, 영화는 보이는 것밖에는 존재하지 않는 세계더군요. 제가 영화의 언어를 배우려면 소설을 쓴 시간만큼을 투자해야 할 것 같았고, 그럴 수는 없기에 소설에 전념해야겠다고 생각했어요.

JFA: 몇년 전 국제여성영화제 관련 행사에서 뵈었을 때 하신 말씀이 기억에 남았는데요. 젠더 관련 질문에 대해, 제가 잘못 기억한 것이 아니라면 작가님께서는 딱히 "젠더론"을 염두에 두고 글을 쓰지는 않는다, 남녀의 구분보다는 존재 자체의 결을 탐색하는 데 주안점을 둔다는 요지로 말씀을 하셨던 것 같아요. 하지만, 앞서 여쭈었던 바와 같이 작품을 통해 다양한 소외의 기제를 다뤄 오셨다는 점에서 작가님의 생각이 궁금한데요. 영미권에서의 SF/판타지에는 최근의 다양한 시도들에도 불구하고 남성중심적 경향이 강한 데 반해, 오늘날 한국 SF (특히 문학)에서는 현재 여성 작가들과 창작자들이 선도적인 역할을 하고 있습니다. 하지만 사실 한국이야말로 가부장제적 사회 구조의 전통이 공고히 자리잡고 있는 곳인 만큼, 특기할 만한 현상인 것 같아요. 그 이유와 의의는 무엇이라고 보시는지요?

김보영: 말씀하셨다시피 한국에서 SF가 철저하게 주류에게 외면받은 비주류였으니까요. 그래서 한국에서 SF는 비주류에게 선택받은 장르가 되었습니다. 역사는 참으로 아이러니합니다. 그리고 여성은 어느 시대와 문화에서든 비주류지요.

전통과 역사의 맹점이라면, 그것이 언제나 이미 지나간 과거의 가치를 담는다는 점입니다. 전통과 역사는 존중받고 계승되어야 하는 동시에 타파되어야 하는 모순적인 과제를 갖고 있지요. 그런데 한국 SF는 계승할 것도 타파할 것도 딱히 없습니다. 덕분에 젊은 작가들이 자유롭게 진보적인 가치관을 설파하는 장이 되지 않았나 합니다.

JFA: 물론 남녀를 불문하고 두터운 팬 층을 거느리고 계시지만, 특히 젊은 여성 독자들에게 작가님의 작품들이 어떠한 면에서 어필한다고 생각하시는지 궁금합니다, 나아가, 젊은 여성들이 SF/판타지적 서사에 끌리는 이유는 무엇이라고 생각하시는지요?

김보영: 앞에서 이어지는 답이겠습니다. 실제로 한국에서 SF가 크게 주목받기 시작한 것은 2015, 6년 페미니즘 운동의 영향으로 출판계가 여성주의 문학을 재조명하면서였습니다. 그때 조명받은 메리 셸리의 『프랑켄슈타인』, 어슐러 르 귄의 『어둠의 왼손』, 게르드 브란튼베르그의 『이갈리아의 딸들』, 마거릿 애트우드의 『시녀 이야기』 등이 대부분 SF 였습니다. 페미니즘 유토피아/디스토피아 소설은 SF 니까요. 그러면서 한국의 주류 문학에서 자신을 위한 서사를

찾지 못했던 여성 독자들이 대거 SF 로 유입되었습니다. 그리고 여성 독자는 한국 독서인구 대부분을 차지하고 있었지요.

젊은 여성 창작자들도 크게 유입되었고, 기존의 한국 SF 작가 다수가 여성인 점도 새로 주목받았지요. 솔직히 저는 그때서야 세상이 내가 여자라고 깨달았다고 느꼈습니다. SF 의 비주류성이 너무나 컸기 때문에 성별까지 언급될 일이 없었어요.

당시 유입된 창작자는 물론 여성만이 아니었습니다. 이산화 작가는 본래 남성향 라이트노벨을 썼는데, 2016 년 넥슨 사상검증 사건 당시 부당하게 작업이 삭제된 노동자를 지지했다는 이유로 – 이것은 당시 극단적 페미니즘 발언으로 해석되었습니다 – 하루만에 출간이 취소되자, 바로 SF 작가로 전향하기도 했습니다.

셰릴 빈트는 "주류 문학에서 자신의 이야기를 찾을 수 없는 사람은 다른 세계로 갈 수밖에 없다. 그곳은 SF 의 세계다."라고 한 바가 있습니다. 그 말을 보았을 때 몹시 기뻤습니다. 저도 제가 정착할 이야기를 찾지 못해 나만의 이야기를 만들어 왔고, 그 이야기가 SF 로 받아들여졌다고 느끼니까요.

USC 의 박선영 교수님께서 한국 노동 운동의 상징과도 같은 소설인, 조세희의 『난장이가 쏘아올린 작은 공(1978)』에도 SF 요소가 있다는 점을 짚어주셨을 때도 크게 기뻤습니다. 이 소설에서 난개발로 쫓겨나는 도시빈민들은 우주인과 클라인 씨의 병 우주론에 대해 이야기하며 달나라 이주를 꿈꿉니다. 소외된 자들이 지금 여기가 아닌 세상을 찾는 경향은 늘 있어왔던 모양입니다.

현재 한국에서 활동하는 SF 소설가 중 가장 원로로 불릴 만한 작가 듀나는 성별을 드러내지 않고 활동하고 있습니다. 현재 한국 최고의 SF 베스트셀러 소설가인 김초엽 작가는 난청 장애인이고, 부커상 최종후보에 오른 정보라 작가는 사회활동가입니다. 최근 SF 문학상을 수상한 최의택 작가는 근위축증 장애인인데, 정보라 작가를 보고 SF 를 쓰기 시작했고 김초엽 작가를 보며 SF 로 장애를 이야기할 수 있다는 희망을 얻었다고 합니다.

우리는 아이러니하게도, 주류가 외면하였기에 현대적인 가치에서 서사를 새로 창조할 수 있었고, 이것이 앞으로도 우리의 역사로 기록되리라는 생각을 하면 기분이 좋습니다.

좋은 말씀 해주시고 질문해주셔서 정말로 감사드립니다.

JFA: 감사합니다

"Those Left on Earth Are Equally Significant": Sang-Keun Yoo's Interview with *Space Sweepers* Director Sung-hee Jo

Translated by Sang-Keun Yoo

BORN IN 1979, SUNG-HEE JO initially studied industrial design at Seoul National Design before shifting his focus to filmmaking. He furthered his education at the Korean Academy of Film Arts, which led to an invitation to the 2009 Cannes Film Festival. His student short, "Don't Step Out Of The House!" (2008), featured at the Cinéfondation sidebar, placed third and won the Grand Prize at the Mise-en-Scène Short Film Festival. Jo's first full-length feature, the indie post-apocalyptic film *End of Animal*, was met with critical acclaim and received invitations from numerous international film festivals, such as Rotterdam IFF, San Francisco IFF, CPH PIX, Vancouver IFF, Dubai IFF (Special Mention), BFI London IFF, and the Cinema Digital Seoul Festival.

Jo's reputation as a promising emerging director in Korea solidified when he made a successful crossover into the commercial sphere. His 2012 film, the fantasy romance *A Werewolf Boy*, had a grand debut, premiering at the Toronto International Film Festival. The film's success subsequently won him the Baeksang Arts Award for Best New Director. Jo's latest

Vol. 34, No. 2, *Journal of the Fantastic in the Arts*
Copyright © 2023, International Association for the Fantastic in the Arts

venture, Korea's debut space sci-fi blockbuster *Space Sweepers* (2021), was released on Netflix where it quickly ascended the ranks of the most-watched shows globally. Jo is currently in the process of preparing a live-action film adaptation of the Japanese anime series *Tokyo Magnitude 8.0*.

* * *

JFA: Greetings, Mr. Jo. It's a privilege to have this interview with you for our special issue on Korean science fiction and fantasy in *the Journal of the Fantastic in the Arts* (*JFA*). Could you offer a brief introduction to our *JFA* readers?

Jo: Hello, I'm Jo Sung-hee, a South Korean filmmaker. It's truly an honor to engage in this dialogue for *JFA*, a respected publication with a rich three-decade history. I'm thrilled to connect with the readers of *JFA* through this medium.

JFA: Your body of work seems to demonstrate a strong affinity for hard science fiction, as evident in films like *A Werewolf Boy* (2012) and *Space Sweepers* (2021). You appear to step away from realism. With *Phantom Detective* (2016), you've ingeniously woven the narrative framework of the 16th-century classic novel, *Tale of Hong Gildong*, into a fantastic tale, despite it not being a traditional SF or fantasy. Could you share your perspective on how you employ the unique elements of SF and fantasy to articulate your narratives?

Jo: Although my filmography is not extensive yet, there's a shared attribute: a departure from stark realism. I don't conform to the notion of, "My world must be fantastical." I simply narrate stories that pique my interest. When I conceive a story, I invariably envisage a world or a scenario distinct from our reality. I surmise this habit might be the reason behind my inclination away from crafting realistic scripts. As I look ahead, I aspire to create an array of films spanning multiple genres, beyond just fantasy or science fiction.

JFA: *Space Sweepers* is often heralded as "South Korea's first space opera film." Historically, hard science fiction films such as *Resurrection of the Little Match Girl* (2002) and *A Mystery of the Cube* (1998) have not resonated with Korean audiences. Nonetheless, the gradual acceptance of the genre is becoming evident with recent films like *The Silent Sea* and *Space Sweepers*. How do you envisage the future of science fiction and fantasy in Korea, and why do you think international audiences are captivated by Korean science fiction? Does SF in Korea, particularly in mixture with traditional narratives like Hong Gil-dong, have a distinct trait or societal role in showcasing the creativity of Korean SF that sets it apart from the global SF tradition?

Jo: Historically, science fiction has largely been the domain of Hollywood. However, as visual effects technology advances and becomes increasingly accessible in Korea, we're seeing a broader spectrum of projects being conceived and produced. When considering past Korean science fiction, these audacious efforts paved the way for the subsequent productions, and I believe they have the potential to captivate audiences globally. Further, as Korean films and dramas continually explore a wider array of genres, I'm confident that the quality and volume of Korean science fiction and fantasy will continue to rise. One distinctive feature of Korean productions is the deep and fervent emotions that are intrinsically Korean. While there's an appeal to being cool, as demonstrated by *Squid Game*, the nuanced yet intense emotional undercurrents of Korean content are relatable to global audiences. I believe there has been a scarcity of opportunities and platforms to exhibit this. However, with the emergence of numerous opportunities via global streaming services, I see

Korean fantasy and sci-fi as an industry that's only just beginning to flourish.

JFA: *Space Sweepers* clearly exhibits your critique of the avarice of Western multinational corporations and the prevailing power disparity in Korea. Simultaneously, by placing Korean astronauts as the saviors of the entire universe and casting Korean heroes at the forefront, you ingeniously challenge the predominantly White perspective of traditional Anglo-American science fiction. The film breaks new ground with its effortless fusion of different languages during the opening space sweepers' combat and features a character speaking Nigerian Pidgin in a Korean film for the first time. The character of Robot Bubs (Ŏptong-i in the original) stands out not only as one of the rare humanoid robots in Korean science fiction films, but also as a character that redefines gender as a human socio-cultural construct, despite not aspiring to become a biological human. I am interested in understanding why you decided to infuse this decolonizing narrative throughout the film.

Jo: Viewing it from the perspective of an audience member rather than a director, I perceive it as a narrative about the forgotten and the marginalized. In every country, in every society, there are pioneers propelling progress, but there are also those who get left behind in their wake. Those with ambitions to transcend their limits, to conquer Mars, are commendable, yet those left on Earth are equally significant. We need people to clear the detritus left by the ambitious ones who have moved on. It's not about dichotomizing between heroes and villains or determining who is worthy of happiness or who is destined for sacrifice. The underlying message of the film is that all can coexist harmoniously.

JFA: Nanotechnology features prominently as a scientific element in *Space Sweepers*. Some SF enthusiasts argue that the depiction of science and technology in such films necessitates accuracy, while many academics believe these details need not mirror reality.

What's your stance on this debate, and do you draw upon any specific references when incorporating science and technology into your films?

Jo: One of the most significant pitfalls in creative endeavors is adherence to a prescriptive rule dictating the specifics of your work. Of all our pursuits, artistic creation should be the most liberating. Take, for example, the diverse range of SF films available. We have *Interstellar*, where black holes are meticulously and realistically portrayed, contrasting sharply with films like *Mars Attacks!*, featuring skeletal aliens brandishing ray guns. I don't see one approach as superior or inferior to the other. Each film is enjoyable and meaningful in its unique way, reflecting the individual sensibilities of their creators. I believe that the realism of the technology isn't as important as the emotional impact on the audience and their level of enjoyment.

The portrayal of science and technology in *Space Sweepers* falls somewhere on the spectrum between hyper-realistic films like *Gravity* and wholly fantastical ones like *Star Wars*. While the movie sprang from the realms of imagination, it grounded itself in current discourse on topics like nanobots and space elevators. Instead of relying on specific references, I amassed a diverse collection of resources and endeavored to utilize them in the most creative ways possible.

JFA: Are there any specific SF or fantasy works that you particularly admire, or that have shaped your perspective as a director?

Jo: The list is extensive, making it difficult to single out just a few. However, when I first embarked on my filmmaking journey, the directors who captivated and inspired me the most were David Lynch, Steven Spielberg, and Bong Joon-ho. I was particularly enamored with David Lynch's work to such an extent that I practiced turning his films into screenplay format, even though they weren't necessarily the ideal candidates for learning commercial screenplay writing.

JFA: Your films often bear a strong semblance to period dramas with *Space Sweepers* being set in a futuristic society, *A Werewolf Boy* in the past, and *Phantom Detective* in the present. Why do you opt to portray a reflection of contemporary society through the lens of the past or future, rather than directly setting your films in the present?

Jo: I am drawn to crafting worlds that diverge from our current reality, and I find joy in collaborating with other artists across direction, art, costume, VFX, etc., to bring something slightly different from our existing reality to life. My affinity for this approach may stem from my childhood passion for drawing. When conceptualizing an idea, I tend to start with an image rather than a theme or story. Undeniably, living in Korea, I can't avoid reflecting the world I perceive and experience here into my work. However, I believe it's also attributed to my preference for imagining things that don't exist over meticulously observing reality.

JFA: Your films often portray unconventional interpretations of humanity, as seen in the human-wolf hybrid character in *A Werewolf Boy* and the human-robot hybrid in *Space Sweepers*. This seems to suggest an attempt to embrace a broader range of beings beyond the traditional definition of humanity. I'd appreciate your further insight on this.

Jo: As you may be aware, characters like werewolves, robots, and humans controlling nanobots aren't new; they've graced Hollywood screens countless times. However, their appearance in Korean cinema is relatively novel. While I have a personal interest in the diversity of non-human beings, other Korean films are also diversifying their character roster with the expansion of genres, featuring zombies, psychics, aliens, etc. I foresee the diversity of non-human characters growing as Korean cinema increasingly connects with global audiences, similar to the trajectory of *Space Sweepers.*

JFA: Your films frequently feature characters that challenge traditional gender roles, such as the female captain in *Space Sweepers* or the female protagonist who tutors a male in *A Werewolf Boy.* In *Space Sweepers,* Robot Bubs, a combat robot with a masculine voice, symbolically undergoes a gender transition by adopting a human female "shell." Could you share your perspective on this subversion of established gender norms and divisions?

Jo: As you've pointed out, challenging established gender roles can be exciting. It's not limited to *Space Sweepers*; many characters across Korean visual media are moving towards disrupting traditional gender images. Audiences no longer view this as groundbreaking, but rather as something more natural. I believe we're in the midst of dismantling stereotypes across all kinds of identities, not just related to gender but also race, nationality, and physical appearance, and my works are reflective of this shift. To add, one technique I employ when creating characters involves combining two seemingly incompatible elements within a single character. For instance, a character might appear tough but enjoys knitting, or appears gentle and quiet but is actually a ruthless killer. In the case of Robot Bubs in *Space Sweepers,* the dichotomy between its violent nature and its desire for a female shell struck me as intriguing, which led to its characterization.

JFA: Could you share your plans for your next movie? Do you intend to explore more SF or fantasy works?

Jo: My next project is a disaster movie. It will be grounded in realism rather than leaning into science fiction. Despite its realistic approach, it will be both frightening and moving. As I mentioned earlier, my long-term plan involves exploring a variety of genres, not just limiting myself to fantasy or science fiction. I appreciate the opportunity to share my thoughts with your readers today. Thank you.

Original Korean text follows.

"지구에 남겨진 사람들도 소중하고 그 야망의 잔재들을 처리하는 사람들도 필요합니다": 조성희 감독과의 대화

(인터뷰/번역: 유상근)

조성희 감독

조성희 감독은 1979 년 수원에서 태어나, 서울대학교에서 산업디자인을 전공한 후 한국영화아카데미에서 영화 연출을 공부했다. 조성희 감독은 단편영화 <남매의 집>이 2009 년 칸 영화제 시네파운데이션 상과 더불어 미쟝센 단편영화제 대상을 수상하며 이름을 알리게 되었다. 그의 첫 장편 <짐승의 끝>은 로테르담 영화제, 샌프란시스코 영화제, 밴쿠버 영화제, BFI 런던 영화제, 서울디지털영화제 등 다수의 국제 영화제에 초청되며 평단의 호평을 받았다. 2012 년 판타지 로맨스 영화 <늑대소년>을 연출하며 평론가와 일반 관객 모두를 만족시키며, 그는 이 영화로 백상예술대상 신인감독상을 수상한다. 넷플릭스에서 공개된 그의 최신작 <승리호>는 전세계적으로 가장 많이 본 넷플릭스 영화 순위에 오르며, 세계적으로 큰 사랑을 받는다. 현재 그는 일본 애니메이션을 기반으로 한 영화를 제작 중이다.

* * *

JFA: 안녕하세요, 감독님. JFA 의 독자분들께 간단한 인사 말씀 부탁드립니다.

조성희: 안녕하세요. 저는 한국에서 영화를 만들고 있는 조성희입니다. 지면으로나마 JFA 독자분들을 만날 수 있게 되어 영광입니다.

JFA: 감독님 작품들을 보면 리얼리즘보다는 <늑대인간>이나 <승리호>같은 하드 SF 에 대한 관심이 많이 보이고, <탐정 홍길동>의 경우에는 SF 나 판타지는 아니지만 홍길동의 서사 구조를 가지고 와 판타지적으로 재구성하셨다는 느낌이 듭니다. 이렇듯 SF 와 판타지의 장르적 특성을 감독님의 메시지를 전달하는 데 유용하게 활용하고 계시는데요, 이에 대한 감독님의 생각이 듣고 싶습니다.

조성희: 제가 아직 영화를 많이 만들지는 않았지만, 이제까지의 작품들은 그리 사실적이지 않다는 공통점이 있습니다. 하지만 저는 '나의 작품 세계는 판타지이다.' 같은 원칙은 없으며, 그저 매번 재미있을 것 같은 이야기들을 할 뿐입니다. 제가 스토리를 구상할 때 항상 지금과는 다른 세상이나 존재를 먼저 떠올리는 습관이 있고, 사실적인 시나리오를 잘 쓰지 못하는 이유도 있는 것 같습니다. 앞으로는 판타지나 SF 뿐 아니라 다양한 장르의 영화를 많이 만들고 싶습니다.

JFA: <승리호>를 두고 흔히들 "한국 최초 우주 SF" (스페이스 오페라)라고 말합니다. 그동안 한국 영화계에서는 유독 <성냥팔이 소녀의 재림>이나 <건축무한육면각체의 비밀>과 같은 하드 SF 가 관객들로부터 외면을 받아왔습니다. 그러나 최근 <고요의 바다>나 <승리호>에서 볼 수 있듯 한국 관객들도 점차 SF 장르를 더 가까이 받아들이고 있는 것 같습니다. 앞으로 한국에서 SF 나 판타지의 미래를 어떻게 보시나요? 더불어 외국의 관객들이 한국 SF 에 열광하는 이유가 무엇일까요? 한국 SF 만의 특징이나 역할이 있을까요? 특히 <홍길동>과 같은 한국 전통 서사가 세계 SF 전통과 다른 한국 SF 의 창의성을 드러내는 데 그 어떤 역할을 할 수 있을까요?

조성희: 이제까지의 SF 는 헐리우드의 전유물이었지만, 한국에서도 시각효과 기술이 발전하고 범용화 됨에 따라 점차 다양한 작품들이 기획되고 만들어지고 있습니다. 과거의 한국 SF 에 대해서 말하자면, 그런 용기 있는 시도들이 있었기에 그 이후 작품들도 탄생할 수 있었고, 그 토양 위에서 지금 전세계인의 사랑을 받게 된 것이라 생각합니다. 게다가 한국 영화와 드라마는 더 다양한 장르의 확장을 계속하고 있습니다. 그래서 저는 한국의 SF 판타지는 그 양과 품질에서 앞으로 더 발전할 것이라 확신합니다.

한국 작품들의 특징은 한국인만의 뜨겁고 강렬한 정서가 아닐까 합니다. 쿨한 것도 근사하지만, <오징어 게임>이 증명했듯이 한국 컨텐츠만의 섬세하면서도 강렬한 감정도 전세계 시청자들이 공감 가능한 것이었습니다. 다만 그동안 많이 보여줄 기회와 통로가 부족하지 않았나 싶습니다. 지금은 많은 글로벌 OTT 를 통해 많은 기회가 열렸기에 한국 판타지 SF 는 이제 막 시작되었다고 생각합니다.

JFA: <승리호>에서는 서구 글로벌 기업의 탐욕과 한국의 차별적 권력구조에 대한 감독님의 비판적 시각이 잘 드러납니다. 이와 동시에 전 우주를 구하는 한국 우주비행사들, 한국적 하어로들이 등장하고 있어 기존 영미권 SF 의 백인중심적 사고를 창의적으로 전유하고 계신데요. 영화 초반부 세계 각국 출신의 우주 쓰레기 수거 함정들 간의 각축전에서 다양한 언어가 자연스레 어우러지는 점이라든지, 한국 영화 최초로 나이지리아 피진어를 사용하는 인물이 등장하는 점도 새로웠구요. 업동이의 경우 "인간형" 로봇을 다룬 SF 중에서 극히 드물게 성소수자로 구현될 뿐 아니라 생물학적으로 딱히 인간이 되고 싶어하는 것이 아닌데도 불구하고 지극히 인간적인 사회 구조적 산물인 젠더를 적극적으로 재전유하고 있다는 측면이 혁신적으로 다가왔습니다. 작품 전체에 걸쳐 이렇듯 탈식민적 프레임을 구축하신 이유에 대한 감독님의 생각이 궁금합니다.

조성희: 작품에 대한 해석은 관객 개개인마다 다른 것이라 생각합니다. 제가 감독이 아닌 관객의 한 사람으로 이 작품을 읽어본다면, 저는 <승리호>를 뒤에 남겨진 사람들, 소외된 사람들에 대한 이야기로 보았습니다. 어느 나라, 어느 사회라도 늘 앞으로 나아가는 개척자도 있지만, 그만큼 가지 못해 뒤에 남겨지는 사람들도 있습니다. 더 높이, 더 멀리 나아가 화성을 개척하려는 사람들도 위대하지만 지구에 남겨진 사람들도 소중하고 그 야망의 잔재들을 처리하는 사람들도 필요합니다. 그 중 누구는 정의롭고 누구는 악당이라거나, 누구는 가치가 있으니 행복할 자격이 있고, 누구는 도태되었으니 희생을 감수해야 되는 것이 아닙니다. 모두 공존할 수 있다는 것이 이 영화의 메시지가 아닐까 합니다.

JFA: <승리호> 에서는 나노 기술이 중요한 과학적 모티프로 등장하고 있는데요, SF 팬들 중에서는 SF 영화에서 과학기술을 차용할 때 그 기제가 현실적인 정확성을 요한다고 생각하는 이들이 존재합니다. 물론 SF 영화 속에 등장하는 과학 기술이 굳이 실제적인 디테일을 정확하게 반영할 필요는 없다고 생각하는 학자들도 많이 있고요. 감독님은 이에 대해 어떻게 보시는지요? 영화 속에서 과학 기술을 활용하실 때 따로 참고하시는 자료들이 있으신가요?

조성희: 창작 활동에서 가장 경계해야 할 것 중 하나는 '작품은 이러이러해야 한다.' 는 어떤 규칙에 지배를 받는 것입니다. 사람이 하는 모든 행위 중에 가장 자유로워야 하는 것이 예술 창작 활동입니다. 세상에는 많은 SF 영화들이 있습니다. 블랙홀을 정말 사실적으로 고증하고 표현한 <인터스텔라>가 있는가 하면, 해골처럼 생긴 외계인이 광선총을 쏘는 <화성침공>도 있습니다. 그 중 어떤 표현방식이 더 우월하거나 나은 것이라 줄 세울 수 없습니다. 둘 다 나름의 재미와 의미가 있으며 모두 예술가들의 독특한 감수성을 반영한 창작물입니다. 중요한 것은 과학기술을 얼마나 사실적으로 구현했느냐가 아니라 관객들이 무엇을 느끼고 얼마나 즐길 수 있는가라고 생각합니다.

<승리호>에 나온 과학기술의 리얼리티는 <그래비티>처럼 사실적인 영화들과 <스타워즈>같은 완전한 판타지 그 중간 어딘가에 위치합니다. 비록 과장된 상상력으로부터 시작된 영화이지만 나노봇이나 우주 엘리베이터 등 지금 실제로 언급되고 있는 것들 모티브로 삼았습니다. 따로 참고하는 자료들이 있다기 보다는 모든 수단과 방법을 다 동원하여 수 많은 자료들을 수집하여 참고하였습니다.

JFA: 감독님이 특히 좋아하시거나 감독님에게 영향을 많이 준 SF 나 판타지 작품이 있나요?

조성희: 작품은 너무 많아서 몇 개만 언급하기 어렵습니다. 다만 제가 처음 영화를 시작할 때 가장 매료되고 열광했던 감독은 데이비드 린치와 스티븐 스필버그, 그리고 봉준호입니다. 데이비드 린치는 그의 영화를 보고 시나리오로 옮겨 적는 연습을 할 만큼 너무 좋아했습니다. (상업적인 시나리오 작법을 공부하기에는 그리 좋은 영화들은 아니었지만).

JFA: 감독님의 작품은 시대극이거나, 시대극의 느낌을 강하게 주는 것 같습니다. <승리호>는 미래 사회를 배경으로 하고 있고 <늑대인간>은 과거, <탐정 홍길동>은 현대를 다루는 데에도 불구하고 시대극의 느낌이 나는데요. 영화의 배경으로 현재를 직접 다루시기보다는 우회적으로 과거나 미래를 통해 오늘날의 자화상을 보여주시는 이유가 있을까요?

조성희: 저는 지금과는 다른 세상을 꾸미는 것에 흥미가 있는 것 같습니다. 연출, 미술, 의상, VFX 등의 예술가들과 지금의 현실과는 어딘가 조금 다른 것을 만들어내는 과정이 즐겁습니다. 제가 어렸을 때부터 그림 그리는 것을 좋아해서 그런지 아이디어를 구상할 때 주제나 스토리보다 어떤 이미지부터 시작하는 것도 그 이유인 것 같습니다. 물론 저 역시 지금의 대한민국을 사는 사람이라 제가 보고 느끼는 세상이 작품에 투영되는 것은 어쩔 수 없지만, 저는 현실을 자세히 관찰하는 것 보다 없는 것을 상상하는 것을 더 즐기는 사람이라 그런 것 같기도 합니다.

JFA: 감독님의 작품에서는 기존 인간관에 대한 다양한 전복 양상을 볼 수 있는데요. 가령 <늑대인간>에서는 사람/늑대의 하이브리드, 승리호에서는 사람/로봇의 하이브리드가 등장합니다. 이와 같이 기존 인간의 정의를 넘어서는 존재들에 대한 다양성을 포용하고자 하는 시도가 드러나는데요. 이에 대한 감독님의 생각이 궁금합니다.

조성희: 아시다시피 늑대인간, 로봇, 나노봇을 조종하는 인간등은 그리 새로운 캐릭터는 아닙니다. 헐리웃 영화에서 수도 없이 등장했지만 한국 영화에서 아직 많지 않았던 것 뿐입니다. 저 개인적으로도 인간이 아닌 다른 존재들의 다양성에 대한 관심도 있지만, 한국 영화의 다른 작품들에서도 좀비, 초능력자, 외계인등, 장르와 더불어 캐릭터의 다양성도 넓어지고 있습니다. <승리호>가 그랬듯 점차 글로벌 관객들을 만나면서 인간 외의 캐릭터도 범위가 커지고 많아질 것이라 기대합니다.

JFA: 감독님 작품을 보면 기존의 성 역할을 뒤집는 캐릭터들이 종종 등장합니다. <승리호>의 여성 선장이라거나, <늑대인간>에서 남성을 조련하는 여성 주인공이 떠오르고요. <승리호>의 업동이는 남성적 목소리를 지닌 전투로봇이 인간 여성의 "외피"를 입는다는 점에서 은유적으로 성전환을 시도하기도 합니다. 기존의 고정된 성역할이나 젠더 구분에 대한 감독님의 전복적 사고가 드러나는 것 같은데요, 이에 대한 감독님의 생각이 궁금합니다.

조성희: 말씀대로 전통적인 성역할을 흐트러트리는 것이 재미있습니다. 비단 <승리호>뿐만 아니라 많은 작품 속 캐릭터들이 기존의 성역할과 이미지를 파괴하는 방향으로 나아가고 있습니다. 관객들도 이제는 그런 것이 파격이라고 여기지 않고 오히려 더 자연스럽게 느끼기도 합니다. 지금은 성별 뿐 아니라 인종과 국적, 외모까지 모든 스테레오 타입들이

희미해지는 과정 중에 있는 것 같습니다. 따라서 작품들에도 이런 현실이 반영되는 게 아닐까 합니다.

조금 더 보태자면 제가 캐릭터를 만들기 위해 쓰는 방법 중 하나는 한 인물 안에 어울리지 않는 두 가지를 집어 넣는 것입니다. 인상은 험악하지만 뜨개질을 좋아한다거나 순하고 조용해 보이지만 사실은 잔인한 살인마라던가 하는 식입니다. <승리호>의 업동이도 아주 폭력적인 로봇이지만 여성의 외피를 원한다는 것이 재미있는 것 같아 그렇게 만들었습니다.

JFA: 차기작에 대한 감독님의 계획이 궁금합니다. 다른 SF 나 판타지 작품에 대한 계획이 있으신가요?

조성희: 바로 다음 작품은 재난 영화입니다. SF 가 아닌 사실적인 영화입니다. 사실적이고 무섭고 감동적인 이야기입니다. 앞서 말씀드렸듯이 판타지나 SF 뿐만 아니라 다양한 장르의 작품을 많이 만들고 싶은 것이 저의 장기 계획입니다.

JFA: 감사합니다.

"This Inexplicable Complexity That Underscores Our Humanity": Sang-Keun Yoo's Interview With *The School Nurse Files* Director Kyoung-mi Lee

Translated by Sang-Keun Yoo

L EE KYOUNG-MI, BORN IN 1973, completed her studies in Russian at the Hankuk University of Foreign Studies before deciding to delve into the world of filmmaking at the Korea National University of Arts. Her journey into short filmmaking commenced with *Myungsook and I* in 2000, and she continued to create a series of short films including *Lies* (2001), *Giant* (2001), *Audition* (2003), and *Feel Good Story* (2004). The latter won the Grand Prize and Audience Award at the Seoul International Women's Film Festival.

She collaborated with Park Chan-wook on *Sympathy for Lady Vengeance* as a scriptwriter and assistant director, marking the conclusion of his renowned Vengeance Trilogy. Following this project, Park extended his support as a producer, a collaboration that resulted in the production of Lee's debut feature, *Crush and Blush*, in 2008. With this film, Lee was rewarded with the Best New Director and Best Screenplay titles at the Blue Dragon Film Awards. Lee's second feature film, *The Truth Beneath*, was released in 2016 and her Netflix series *The School Nurse Files* was released in 2020.

* * *

Vol. 34, No. 2, *Journal of the Fantastic in the Arts*
Copyright © 2023, International Association for the Fantastic in the Arts

JFA: Greetings, Lee. Given the escalating global interest in Korean cultural content, it's truly a privilege to have you here for the *Journal of the Fantastic in the Arts*'s (*JFA*) special issue on Korean science fiction and fantasy. Would you mind sharing a few words with our *JFA* readers?

Lee: I'm truly delighted to connect with *JFA*'s readership in this opportunity. I appreciate your interest in my creative endeavours.

JFA: Your filmography consistently showcases an imaginative defiance of conventional genre classifications. For instance, while Netflix's *School Nurse Files* is generally categorized as fantasy, one could also perceive it as an action-hero film that delves into corporate corruption. Similarly, the short film *The Lady from 406* intertwines everyday societal issues with elements of the occult, transitioning from a realistic narrative to fantasy towards the conclusion. *The Truth Beneath* grapples with political and social issues while incorporating fantastical components, such as the shamanistic sequence and the music video scene featuring the two girls. Numerous SF and fantasy scholars in the English-speaking world have posited that the demarcation between hard science fiction and fantasy is becoming increasingly blurred over the past few decades. In contrast, in Korea, the divide between realism, hard science fiction, and fantasy tends to be more rigidly delineated. I'm interested to hear your insights regarding this perceived dichotomy in genre divisions. Furthermore, how would you classify your films within these genre classifications?

Lee: My cinematic journey began with *Crush and Blush*, a comedy, followed by *The Truth Beneath*, a thriller. You might categorize my short film *The Lady from 406* as a blend of fantasy and horror, while *The School Nurse Files* might be deemed a fantasy-action hero piece. Each of my creations is unique, often flouting genre conventions. But I'm not alone in this. Like many Korean filmmakers, my love for cinema began with an appreciation for Hollywood films and international genre films. Our unique cultural and political contexts further color our narratives, which I believe resonate in an intriguing way with international audiences. This intercultural exchange is where art truly transcends language barriers. It's been my observation that Korean filmmakers who have found international acclaim are those who bend genre norms and imprint their distinctive personalities onto their work. However, the genre of science fiction is still stringently defined in Korea. This could be due to the scarcity of SF works originating from our country and our familiarity with high-tech American SF movies.

Returning to your question about my own films' genres, while I have experimented with a multitude of genres, the prevailing emotion that permeates my body of work is horror, often encapsulated in comedy, thrillers, or fantasy. Take *The School Nurse Files*, for example, based on an existing novel. While the original narrative was light-hearted and sincere, my adaptation infused it with a horror component. My intent was to evoke a dichotomy of feelings, encapsulated in phrases like "disgusting yet adorable" and "terrifying yet amusing." I appreciate the awkward, discordant sensation that arises when seemingly incompatible emotions intertwine. The Korean term for "utp'ŭda" [웃프다; laughable] conveys a similar sentiment. To me, human emotion is a perplexing chemistry that defies conventional wisdom, and it is this inexplicable complexity that underscores our humanity.

JFA: While your works invariably incorporate elements of fantasy, they don't necessarily adhere to hard science fiction with a focus on science and technology. Instead, they explore how religion, particularly cults, superstition, and shamanism, profoundly influences the characters' thought processes and lifestyles. As touched upon in the previous question, Ahn Eun-young's decorative cabinet in *The School Nurse Files* holds myriad religious artifacts, be they Taoist, Buddhist, or Christian. The protagonist in *The Truth Beneath* seeks counsel from a shaman, and Hee-ji from *The Lady from 406* appears to be a cult follower. Yet, in your films, these components seem more grounded in reality than they are fantastical or surreal. Can we interpret this as your attempt to portray such seemingly surreal elements as inherent aspects of everyday life?

Lee: I believe religion is one of the key facets in understanding Korean culture. Shamanism is deeply ingrained in our society. We Koreans covertly rely on it while overtly disavowing it. Shamanism isn't confined to the general populace in Korea; it's not uncommon to discover strong shamanistic influences among those occupying political and economic echelons. Not only shamanism, but also cults, have a rich history in Korea, with roots dating back to the 1940s and 50s. These sects continue to diverge and grow, enriching their doctrines over time. It might sound somewhat preposterous, but it's possible that successful K-content was heralded by K-religion before K-pop became a global sensation. Consequently, I view cults as elements so intertwined with the reality of life that they take on an aura of authenticity.

JFA: Within the Korean film industry, hard science fiction such as *Resurrection of the Little Match Girl* (2002) and *A Mystery of the Cube* (1998) have historically been less well-received by audiences, in contrast to the popularity of fantasy genres, as exemplified by *Korean Ghost Stories* (Chŏnsŏrŭi Kohyang; 1977-1989, 1996-1999, 2008-2009). However, recent trends suggest a growing acceptance of science fiction among Korean audiences, as seen with films like *The Silent Sea* (2021) and *Space Sweepers* (2021). How do you envision the future of science fiction and fantasy within the Korean film industry?

Lee: When it comes to Korean genre cinema, SF often receives the harshest critique. It's a genre that necessitates technical perfection, which is challenging to achieve with budgets constrained by the limitations of the Korean market and its inability to match Hollywood. However, as K-content expands in popularity and scalability, I perceive significant potential for the genre in Korea. As our audiences and creators continue to elevate their standards and expectations, there's a vast unexplored terrain within the genre.

JFA: Of late, there's been a surge in international interest in Korean science fiction and fantasy, facilitated by global streaming platforms. What do you attribute this to, and how would you define Korean science fiction and Korean fantasy? Furthermore, do you believe such definitions carry any substantial meaning?

Lee: I can't pinpoint the exact reason for this burgeoning interest, but I believe Korean fantasy is still evolving. Just as Bong Joon-ho's *Memories of Murder* effectively localized the American thriller genre by infusing it with Korean sensibilities, characters, and settings, I hope that Korean science fiction will similarly captivate international audiences.

JFA: Many of your past films, not just *The School Nurse Files*, seem to carry an undercurrent of female empowerment. Characters like Kim Yeon-hong in *The Truth Beneath* and Yang Mi-sook in *Crush and Blush* can be viewed as female protagonists in their own rights. They often depict women challenging and toppling societal structures, portraying the realistic fears of women living alone and the discrimination they face in a male-dominated society. Moreover, you frequently explore the theme of maternal frenzy following the loss of a daughter, which often culminates in a show of solidarity between women, be it the camaraderie between the girls and the nurse in *The School Nurse Files* or the bond between Choi Mi-ok and Kim Yeon-hong in *The Truth Beneath*. Your films also tend to feature adult female characters protecting younger women, whether they are daughters or schoolgirls. Could you share your insights on this recurring theme in your works?

Lee: Perhaps my own gender gives me a greater degree of comfort and confidence when portraying female characters. I attended all-girls schools through middle and high school, and although my university was co-ed, my adolescent years were predominantly spent in the company of girls. Consequently, I had ample opportunity to engage with women. I didn't consciously set out to tell stories about female solidarity, but it took someone else's perspective to make me realize that my stories always involve an adult woman, the protagonist, and her relationship with a younger woman.

My interest lies less in redemption narratives and more in stories where those yet unsaved encounter one another. I believe that's a more realistic depiction of our society. The society I grew up in was far more steeped in gender inequality than it is today, and this instilled in me a certain insecurity about my future if I failed to adhere to societal expectations, such as marrying at the "appropriate" age. This was partly due to the lack of real-life role models to look up to. Female artists tend to dwell on women who are older than us because they represent our future, and likewise, we reflect on girls younger than us because they mirror our past. This, I believe, is the source of the solidarity the audiences can see in my films. It's intriguing to consider how different the narratives might be if we had more stories of women taking the lead and making history.

JFA: Do you perceive young female viewers as your primary audience? If so, why do you believe your work resonates with them? Additionally, what draws young women to fantasy narratives?

Lee: I am truly grateful for the affection I receive from younger audiences; it feels as though it extends my own life in a way. As to why young women might be drawn to fantasy narratives, I can only hypothesize that perhaps their reality feels constrained and dispiriting. In South Korea, the gender conflict among individuals in their 20s and 30s is particularly severe. With declining marriage and fertility rates, the disparity between the visions held by women and men seems increasingly insurmountable. If it's indeed the case that my work holds a particular appeal for young women, I cannot definitively say why. However, I suspect that the range of emotions I've navigated throughout my own life within a somewhat frustrating Korean society might resonate with young women currently facing similar situations.

JFA: Do you have a favorite SF or fantasy work that holds particular significance or has inspired you?

Lee: While working on *The School Nurse Files*, I drew inspiration from Lovecraft's Cthulhu Mythos, 50s Hollywood low-budget horror films featuring blob-like entities, and the Japanese video game *Dragon Quest*, renowned for its depiction of slime-like monsters.

JFA: After graduating from the Department of Russian at Hankuk University of Foreign Studies, it's understood that you continued to work in jobs requiring Russian for some time prior to your debut. Has Russian literature or filmography had any influence on your directorial work?

Lee: I wouldn't say directly. Russian literature and art are unquestionably magnificent. I am certain I'm not the only creator to have been inspired, moved, and comforted by Russian literature, music, art, and cinema. However, to delve a bit into my personal experience, I think the impact of my time studying Russian and earning my living using that language has less to do with Russian art per se, and more with the loneliness and despair I felt while pursuing a career that wasn't quite right for me—interpreting and translating. These feelings have since been channeled into my artistic work.

JFA: It's been reported that you're preparing a new film, *A Bride*, which falls into the horror-fantasy genre. Can you share some insights into what we might expect from this project? Additionally, do you have plans for a second season of *The School Nurse Files* or any other SF or fantasy projects?

Lee: At the moment, I am not certain whether my next venture will be *A Bride*, which I've just completed writing, or if it will be another series. I think I'll proceed with whichever project is ready to go into filming first. Thank you.

Original Korean text follows.

"사람의 감정은 우리가 상식적으로 이해할 수 없는 복잡한 화학작용": 이경미 감독과의 대화

(인터뷰/번역: 유상근)

이경미 감독

이경미 감독은 1973 년 12 월 서울에서 출생 후, 한국외국어대학교 러시아어과와 한국예술종합학교 영상원 영화과를 졸업했다. 2003 년 단편영화 <오디션>을 시작으로, 2004 년 한예종 졸업작품으로 만든 <잘돼가? 무엇이든>이 미장센 단편영화제를 비롯 다수의 영화제에서 호평을 받으며 이름을 널리 알리게 된다. 박찬욱 감독의 영화 <친절한 금자씨>에서 스크립터 역할을 맡은 것으로 박찬욱 감독과 인연을 시작하여, 이경미 감독의 첫 장편영화 <미쓰 홍당무> 역시 박찬욱 감독이 제작을 맡으며 함께 협업한다. 이후 이경미 감독은 <미쓰 홍당무>를 통해 청룡영화상을 비롯해 그 해의 신인감독상 3 개를 받게 된다. 이후 2016 년 두 번째 장편영화 <비밀은 없다>로 부산영화평론가협회상 대상, 한국영화평론가협회상 감독상을 거머쥔다. 2020 년에는 넷플릭스 오리지널 시리즈 <보건교사 안은영>을 통해 첫 TV 드라마 연출을 시도했다.

* * *

JFA: 안녕하세요. JFA 의 독자분들께 간단한 인사 말씀 부탁드립니다.

이경미: 안녕하세요. 이렇게 지면으로 인사드리게 되어 반갑고 기쁩니다. 그리고 제 작품에 대해서 관심을 가져주셔서 고맙습니다.

JFA: 감독님의 작품들을 보면 항상 기존의 전통적 장르 구분을 뛰어넘는 탈–장르적 상상력을 보여주셨다고 생각합니다. <보건교사 안은영>은 엄격하게 말해 판타지 장르에 속한다고 할 수 있지만, 액션 히어로물에 속한다고 볼 수도 있고, 한편으로는 사건 뒤에 숨어 있는 거대 기업의 비리를 파헤치는 르포로 다가오기도 합니다. 단편 <아랫집>의 경우에도 일상에서 흔히 접할 수 있는 사회 문제를 다루고 있지만, 사이비 종교도 등장하고, 특히 엔딩 장면에서는 리얼리즘 영화에서 판타지 장르로 넘어가는 듯한 느낌도 듭니다. <비밀은 없다> 역시 정치사회적 문제를 다루고 있지만, 무당이 등장하는 장면이라거나 두 소녀의 뮤직비디오 씬

등을 볼 때 환상적인 요소들이 많이 느껴지는데요. 영미권의 많은
SF/판타지 학자들은 하드 SF 와 판타지의 구분이 더 이상 불가능하며, 그
경계가 지난 수십년간 계속 해체되어 왔다고 지적하고 있는데 반해
한국에서는 아직 리얼리즘/하드 SF/판타지의 구분을 보다 엄격하게
정의하고 있습니다. 이런 관점에서 기존의 장르 구분에 대한 감독님의
생각이 궁금합니다. 더불어, 감독님께서는 스스로의 영화를 어떤 장르에
속한다고 생각하시는지, 기존의 장르 구분에 대해 어떤 생각을 가지고
계신지요?

이경미: 저의 데뷔작 <미쓰 홍당무>는 코미디고 다음 작품 <비밀은
없다>는 스릴러입니다. 단편 <아랫집>은 판타지 호러고 <보건교사
안은영>은 판타지 액션 히어로물 정도라고 이야기할 수 있을 것
같습니다. 제가 만든 작품의 장르는 각각 다른데 또 들여다보면 기존의
장르물 컨벤션을 충실하게 따르지도 않다는 점을 느끼실 수 있습니다.
그런데 제 작품만 그런 것은 아닙니다. 한국 영화감독들은 (저를
비롯해서) 어렸을 때부터 헐리우드 영화를 즐겨보면서 자랐고 다른
나라의 장르 영화들을 보면서 영화 만드는 꿈을 키웠습니다. 거기에
우리의 정치적 문화적 배경이 더해지면서 차별점이 생긴다고 생각합니다.
우리의 정서와 해학이 해외 관객들에게 흥미롭게 전달된다고 느낄 때
기분이 좋습니다. 예술이 언어의 장벽을 뛰어넘는 순간이라고
생각합니다.

한국 영화감독 중에서도 해외에서 많은 사랑을 받는 감독들은 장르
컨벤션을 비틀고 거기에서 고유한 개성을 창조한 예술가들이라고 저는
생각하고 있습니다. 그런데 SF 에 대해서 만큼은 아직 한국에선 엄격한
편입니다. 제 생각에는 한국의 SF 장르물이 아직 많지 않은 편이고
우리는 뛰어난 테크닉을 겸비한 미국의 대형 SF 영화에 매우 익숙해져
있기 때문인 것 같습니다.

이제 제 영화의 장르에 대한 질문으로 돌아가자면 저는 여러 장르를 다
시도해보고 있습니다. 그런데 제 생각에 저의 모든 작품을 관통하는
감정은 공포라고 생각합니다. 그 공포를 코미디로 포장하고, 스릴러로
포장하고, 판타지로 포장한다고 생각합니다. <보건교사 안은영>의
경우는 원작 소설이 있습니다. 원작은 발랄하고 정직하고 명랑한
이야기인데 제가 각색하고 연출을 하면서 '호러' 요소가 가미됐습니다.
저는 "징그러운데 귀엽고" "무서운데 웃긴" 정서를 느끼게 해주고
싶었습니다. 복합될 수 없는 두 가지 감정이 부딪혀 섞일 때 발생되는

난처하면서 색다른 기분을 느끼는 것을 좋아합니다. 한국말로 '웃프다'는 신조어도 비슷한 예입니다. 슬픈데 웃긴 거죠. 사람의 감정은 우리가 상식적으로 이해할 수 없는 복잡한 화학작용이라고 생각합니다. 그것이 사람을 진정 사람답게 보여주는 순간이기도 하다고 생각합니다.

JFA: 감독님의 기존 작품들이 모두 환상예술적인 측면이 있지만, 엄격히 말해 하드 SF 적(예를 들어 과학기술에 대한 관심)이라기보다는 종교, 특히 사이비 종교나, 미신, 무속 신앙 등이 등장인물들의 사고 방식과 삶에 얼마나 큰 영향을 주는지가 잘 드러나고 있습니다. 앞선 질문에서 언급한 바와 같이 안은영의 장식장을 보면 도교, 불교, 기독교 가릴 것없이 각종 종교관련 물건들이 전시되어 있고, <비밀은 없다>의 김연홍 역시 무당을 찾아가는데요, <아랫집>의 희지 역시 사이비 종교 회원인 것으로 보입니다. 그럼에도 불구하고 감독님 작품에서는 이러한 요소들이 초현실적이거나 비현실적이라기 보다는 오히려 리얼하게 보이는데요. 우리의 일상에 이미 이러한 비현실적 요소들이 현실의 일부로 들어와 있다고 봐도 될까요?

이경미: 한국을 이해할 수 있는 몇 개의 키워드 중에 종교는 매우 중요한 비중을 차지한다고 생각합니다. 우리에게 무속신앙은 아주 밀접하게 연결되어 있습니다. 무속신앙을 터부시하면서 어둠 속에선 대단히 의지를 많이 합니다. 우리나라에서 무속신앙은 서민들만의 것이 아닙니다. 정치,경제 분야의 실권자들 사이에서도 무속신앙이 깊이 연결되어 있는 경우를 심심치 않게 발견하지요. 한국은 무속신앙 뿐만이 아니라 사이비 종교의 역사도 깊습니다. 해방전후 시기를 뿌리에 두고 분파를 거듭하며 교리를 발전시키면서 확장해오고 있습니다. 조금 우스갯소리 같기도 하겠지만 성공적인 K-컨텐츠의 선두는 K-팝 이전에 K-종교가 있을지도 모릅니다. 이렇듯이 저는 사이비 종교를 매우 현실에 기반을 둔 생활 요소 중 하나라고 생각하고 있어서 리얼하게 보일 수도 있습니다.

JFA: 그 동안 한국 영화계에서는 유독 <성냥팔이 소녀의 재림>이나 <건축무한육면각체의 비밀>과 같은 하드 SF 가 관객들로부터 외면을 받아왔습니다. 반면 <전설의 고향>같은 판타지 장르들은 큰 사랑을 받아왔는데요. 물론 최근 <고요의 바다>나 <승리호>에서 볼 수 있듯 한국 관객들도 점차 SF 장르를 더 가까이 받아들이고 있습니다. 앞으로 한국 영화계에서 SF 나 판타지의 미래를 어떻게 보시나요?

이경미: 한국의 장르물에서 유독 혹독하게 평가되어지는 장르가 SF입니다. SF는 기술적인 완성도가 중요하게 받쳐줘야하는 장르인데 한국 시장만을 타겟으로 소화할 수 있는 예산의 최대치로는 헐리우드의 에스에프를 따라갈 수 없습니다. 하지만 K-콘텐츠가 인기가 많아지고 확장성이 넓어지면서 소화할 수 있는 시장도 커진다면 한국 SF 장르가 가진 잠재력은 이미 크다고 생각합니다. 한국 관객들과 창작자의 눈은 점점 높아지고 SF 장르는 아직 시도되지 않은 것들이 무궁무진하기 때문입니다.

JFA: 최근 글로벌 OTT 플랫폼을 통해 한국 SF와 판타지에 대한 세계 관객들의 관심이 커지고 있습니다. 그 원인을 무엇이라고 보시나요? 더불어 한국적인 SF, 한국적인 판타지를 어떻게 정의할 수 있을까요? 나아가, 그런 정의에 의미가 있을지요?

이경미: 관심이 커지는 원인은 모르겠습니다. 한국적 판타지는 지금도 시도 중에 있다고 생각합니다. 예를 들어 봉준호 감독님이 미국 스릴러 장르를 가져와 한국 배경과 인물들에 한국적인 정서를 넣어 한국 사람들이 친근하게 느낄 수 있도록 만드신 <살인의 추억>이 다른 나라 관객들에게 신선하게 어필이 된 것처럼 우리나라 SF 장르물도 그런 날이 올 것이라고 기대하고 있습니다.

JFA: 감독님의 전작들을 보면 비단 <보건교사 안은영>뿐 아니라 많은 작품들이 여성 히어로물적인 느낌이 납니다. <비밀은 없다>의 김연홍이나 <미쓰홍당무>의 양미숙 역시 어떤 점에 있어서는 여성 히어로라고 볼 수 있는데요. 다른 한편으로는 혼자 사는 여성들이 느끼는 공포와 남성중심적 가부장제 하에서의 차별에 대한 리얼한 묘사가 돋보이면서 그러한 사회 구조에 저항하고 이를 전복하는 여성 히어로에 대한 일관된 관심이 드러나는데요. 이와 더불어 전작에서 다루신 딸을 잃은 엄마의 광기라는 주제에서 보듯 여성 간의 연대라는 코드가 자주 등장하는 것 같습니다. <보건교사 안은영>에서 양호실에 모인 여학생들과 보건교사와의 관계라든지, <비밀은 없다>에서 최미옥과 김연홍의 연대가 그러한 케이스에 속할 텐데요. 딸이 되었건, 여학생이 되었건, 자신보다 어린 여성을 지켜주는 어른 여성 캐릭터가 자주 등장하는 것 같습니다. 이 같은 주제 의식에 대한 감독님의 생각이 궁금합니다.

이경미: 제가 여성이라서 그런지 남성보다는 여성 이야기가 자신 있습니다. 저는 여자 중학교, 여자 고등학교를 나왔습니다. 물론

대학교는 남녀공학이었지만 청소년기를 여자들끼리 보내다보니 여자들을 접할 기회가 월등히 많기도 했습니다. 여성 간의 연대를 이야기하겠다는 의도나 계획이 있었던 것은 아닙니다. 그런데 제가 만드는 이야기들마다 어른 여자 (주인공)과 어린 여자와의 관계가 늘 등장한다는 점을 저도 누군가 지적해줘서 깨닫게 됐습니다. 저는 '구원' 서사에는 크게 관심이 없습니다. 오히려 구원받지 못한 사람들이 만나는 이야기를 더 좋아합니다. 그게 아주 현실적인 우리들의 이야기라고 생각하는 것 같습니다. 제가 살아온 한국 사회는 남녀불평등이 지금보다도 훨씬 심했습니다. 저처럼 적정 나이에 결혼을 하지 않고 사회생활을 이어갈 경우의 미래는 상당히 불안할 수밖에 없었습니다. 왜냐하면 나의 미래를 꿈꾸게 해줄 만한 현실에서의 모델이 별로 없었기 때문입니다. 그렇기 때문에 우리는 우리보다 나이가 많은 여자들에 대해서 생각이 많아지게 됩니다. 그들이 우리의 미래의 모습이기 때문입니다. 그리고 우리보다 어린 여자들에 대해서도 생각이 많아지게 됩니다. 우리의 과거가 반영되기 때문입니다. 저는 거기에서 연대가 비롯된다고 생각합니다. 만약에 우리들이 주도권을 잡고 역사를 만들어온 성공의 경험이 이어지고 있다면 조금 달랐을지도 모르겠다는 생각도 해봅니다.

JFA: 젊은 여성 관객들을 주된 팬층으로 보시는지, 또 만약 그렇다면 왜 그들에게 감독님의 작품들이 어필한다고 생각하시는지 궁금합니다. 또, 한국의 동세대 남성들에 대한 여성들의 인식은 보통 어떻다고 보시는지요?

이경미: 젊은 관객들에게 사랑받는다는 것은 정말 기쁜 일입니다. 그만큼 제 수명이 늘어나는 기분이 들 거든요. 젊은 여성들이 판타지 서사에 특히 끌리는 지는 제가 잘 모르겠습니다. 만약 그것이 사실이라면 제 생각에는 현실이 답답하고 암울하기 때문이 아닐까 싶기도 합니다. 한국의 20-30 대는 젠더 갈등은 심각합니다. 결혼과 출산율은 급격하게 떨어지고 있고요. 여성과 남성의 비전 간의 간극이 좁혀지기 힘듭니다. 특히 젊은 여성들이 제 작품을 좋아한다는 것이 사실이라면 제가 이유를 정확히 알 순 없지만 제가 답답한 한국사회를 살아오면서 마음속에 품고 있던 다양한 감정들이 지금을 살고 있는 젊은 여성들과 통한 게 아닐까 싶기도 합니다.

JFA: 특별히 좋아하거나 영감을 받은 SF 혹은 판타지 작품이 있으신가요?

이경미: <보건교사 안은영>을 만들 때 러브 크래프트의 크툴루 신화를 참고했고 헐리우드 50년대 비급 호러무비 블럽(blob)물 (이후 현대에 이르기까지 응용 발전되어온)을 참고했습니다. (슬라임 형태의 괴물들이 나오는) 그리고 일본식 플레임 게임인 드래곤 퀘스트를 참고했습니다.

JFA: 외대 러시아어과를 졸업하신 후에, 이후에도 입봉 전까지 러시아어를 사용하는 일을 오래 하셨다고 들었습니다. 혹시 러시아의 문학작품이나 영화 등이 감독님의 작품 세계에 영향을 준 바가 있나요?

이경미: 그렇진 않은 것 같습니다. 러시아 문학, 예술은 정말 위대합니다. 저 뿐만이 아니라 수많은 예술가들이 러시아 문학과 음악, 미술 영화로부터 영감을 받고 기쁨과 위안을 얻으며 창작을 할 것입니다. 그런데 저의 개인적인 이야기로 조금 들어가자면 제가 러시아어를 공부하고 그 기술로 밥벌이를 하던 시절이 지금 영화감독으로서의 저에게 준 영향은 러시아의 예술 작품들보다도 저와 맞지 않은 일 (통역, 번역)을 억지로 하면서 견뎌야했던 고독과 절망이 지금 저의 예술 작업에 동력이 됐다고 생각하고 있습니다.

JFA: 새로운 영화를 준비중이시라고 들었습니다. 새 영화 <새색시>가 호러 판타지 장르물이라는데, 어떤 작품이 될지 조금 더 설명을 들을 수 있을까요? 이외에도 <보건교사 안은영> 시즌 2 라든가 혹은 다른 SF 나 판타지물에 대한 계획이 있으신가요?

이경미: 다음 작품이 이제 막 각본 작업을 마친 <새색시>가 될지 다른 시리즈가 될지 아직 모르겠습니다. 먼저 촬영이 진행되는 프로젝트를 할 것 같습니다. 구체적인 내용은 아직 말씀드리기 어렵네요.

JFA: 감사합니다.

이경미: 감사합니다.

Cli-Fi, Noir, and The Nonhuman Subject in Netflix's *The Silent Sea* (2021)

Katrina Younes

Introduction

NETFLIX'S *THE SILENT SEA* (2021) is a South Korean television series that fuses elements of American noir and its subgenres, such as the hardboiled literary root of film noir, and climate fiction (cli-fi, a subgenre of science fiction) to address the dark and uncanny issues of environmental degradation. My analysis of *The Silent Sea* develops the scholarship exploring the links and conversations happening between contemporary South Korean noir and early American noir. In doing so, one can better grasp how, with this series as an example, South Korean popular culture utilizes American noir conventions to have a meaningful conversation about the reality of the climate crisis.[1] The television series is directed by Choi Hang-yong, who also wrote and directed the South Korean film *The Sea of Tranquility* (2014), which the 2021 series is based on. The television series stars Bae Donna (as astrobiologist Doctor Song Ji-an), Gong Yoo (as the exploration team leader Han Yoon-Jae), Lee

Joon (as the team's head engineer Lieutenant Ryu Tae-seok), Kim Sun-young (as the team's Doctor Kim Sun), and Lee Moo-saeng (as the mysterious survivor of the Balhae accident, Luna 073). The series is set in a near-future Earth suffering from extreme desertification, leading to government-sanctioned measures rationing water usage. Doctor Song Ji-an and the rest of the personnel are selected for a mission to the moon whereby they must attend to an abandoned research facility, Balhae station. Five years prior, there was an incident at the station that killed 117 personnel, including Doctor Song's sister. The team's sole mission is to retrieve a sample of unknown content before the higher-ups permanently close the station. While at the station, Doctor Song transforms into a private investigator who insists that the officials commanding the mission have concealed information regarding their objective for the team, the facility and research conducted within, as well as the circumstances surrounding the accident five years ago. Doctor Song's string of investigations leads to others working with her to unravel the secrets of their mission, the accident, and the sample. It is discovered that the sample consists of a new element that mimics water, but it multiplies like a virus when it comes in physical contact with living cells. Eventually, after multiple fatalities and betrayals, the team discovers a human/nonhuman hybrid girl on the station (Luna 073) who is immune to the effects of this water-mimetic substance.

The Silent Sea fuses conventions from the cli-fi and American noir genres to tell viewers a story about an Earth ravaged by drought. Some of the characters act as eco-investigators, meaning they are private investigators situated in a cli-fi setting (1) trying to solve a mystery concerning humans' perpetuation of climate change and (2) are placed in a landscape ridden with environmental degradation. The series relies on conventions of noir, such as realism, crime, and violence, to situate the futuristic world of the show in our reality with the hope of making more prominent the violence we enact against our environment and the impending destruction we will face if we do not halt our vicious actions.

Noir can be understood in its origins as both an aesthetic and as a social commentary on American life in the mid-twentieth century. For example, many noir texts, and those of its sub-genres (such as the hardboiled and neo-noir), focus on conventions such as urban crime and decay, mystery, violence, and so on. Film noir, which grew alongside the hardboiled narratives, contains many flashbacks, dim lighting, and a bleak setting. Noir, from both a cinematic and literary tradition, is concerned with crime, mystery, fragmentation, thrill, and realism. The various elements explored by American noir scholars such as Stewart King and Homer B. Pettey include an analysis of how the hardboiled private investigator and the dangerous femme fatale reflect gender and sexual norms of the era, or how the anti-hero reflects a conception of the individual as isolated or fragmented. Regardless of the focus, whether it is an exploration of the representation of race or sexuality, the overall depiction, Pettey argues in "Hard-boiled Tradition and Early Film Noir," reflects a "harsh, bleak reality" (61). As noir continued to develop into the neo-noir age, contemporary iterations of the genre highlight the study of noir and its sub-genres to include the representation of environmental degradation. The bleakness of noir is utilized to demonstrate an awareness of the decaying natural environment and our bleak future as consequence.

The Silent Sea couples the bleak noir conventions with cli-fi conventions such as the depiction of a dystopian/utopian society resulting from the impacts of climate change, which is a key focus for many climate fiction narratives, a sub-genre of science fiction. In short, *The Silent Sea* depicts what Timothy Morton calls a "dark ecology," in his book of the same name, that renders nature as ruined or destroyed as a result of anthropogenic climate change;

the series relies on a fusion of noir and cli-fi conventions with the hope that humanity may halt the violence humans inflict on the nonhuman, and the potential violence that a destroyed nature may wreak upon humanity in return. Because eco-catastrophes are often experienced on a global level, especially when they pertain to water usage and drought, it is important to consider how this series adopts a global perspective—how it links South Korean and American conventions—to highlight the widespread effects of climate change. The series adapts noir conventions from the American cinematic and literary tradition to communicate a dark nature as defined by the eco-catastrophe of drought. In *Dark Ecology*, Morton argues that a rendering of nature in positive terms, as that which is harmonious, renders that which is toxic and destructive in nature invisible. *The Silent Sea* brings to light a dark nature in its conception of lunar water, dismantling the romantic construction of nature as beautiful and demonstrating to us the dangerous natural forces that often manifest because of human activities. This dark destructive nature, which we ourselves make manifest, ironically comes to threaten our lives.

Because *The Silent Sea* depicts space exploration and the dystopic effects of climate change by fusing elements of speculative fiction with mystery, violence, and thrill, one might name the series as a "crimate" television series, a term that Stewart King coined in "*Crimate* Fiction and the Environmental Imagination of Place." King argues that crimate fiction is about texts that "investigate and interrogate issues of environmental damage" (1235). King echoes Marta Puxan-Oliva from her chapter on "Crime Fiction and the Environment" when he notes that these texts depict and discuss "ecological crises and abuses" and attempt to bring to light "the criminal acts they involve" (1236). King further argues that "environmental (crime) fictions are fundamentally concerned with entangled relationships between the human and nonhuman in specific places" (1236). In short, we can expand upon our ecocritical approaches when examining expression of environmental concern, and one way of doing so is by using the conventions of noir as tools for "discussing ecological crises and abuses [...] exposing the criminal acts they involve in their violent effects on people and the environment" (1236).

In *The Silent Sea*, viewers are exposed to the criminality involved in capitalist endeavours on the principle of growth and the perpetual exploitation of natural resources (on Earth and in outer space). The sample, in mimicking water, is both familiar and unfamiliar. In being literally unearthly, it is that which does and does not belong (to us), or that which involves, as Jonathon Turnbull argues in "Weird," an "(un)earthly belonging" (275). Depicting lunar water as unassimilable to terrestrial water, the show demonstrates that not everything in the natural world is scalable and, as such, not everything on Earth, or in outer space, is a resource that should be exploited for our own gains. In ignoring the dangers of an exploitative mindset, we become criminals perpetuating the destruction of our world, and other worlds and celestial objects.

As I address in the next section, the merging of noir with cli-fi elements reinforces the most common forms of science fiction in South Korea, providing viewers with a new way to understand the nonhuman and our relationship with it. In better grasping nature and altering our construction of it, we can better grasp the threats we pose to ourselves as human beings and to others living on Earth if we do not alter our recurring exploitative behaviour.

Noiring Science Fiction

Science fiction as a genre in South Korea focuses primarily on a near-future reality. Dong-Won Kim explains in "Science Fiction in South and North Korea: Reading Science and Technology as Fantasized in Cultures" that science fiction was "first introduced to

Korea in the early twentieth century by Korean students in Japan" (310). It was largely neglected before the early 1990s. In the mid-1990s, some young Koreans began to write science fiction regularly and "internet websites became important and useful crossroads where South Korean science fiction writers and readers could meet" (311). But, as Kim explains, writers of science fiction in South Korea are not widespread, "and the quality of their work does not meet the expectations of South Korean readers who are familiar with Western science Fiction" (311). One key convention of South Korean science fiction texts is describing "the very near future, one or two generations beyond the present; very few deal with society in the far-distant future" (314). For Kim, this is because "South Korean writers' favourite subjects for science fiction are actually present-day issues such as environmental pollution or conglomerates' dominance in the economy and society" (314). Moreover, such writers rarely focus on "new imaginary science or technology" (315). *The Silent Sea* remains true to the South Korean science fiction convention of setting largely pessimistic narratives in near-future dystopic realities, and it does so by merging such South Korean science fiction conventions with the realism of American noir and its sub-genres.

Seo-Young Chu echoes Kim's comments in "Science Fiction and Postmemory Han in Contemporary Korean American Literature" when defining science fiction as that genre whose objects of representation are not "altogether imaginary" (99). Chu argues:

> Instead of defining science fiction as a non-mimetic genre that achieves the effect of cognitive estrangement through 'an imaginative framework,' I define science fiction as a mimetic genre whose objects of representation are non-imaginary yet cognitively estranging. Such referents include virtual entities (such as cyberspace), realities

imperceptible to humans (such as the fourth dimension), and events so violent that they elude immediate understanding (trauma). (99)

In other words, Chu is defining Korean science fiction worlds as not the "imaginary referents" they often are in American science fiction, but rather as encompassing a "narrative realm where *literal* and *figurative* share ontological status"; such science fiction can thus "accommodate referents that are themselves neither purely literal nor purely figurative" (100). Like Kim, Chu understands science fiction in the South Korean literary tradition as that which depicts a reality in the near future.

Science fiction stories are focused on the future, whether in space, a utopian/dystopian world or in a different universe/world/dimension. Like noir, science fiction contains conventions that are fluid and adaptable, existing in a "dialectical relationship" with its surroundings. In other words, it is not a static genre. Broadly speaking, science fiction puts together our imagined futures as well as fragments of our present-day situations. In other words, the genre is rooted in past and present daily life as well as the future. To quote Fredric Jameson in *Archaeologies of the Future*, science fiction "registers some nascent sense of the future and does so in the space on which a sense of the past had once been inscribed" (Jameson 286). As Kim and Chu have noted in relation to South Korean science fiction, American science fiction is largely concerned with unearthing a possible future in our present reality.

Because of noir's realism, it can be utilized in situating the eco-catastrophe of *The Silent Sea* in, not a far-off future, but rather a near-reality. For example, Jameson notes how noir contains some "kind of run-down urban space, impersonal yet threatening alike" and that "it is in film noir that we find the most 'realistic' development of the narrative unit in question, a development which offers some useful clues as to its ultimate historical meaning or content" (317, 322). The urban decay in noir is important in highlighting the dystopian wastelands of a past and a present. The past conventions of noir issue slowly forth "like the growth of an organism" transforming the traditional violence of the urban city into an "unimaginable yet inevitable 'real' future" (Jameson 287-288). Noir's conventional realist setting, and depiction of a violent urban underworld, is not re-envisioned but "regenerated"[2] in the black-and-white lunar setting of *The Silent Sea* to enhance and complicate a cli-fi narrative and near-future dystopic reality. *The Silent Sea*'s regeneration of noir places it in conversation with science fiction across time, which demonstrates to readers that the imagined future is not always in disregard of the imagined past.

Noir and the Hardboiled Sub-Genre of Noir

One reason why noir, which can include the conventions found in detective fiction, works well when fused with near-future science fiction narratives is because the former, as Jooyeon Rhee argues in "The Development of Detective Fiction in Korea," shows the inextricable connection between "the traumas and pleasures of modern life that manifests in crimes in urban settings" (188). Noir narratives often reflect "negative psychological effects of modern life," and crimes and violence are often "consequences of the modernizing process, mostly in Euro-American contexts, that affected social lives and psychology of people in the consumption-driven and alienated urban environment" (188). Perhaps a classic example of a Korean film noir that takes up elements of art cinema and Hollywood noir conventions is *Oldboy* (2003). Directed by Park Chan-wook, the film, as Chelsea McCracken notes in "*Oldboy* and Korean Film Noir," uses "elements of mainstream genres, but adapt[s] them in stylish new ways, and in so doing [is] able to make films that are both commercially and critically successful" (167). During the 2000s, when *Oldboy* was filmed, Korean cinema "was increasingly affected by international distribution" (McCracken 169). South Korean texts' genre-bending has thus long existed prior to *The Silent Sea*: "the use of noir conventions is either ignored or taken for granted, as an uncomplicated element mixed into genre hybrids" (McCracken 169).

Noir conventions are utilized in various other genres largely because of their adaptability. Key here is noir's tendency to represent isolated (criminal) incidents as symptoms of larger social or systemic problems. As Anthony Hoefer explains in "Violence, Spectacular and Slow: Ecology, Genre, and Murder in Biguenet's *Oyster* and Rash's *One Foot in Eden*":

> Despite their common associations, noir (whether film or fiction) requires neither a mystery nor a detective, but simply a crime or an act of violence—and, most often, one that is spectacular, even lurid. However, noir is distinct from other crime fiction in the way it contextualizes even the most spectacular violence: from its cynical perspective, a particular criminal scheme or a singular act of violence is almost always the consequence of systemic corruption and injustice. Noir is interested in crime and violence as the manifestation of something sprawling, pervasive, and unseen, rather than the result of singular, individual evil. In noir, the lurid and the spectacular offer access to something otherwise unintelligible—the complexities and contradictions produced by (late) modernity. The genre's shared textures, of course, are not just strategies for accessing complicated truths; they are exciting, titillating, and fun. (489-490)

Hoefer demonstrates how when one pulls away the veil that is noir's excitement and thrill, one can see the malleability involved in how we understand and represent violence This, in turn, allows for an examination of how such urban violence centered on guns and car chases can be translated into a conversation about violence against the environment in cli-fi texts. The investigator or detective is not a necessary element. Rather, what is critical in noir is violence: it can be criminal, illegal, or legal, but regardless, as Hoefer says, it is "always the consequence of systemic corruption and injustice." The investigator(s) navigate spaces of violence, whether it is a human-driven act of violence against another human or/and nonhuman, or a capitalist industrialist's harmful practices against a community. Noir uses its cynical overtone to offer "a skepticism about narratives of national progress and development that aligns it with the project of representing" violence (Hoefer 502). By focusing on the different manifestations of violence in noir, we can begin to understand why this key convention of the genre is useful when expanded upon to analyze the different representations of violence in relation to, and against, the nonhuman in *The Silent Sea*.

Much like Hoefer, Lucas Hollister is interested in questions such as "what is violence? How do we conceptualize networks and causalities of violence? How do we understand the distribution of victimization and guilt? What conclusions are we to draw from the violence that marks our political, economic, and social conditions?" (1012). Morton's ideas in *Dark Ecology* are taken up by scholars such as Hollister because they reshape the way violence and climate change function in thrill-packed noir narratives. Hollister opens his 2019 essay by quoting Morton's argument that "the darkness of ecological awareness is the darkness of noir" (9). Hollister relies on Morton's book to connect ecological awareness with the crime fiction trope of violence. With the help of such scholarship, we can see how noir resonates in ecological criticism, which in turn affects "our interpretations of noir or crime fictions" by "destabilizing" such fictions (1022).

The Silent Sea, as analyzed below, provides viewers with a noirish landscape ridden with the effects of climate change perpetuated by human aggressors. Evidenced by Hollister's recognition of how "crime fiction can be made black and greener," we begin to see how crime fiction and the fluid representation of violence can be useful in examining *The Silent Sea* as a noirish cli-fi tale. This way of seeing violence, in a "greener" light, reduces the "bloody thrills" that the popular genre promises and makes realities easier to represent and act upon (Hollister 1020).

Noiring *The Silent Sea*: The Eco-Investigative Narrative

The investigative focus of the team in *The Silent Sea* is multifold: the members—including the two undercover spies—are searching for a mysterious sample and for clues and answers regarding the accident that occurred on the station years ago. In a certain sense, the entire investigative narrative contrasts with the traditional linear narratives in noir texts. *The Silent Sea* de-centers realms and connections. There is no single private investigator in the series since all the team members work in a collective to unravel the mysteries of the sample and the station. Moreover, there is no single beginning, middle/centre, or end to the narrative. There is no explanation of the cause of the drought or when the experiments were conducted on lunar water, and there is no clear ending or definitive conclusion to the future of water, lunar water, or the two surviving female doctors and Luna 073. Thus, the fusion of mystery, crime, and ecological concerns re-envisions both the classic American noir genre and contemporary cli-fi narratives. The fusion of conventions of both genres forms an eco-investigative narrative that situates a fictitious dystopic world within realism, providing viewers with a useful and unique avenue through which to make clear the impending effects of climate change.

Broadly speaking, *The Silent Sea* puts on display various conventions and elements of film noir: there is an investigator with intellectual power, an urban setting, flashbacks, and there are stories based on crimes and violence. The series initially follows a collective of government-ordered investigators. However, as the series develops, they transform into a rebellious collective of private investigators, in the sense of being independent of any police or government bodies. In other words, as the government-capitalist exploitative practices become clear to these characters, they form a new investigative collective in retaliation against their original commanding bodies. Furthermore, despite the primary setting being on the moon, the station and its interior are reminiscent of the type of urban setting seen back on Earth. In addition, nearly every episode of the series begins with a flashback. For example, the first episode begins with a scene of crash-landing on the moon and works its way back in retrospect to explain why there is a team heading there.

Lastly, although no official illegal acts lead to the team's investigation of lunar water and the incident on the station from years ago, they discover that government-sanctioned actions pertaining to the previous research, the other members on the station, and the studies conducted on the human/nonhuman clone Luna (73 times) are inhumane and criminal (albeit legally sanctioned) acts. For example, beyond lunar water and scientific studies, Director Choi blackmails the team leader to complete this mission so that his daughter will live, positioning herself as a type of gangster who controls Yoon Jae's daughter's life. As the series progresses, there are other crimes that unfold, specifically the murder of E2 by Ryu. Thus, there is both an eco-mystery that does not necessarily pertain to illegal behaviours, and traditional crimes we often see in film noir. The murder and acts of betrayal do not overshadow the tone of the series, which is like the tone of film noir in the Post-World War II American context; the tone of *The Silent Sea* reflects "the malaise and disillusionment" of our contemporary society, which is focused on exploitation of natural resources (McCracken 171).

Unlike noir, the violence in the series is largely slow. While the first episode opens with a tense and thrilling scene, with the team's spacecraft malfunctioning and the team having to land on the moon, the rest of the narrative progresses rather slowly. The series transforms the fast-paced style of American noir narratives to make room for the slow violence embedded within the eco-crimes. Rob Nixon defines slow violence as "violence that occurs gradually and out of sight, a violence of delayed destruction that is dispersed across time and space, an attritional violence that is typically not viewed as violence at all" (2). He urges an engagement with "a different kind of violence, a violence that is neither spectacular nor instantaneous, but rather incremental and accretive, its calamitous repercussions playing out across a range of temporal scales" (2). As per Nixon's book, one needs to rethink the "accepted assumptions of violence to include slow violence" and that "such a rethinking requires that we complicate conventional assumptions about violence as a highly visible act that is newsworthy because it is event focused, time bound, and body bound" (3). The slowness of the narrative is indicative of both the slow violence involved in droughts and climate change and the slow dying moments of those infected by the deadly lunar water. The violence and thrill of noir is both evident and out-of-sight in *The Silent Sea* insofar as the drownings from lunar water are extremely violent, but the mental images of the drowning victim are tranquil and slow as they imagine drowning in a calm and near-black body of water.

In addition to key elements such as flashbacks and mysteries, the series paints largely black-and-white scenes on the moon, which alludes to black-and-white noir films. Another key element to American crime and noir is, as mentioned above, the overall pervasive mood of the narrative. *The Silent Sea*'s urban and lunar setting is bleak and dark. These images are devoid of substantial colour as the series relies primarily on black and white to set the overall noir mood of the narrative. However, in stark contrast to noir films, the black-and-white setting of the series is not an effect added post-filming, but rather simply the colours of space, the moon, and the station. The more realistic colour palette of *The Silent Sea* conveniently creates a noir setting and further highlights the bleak future in store for us if we do not halt our exploitative actions against the natural environment. In short, *The Silent Sea*'s eco-investigative narrative fits neatly into McCracken's definition of film noir, in which the narrative and the pervasive mood are interrelated elements (170).

Watery Violence and Weird Mysteries

Rather than having an organized, underground crime unit, *The Silent Sea* depicts government officials and committees (such as the National Committee for Human Survival Measures), who limit water usage by discriminating against different tiers of people, as criminals. The drought is a universal issue in the series, with news broadcasts communicating the climate issue in English, French and Korean. There is a stark contrast between reality as depicted in the news and the protests that are unfolding on South Korean land. The protestors are advocating for fairness of water consumption, insinuating that the higher-ups are exploiting the ecological catastrophe by determining who can access what amount of water. In short, there are different types of "members" or classes, and limits on how much water each person from each class can obtain. These legally sanctioned actions rely on the drought as an excuse to allow some people to die from dehydration while the privileged continue to thrive. The crimes of mobsters, gangsters, and other people typically viewed as acting outside of the law in harmful ways are transformed into the crimes of the ruling, government class. In expanding the genre of American noir into this cli-fi series, there is a development of who can be categorized as a criminal and victim. People subject to inhumane government regulations are victims of such. However, the nonhuman is another victim of not just the higher-ups, but the actions of society as a whole.

The core investigator, Doctor Song, has a positive relationship with nonhumans. When viewers are first introduced to her, she is in an enclosure with a tiger, which responds positively to her presence. In addition to having a positive relationship with the tiger, the doctor treats other animals with kindness, offering water to a dog, for example. Immediately, viewers credit Doctor Song, who asks for help of other members as collective investigators, with positive attributes. Specifically, Doctor Song can perceive the nonhuman as subjects, as opposed to objects to be exploited. In this concluding analysis, there is an examination of nature fighting back and the idea of Luna as warning of humanity's bleak future.

Lunar water, a nonhuman, fights back against its exploitation by humans. This is evidenced by its ability to infinitely and rapidly multiply when in contact with human blood/living cells, eventually leading to the death of the host. Take for example Soochan's death in episode two: after coming into direct physical contact with Lunar water, he begins to violently vomit water. Although he is not spewing up blood, the scene of gushing water is an uncanny scene of abjection. The spectacle of bloody violence and thrill found in early American noir, specifically as these acts of violence are perpetuated by human criminals, mobs, and so on, is transformed in *The Silent Sea* into the weird, uncanny, and abject one that considers the retaliatory potential of nature. Lunar water's sense of agency, evidenced by its ability to kill a human host, breaks down the conventional boundaries separating a subject from an object. Lunar water's ability to fight back highlights how such conventional boundaries, built upon the exploitation of natural resources, need to be abolished. Lunar water helps viewers to reconsider the view of natural resources as objects to be infinitely exploited for the benefit of humankind: it forces us to reexamine these socially and culturally created boundaries and allows us to better perceive how such ideas perpetuate environmental disasters. While lunar water is fighting back against the humans' exploitation of it, a human/nonhuman hybrid, Luna 073, demonstrates an ambiguous answer to whether humans will leave the lunar water alone (thus rewarding its resilience) or continue to exploit it as an object. Luna is a weird and uncanny nonhuman, as well as a victim of government, corporate, and everyday citizens' greed. We can thus understand her character through a posthuman analysis. Posthumanism is generally concerned with how emerging technologies and other advances reshape what it means to be human. The infliction of scientific tests on Luna 073 creates a character who helps viewers reconsider what it means to commit acts of violence against natural environments. Luna 073 is not integrated into a machine, as some posthuman theories focus on, but she has biologically evolved with enhanced capabilities that transform her into a weapon, perpetuating the criminal acts of exploitation by Earth officials. Luna 073 is the only clone (out of 73) who has survived the experimentation process pertaining to the usability of lunar water by humans. Not only is Luna 073 immune to the effects of lunar water, thus being able to consume it (as per the intention of the government officials), but she is also a superhuman because of it: she is extremely fast, strong, and able to heal her own wounds.

Luna 073 is both a conventional subject (a human) and an object (in being exploited as a scientific experiment to ensure immunity to the deadly effects of lunar water). Unlike lunar water, Luna does not fight back, but is rather trying to survive on a station now occupied by the investigative team. When eventually Doctor Song initiates good relations with Luna, the remaining team members (Doctor Song and Doctor Hong Ga-Young), all female, escape the overflowing lunar water on the station and take refuge on the moon. At the conclusion of the series, viewers encounter Luna staring at Earth. While lunar water is a victim that fights back, Luna 073 is a present victim and a warning of future victims. The final scene highlights the ambiguous future in store for humanity if they continue to exploit the nonhuman to reproduce the exact or similar conditions that resulted in their current circumstances. This is demonstrated by Luna's gender and age: she is a young female, a beacon of hope for a future in which children can grow and flourish, but she is also a weird clone, a warning of imminent, and additional, environmental crises if humans continue their exploitative behaviour.

Conclusion

The fusion of American noir and crime fiction conventions with cli-fi provide scholars, readers, and viewers with an avenue to rethink what the former genre can look like in a South Korean popular culture text, and the ways in which it is useful in making cli-fi narratives more realistic to elicit action from viewers. In *The Silent Sea*, the near-future setting is infused with the conventions of noir as the investigative team follows clues pertaining to a mysterious nonhuman object of human greed: lunar water that can both solve the Earth drought crisis and kill any human who comes into physical contact with it. The darkness of climate change is heightened by utilizing the darkness of American noir, making the reality of climate change's effects, such as droughts, more realistic than relying purely on the genres of cli-fi or science fiction. Conventions of crime and violence found within some sub-genres of American noir are utilized not only to draw the viewer's attention to our climate crisis, but also to rethink our exploitative relationship with natural resources. In short, not only do viewers encounter a bleak reality fitting both a cli-fi and noir text, but they also encounter an alien nonhuman (lunar water) as it fights back against humans' exploitative practices. In short, *The Silent Sea*'s expedition team becomes an eco-investigative team that tries to unravel the mysteries behind government funding of researching lunar water to better understand the subject of the experiments as a subject, as opposed to an object. The ending of the series contains a warning: seeking other ways to exploit the nonhuman as an object with infinite resources for our use will result in an endless loop of destruction.

Notes

1. Not only does the series adapt American conventions, but one can also discern thematic and structural similarities between the series and American science fiction films such as Douglas Trumbull's *Silent Running* (1972) and Duncan Jones's *Moon* (2009).

2. I am borrowing Donna Haraway's idea, from her essay "Cyborg Manifesto," that "We all have been injured, profoundly. We require regeneration, not rebirth" (67).

Works Cited

Choi Hang-yong, dir. *The Silent Sea*. Netflix, 2021.

Chu, Seo-Young. "Science Fiction and Postmemory Han in Contemporary Korean American Literature." *MELUS*, vol. 33, no. 4, 2008, pp. 97-121.

Haraway, Donna. *A Cyborg Manifesto: Science, Technology, and Socialist-Feminism in the Late Twentieth Century*. University of Minnesota Press, 2016.

Hoefer, Dyer Anthony "Violence, Spectacular and Slow: Ecology, Genre, and Murder in Biguenet's *Oyster* and Rash's *One Foot in Eden*." *Mississippi Quarterly*, vol. 68, no. 3-4, pp. 487-490.

Hollister, Lucas. "The Green and the Black: Ecological Awareness and the Darkness of Noir." *PMLA*, vol. 134, no. 5, pp. 1012-1027.

Jameson, Fredric. *Archaeologies of the Future*. Verso, 2005.

Kim, Dong-Won. "Science Fiction in South and North Korea: Reading Science and Technology as Fantasized in Cultures." *East Asian Science, Technology and Society*, vol. 12, 2018, pp. 309-326.

Kim, Won-Chung. "Environmental Literature and the Change of its Canon in Korea." *CLCWeb*, vol. 16, no. 6, 2014, pp. 1-9.

King, Stewart. "Crimate Fiction and the Environmental Imagination of Place." *The Journal of Popular Culture*, vol. 54, no. 6, 2021, pp. 1235- 1253.

McCracken, Chelsea. "*Oldboy* and Korean Film Noir." *Asian Cinema*, vol. 23, no. 2, 2012, pp. 167-182.

Morton, Timothy. *Dark Ecology.* Columbia University Press, 2016.

Nixon, Rob. *Slow Violence and the Environmentalism of the Poor.* Harvard University Press, 2011.

Park, Sunyoung. "Decolonizing the Future: Postcolonial Themes in South Korean Science Fiction." *Routledge Handbook of Modern Korean Literature*, edited by Yoon Sun Yang, Routledge, 2020, pp. 56-67.

Pettey, B. Homer. "Hard-Boiled Tradition and Early Film Noir." *Film Noir*, edited by Homer B. Pettey and R. Barton Palmer, Cambridge UP, 2014, pp. 58-79.

Puxan-Oliva, Marta. "Crime Fiction and the Environment." *The Routledge Companion to Crime Fiction*, edited by Janice Allan, et al., Routledge, 2020, pp. 362-370.

Rhee, Jooyeon. "The Development of Detective Fiction in Korea." *Routledge Handbook of Modern Korean Literature*, edited by Yoon Sun Yang, Routledge, 2020, pp. 188-199

Smart, Alan and Josephine Smart, editors. *Posthumanism.* University of Toronto Press, 2017.

Turnbull, Jonathon. "Weird." *Environmental Humanities*, vol. 13, no. 1, pp. 275-280.

www.ingramcontent.com/pod-product-compliance
Lightning Source LLC
LaVergne TN
LVHW030632080426
835511LV00020B/3443